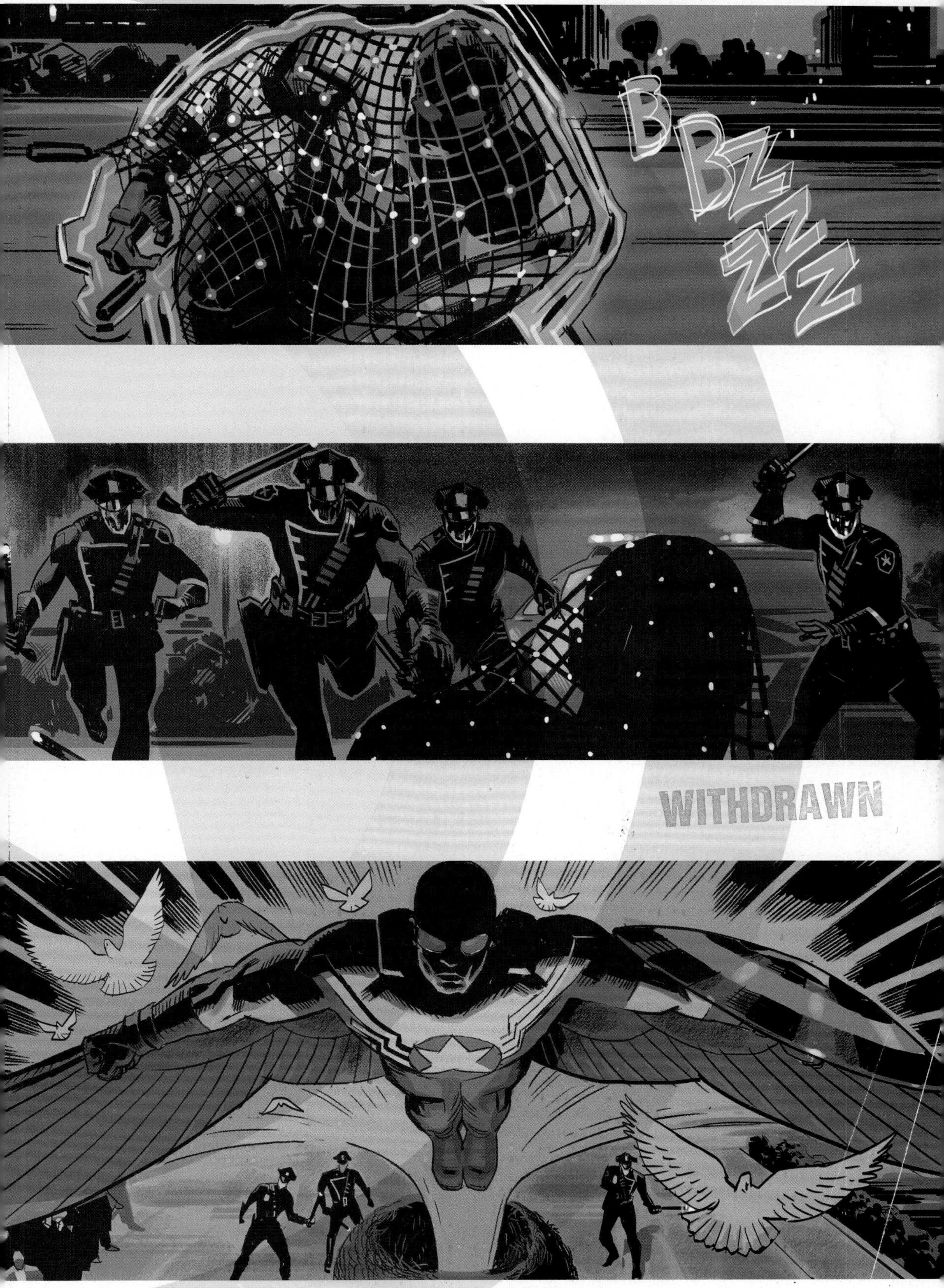
BBZZZZ

CIVIL WAR II

writer **NICK SPENCER**

artists **ANGEL UNZUETA** (#9-10) &
DANIEL ACUÑA (#11-13)

colorists **CRIS PETER** (#9-10) &
DANIEL ACUÑA (#11-13)

letterer **VC'S JOE CARAMAGNA**

cover art **ANGEL UNZUETA** (#9) &
DANIEL ACUÑA (#10-13)

assistant editor **ALANNA SMITH**
editor **TOM BREVOORT**

Captain America created by Joe Simon & Jack Kirby

collection editor SARAH BRUNSTAD
associate managing editor KATERI WOODY
editor, special projects MARK D. BEAZLEY
senior editor, special projects JENNIFER GRÜNWALD
vp production & special projects JEFF YOUNGQUIST

svp print, sales & marketing DAVID GABRIEL
editor in chief AXEL ALONSO
chief creative officer JOE QUESADA
publisher DAN BUCKLEY
executive producer ALAN FINE

CAPTAIN AMERICA: SAM WILSON VOL. 3 — CIVIL WAR II. Contains material originally published in magazine form as CAPTAIN AMERICA: SAM WILSON #9-13. First printing 2017. ISBN# 978-1-302-90319-0. Published by MARVEL WORLDWIDE, INC., a subsidiary of MARVEL ENTERTAINMENT, LLC. OFFICE OF PUBLICATION: 135 West 50th Street, New York, NY 10020. Copyright © 2016 MARVEL No similarity between any of the names, characters, persons, and/or institutions in this magazine with those of any living or dead person or institution is intended, and any such similarity which may exist is purely coincidental. **Printed in the U.S.A.** ALAN FINE, President, Marvel Entertainment; DAN BUCKLEY, President, TV, Publishing & Brand Management; JOE QUESADA, Chief Creative Officer; TOM BREVOORT, SVP of Publishing; DAVID BOGART, SVP of Business Affairs & Operations, Publishing & Partnership; C.B. CEBULSKI, VP of Brand Management & Development, Asia; DAVID GABRIEL, SVP of Sales & Marketing, Publishing; JEFF YOUNGQUIST, VP of Production & Special Projects; DAN CARR, Executive Director of Publishing Technology; ALEX MORALES, Director of Publishing Operations; SUSAN CRESPI, Production Manager; STAN LEE, Chairman Emeritus. For information regarding advertising in Marvel Comics or on Marvel.com, please contact Vit DeBellis, Integrated Sales Manager, at vdebellis@marvel.com. For Marvel subscription inquiries, please call 888-511-5480. **Manufactured between 11/18/2016 and 12/26/2016 by SOLISCO PRINTERS, SCOTT, QC, CANADA.**
10 9 8 7 6 5 4 3 2 1

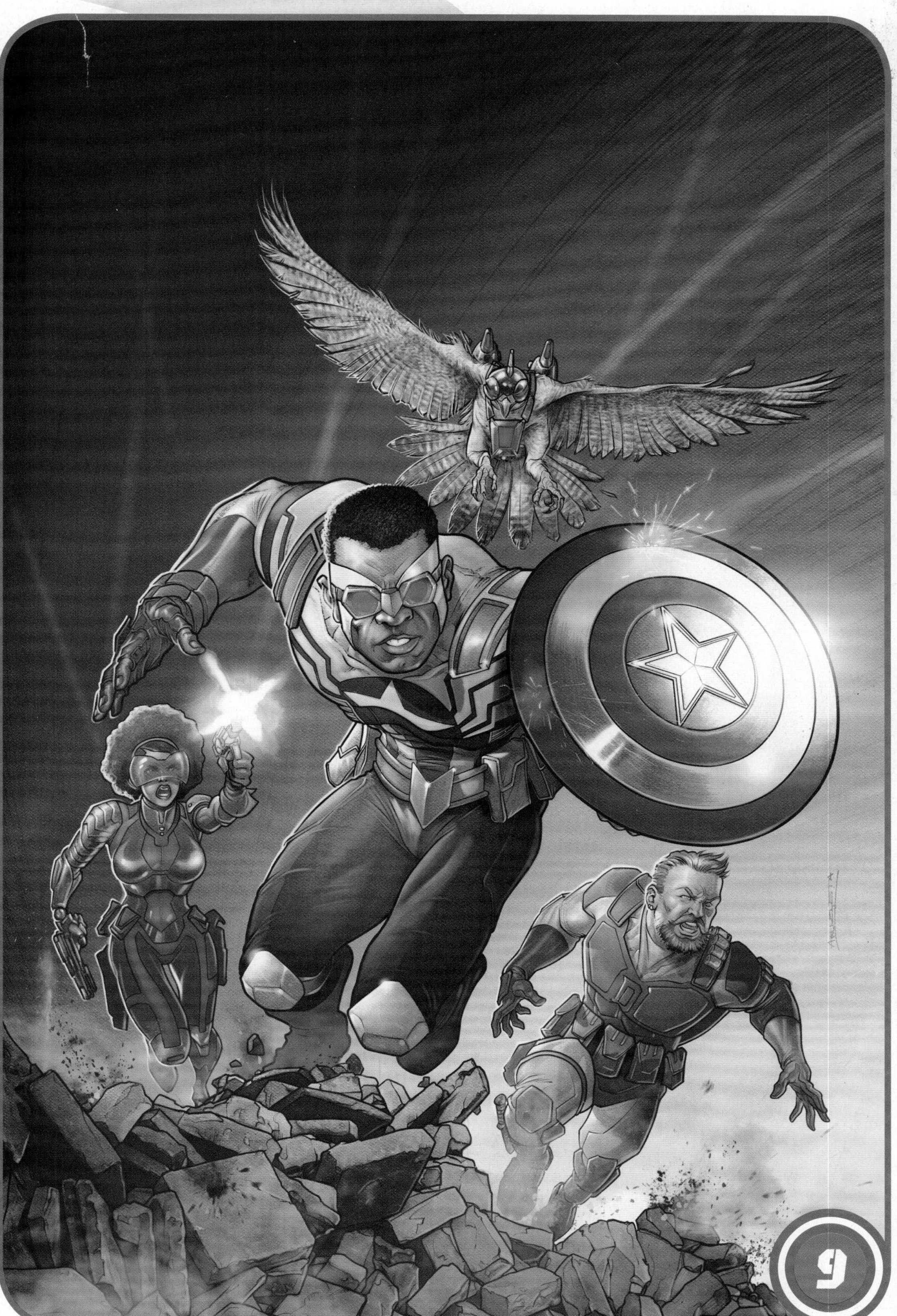

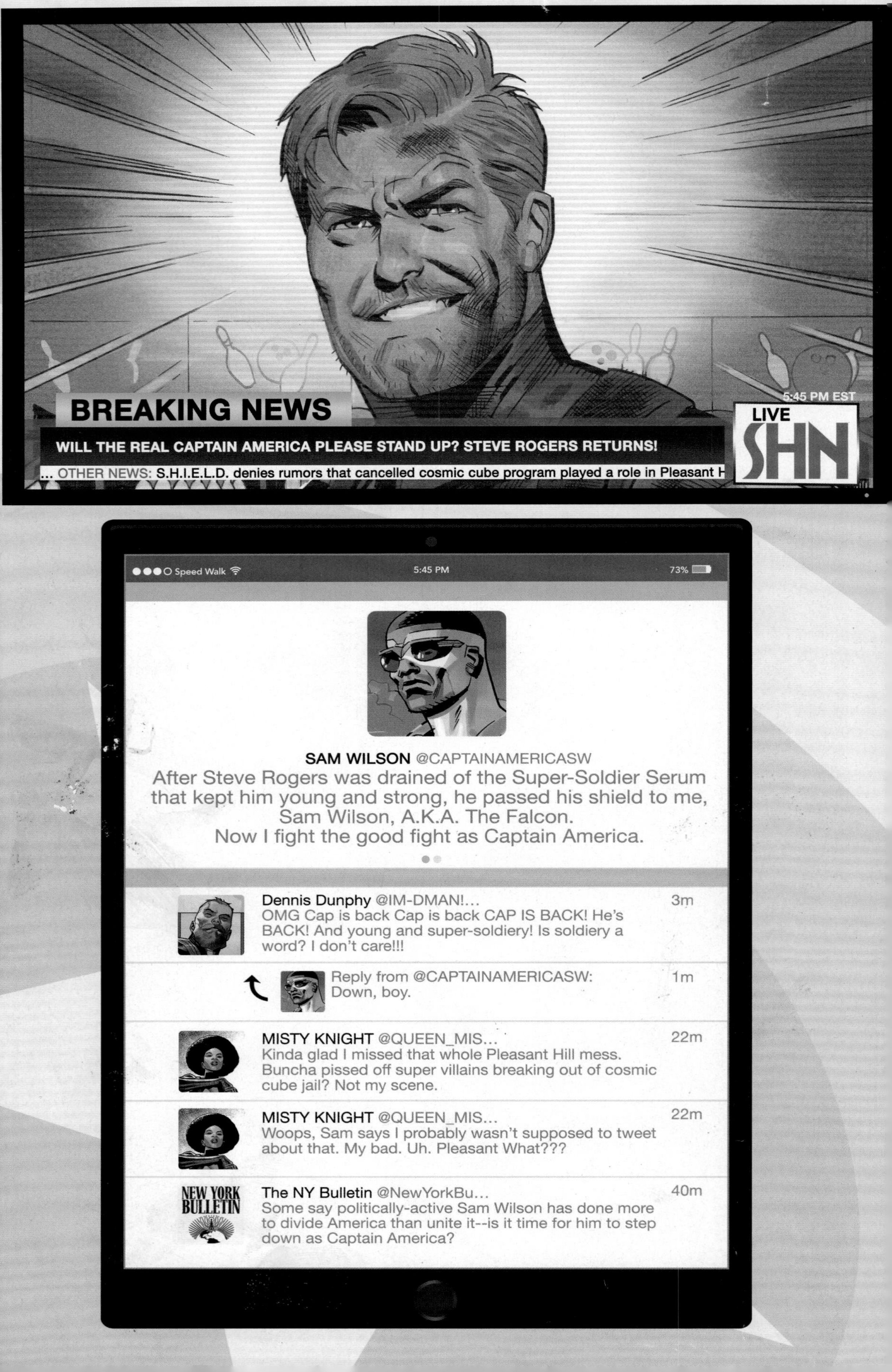

BREAKING NEWS
WILL THE REAL CAPTAIN AMERICA PLEASE STAND UP? STEVE ROGERS RETURNS!
... OTHER NEWS: S.H.I.E.L.D. denies rumors that cancelled cosmic cube program played a role in Pleasant H
5:45 PM EST
LIVE
SHN
Speed Walk
5:45 PM
73%
SAM WILSON @CAPTAINAMERICASW
After Steve Rogers was drained of the Super-Soldier Serum that kept him young and strong, he passed his shield to me, Sam Wilson, A.K.A. The Falcon.
Now I fight the good fight as Captain America.
Dennis Dunphy @IM-DMAN!... 3m
OMG Cap is back Cap is back CAP IS BACK! He's BACK! And young and super-soldiery! Is soldiery a word? I don't care!!!
Reply from @CAPTAINAMERICASW: 1m
Down, boy.
MISTY KNIGHT @QUEEN_MIS... 22m
Kinda glad I missed that whole Pleasant Hill mess. Buncha pissed off super villains breaking out of cosmic cube jail? Not my scene.
MISTY KNIGHT @QUEEN_MIS... 22m
Woops, Sam says I probably wasn't supposed to tweet about that. My bad. Uh. Pleasant What???
NEW YORK BULLETIN
The NY Bulletin @NewYorkBu... 40m
Some say politically-active Sam Wilson has done more to divide America than unite it--is it time for him to step down as Captain America?

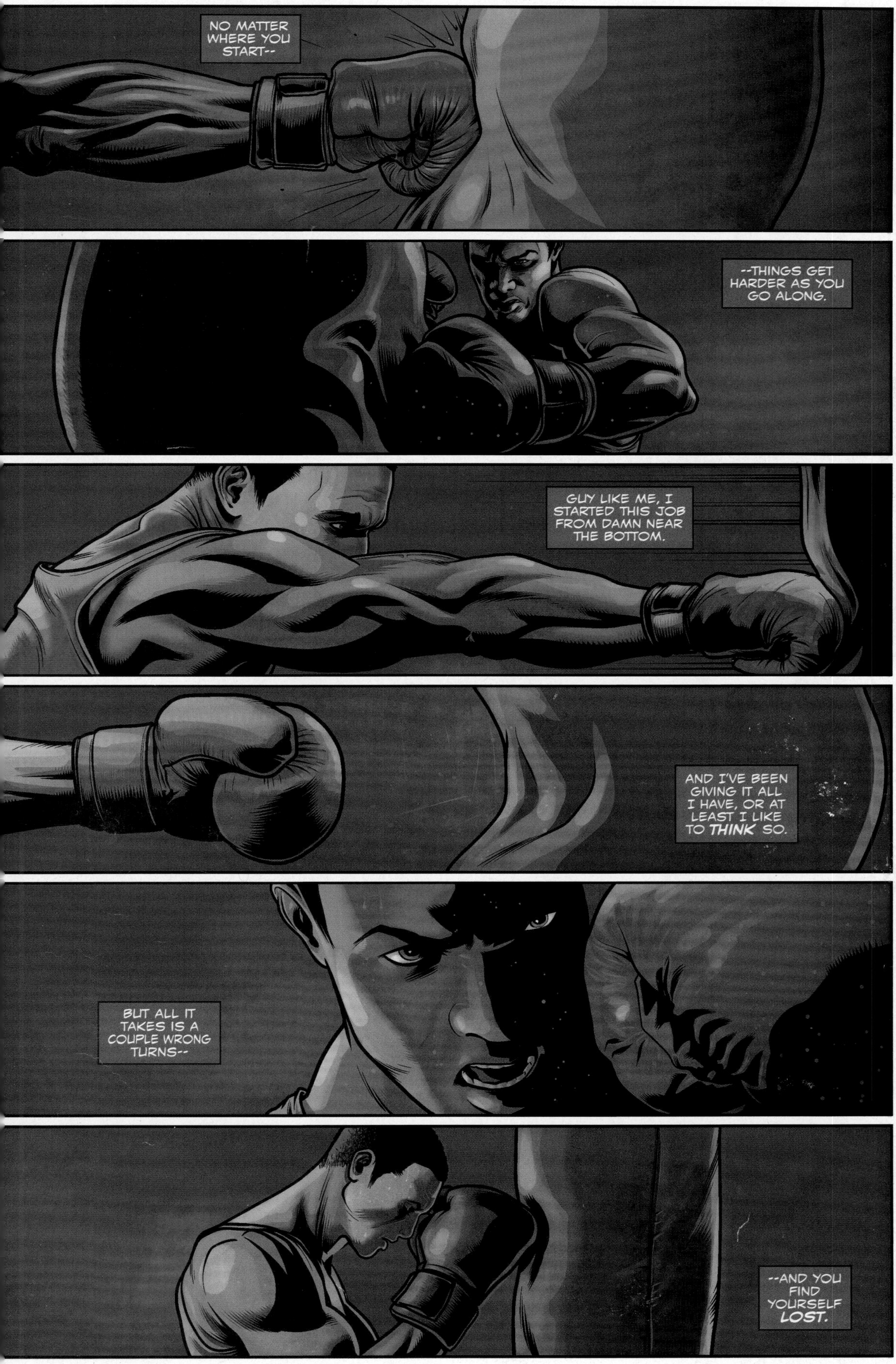

NO MATTER WHERE YOU START--
--THINGS GET HARDER AS YOU GO ALONG.
GUY LIKE ME, I STARTED THIS JOB FROM DAMN NEAR THE BOTTOM.
AND I'VE BEEN GIVING IT ALL I HAVE, OR AT LEAST I LIKE TO *THINK* SO.
BUT ALL IT TAKES IS A COUPLE WRONG TURNS--
--AND YOU FIND YOURSELF *LOST.*

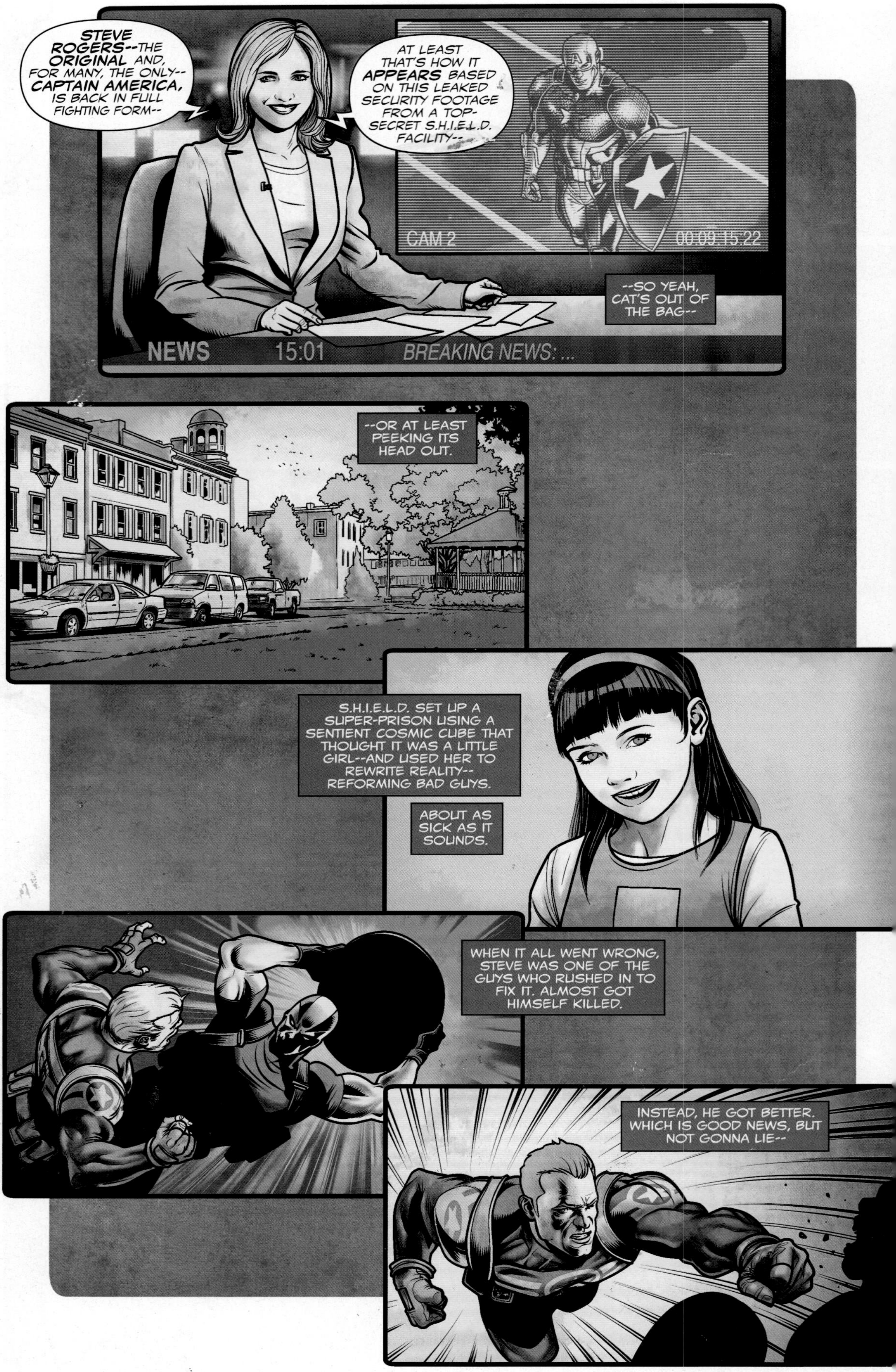
STEVE ROGERS--THE ORIGINAL AND, FOR MANY, THE ONLY--CAPTAIN AMERICA, IS BACK IN FULL FIGHTING FORM--
AT LEAST THAT'S HOW IT APPEARS BASED ON THIS LEAKED SECURITY FOOTAGE FROM A TOP-SECRET S.H.I.E.L.D. FACILITY--
CAM 2
00.09.15.22
--SO YEAH, CAT'S OUT OF THE BAG--
NEWS
15:01
BREAKING NEWS: ...
--OR AT LEAST PEEKING ITS HEAD OUT.
S.H.I.E.L.D. SET UP A SUPER-PRISON USING A SENTIENT COSMIC CUBE THAT THOUGHT IT WAS A LITTLE GIRL--AND USED HER TO REWRITE REALITY--REFORMING BAD GUYS.
ABOUT AS SICK AS IT SOUNDS.
WHEN IT ALL WENT WRONG, STEVE WAS ONE OF THE GUYS WHO RUSHED IN TO FIX IT. ALMOST GOT HIMSELF KILLED.
INSTEAD, HE GOT BETTER. WHICH IS GOOD NEWS, BUT NOT GONNA LIE--

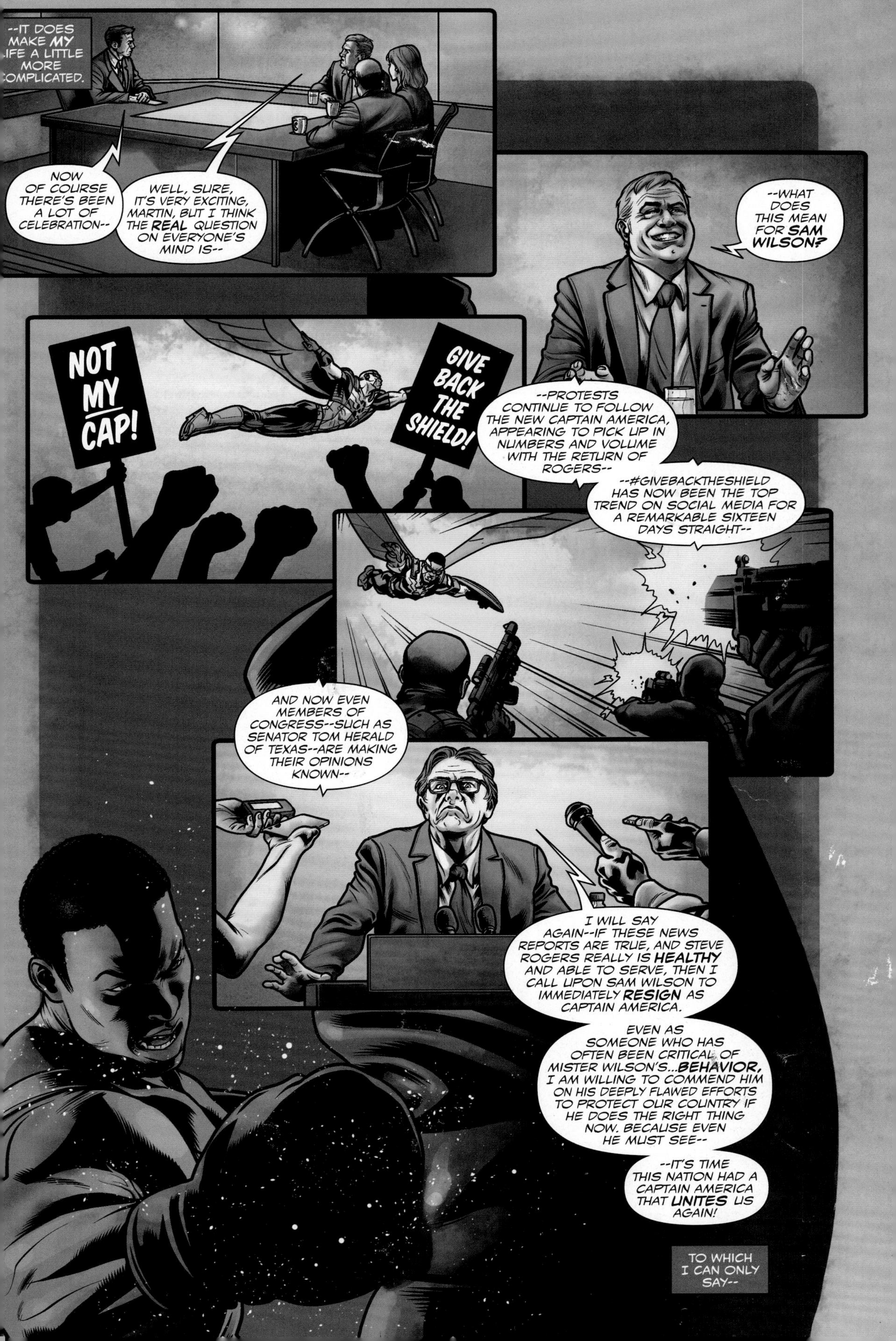
--IT DOES MAKE MY LIFE A LITTLE MORE COMPLICATED.
NOW OF COURSE THERE'S BEEN A LOT OF CELEBRATION--
WELL, SURE, IT'S VERY EXCITING, MARTIN, BUT I THINK THE REAL QUESTION ON EVERYONE'S MIND IS--
--WHAT DOES THIS MEAN FOR SAM WILSON?
NOT MY CAP!
GIVE BACK THE SHIELD!
--PROTESTS CONTINUE TO FOLLOW THE NEW CAPTAIN AMERICA, APPEARING TO PICK UP IN NUMBERS AND VOLUME WITH THE RETURN OF ROGERS--
--#GIVEBACKTHESHIELD HAS NOW BEEN THE TOP TREND ON SOCIAL MEDIA FOR A REMARKABLE SIXTEEN DAYS STRAIGHT--
AND NOW EVEN MEMBERS OF CONGRESS--SUCH AS SENATOR TOM HERALD OF TEXAS--ARE MAKING THEIR OPINIONS KNOWN--
I WILL SAY AGAIN--IF THESE NEWS REPORTS ARE TRUE, AND STEVE ROGERS REALLY IS HEALTHY AND ABLE TO SERVE, THEN I CALL UPON SAM WILSON TO IMMEDIATELY RESIGN AS CAPTAIN AMERICA.
EVEN AS SOMEONE WHO HAS OFTEN BEEN CRITICAL OF MISTER WILSON'S...BEHAVIOR, I AM WILLING TO COMMEND HIM ON HIS DEEPLY FLAWED EFFORTS TO PROTECT OUR COUNTRY IF HE DOES THE RIGHT THING NOW. BECAUSE EVEN HE MUST SEE--
--IT'S TIME THIS NATION HAD A CAPTAIN AMERICA THAT UNITES US AGAIN!
TO WHICH I CAN ONLY SAY--

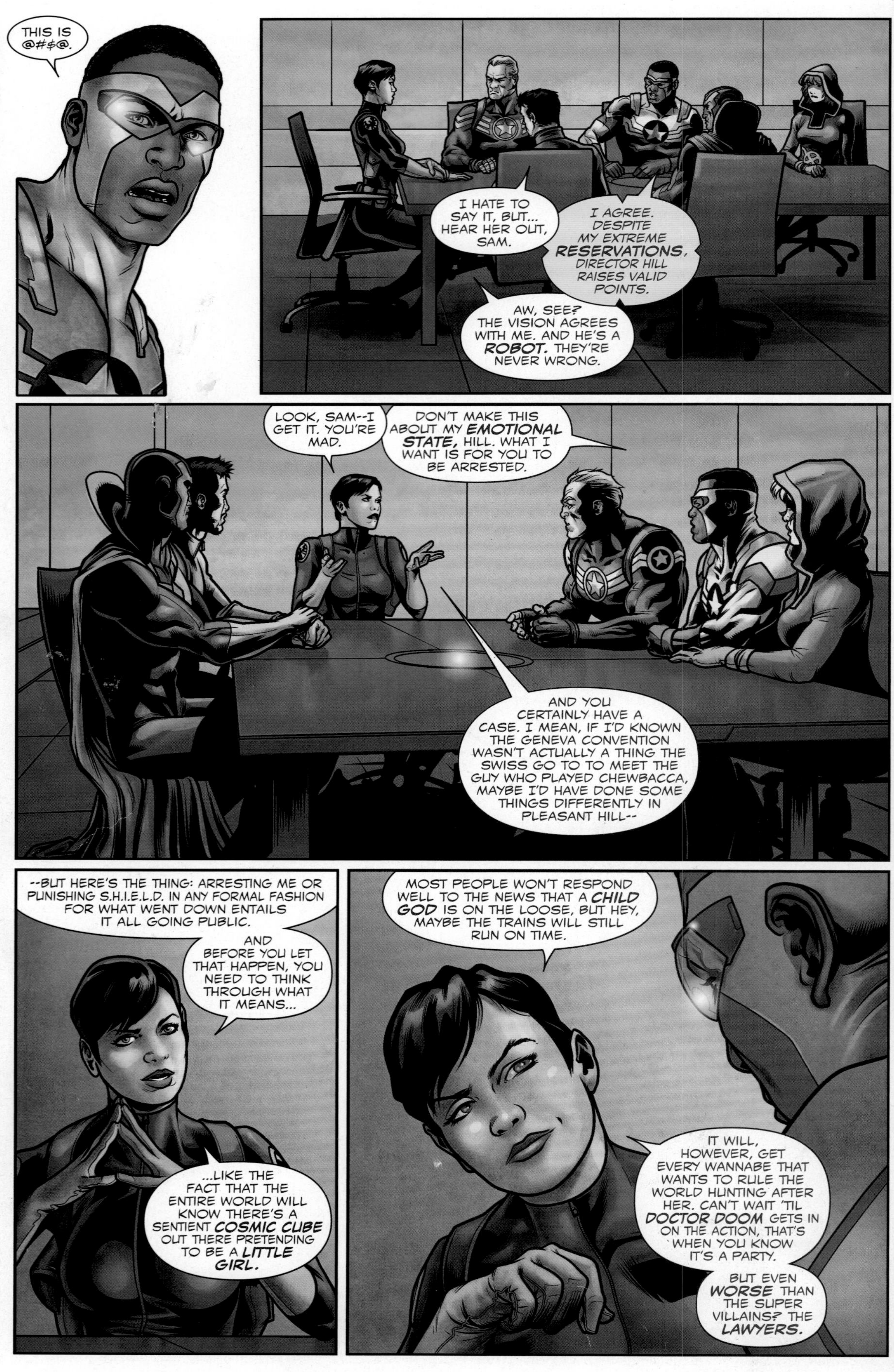
THIS IS @#$@.
I HATE TO SAY IT, BUT... HEAR HER OUT, SAM.
I AGREE. DESPITE MY EXTREME RESERVATIONS, DIRECTOR HILL RAISES VALID POINTS.
AW, SEE? THE VISION AGREES WITH ME. AND HE'S A ROBOT. THEY'RE NEVER WRONG.
LOOK, SAM--I GET IT. YOU'RE MAD.
DON'T MAKE THIS ABOUT MY EMOTIONAL STATE, HILL. WHAT I WANT IS FOR YOU TO BE ARRESTED.
AND YOU CERTAINLY HAVE A CASE. I MEAN, IF I'D KNOWN THE GENEVA CONVENTION WASN'T ACTUALLY A THING THE SWISS GO TO TO MEET THE GUY WHO PLAYED CHEWBACCA, MAYBE I'D HAVE DONE SOME THINGS DIFFERENTLY IN PLEASANT HILL--
--BUT HERE'S THE THING: ARRESTING ME OR PUNISHING S.H.I.E.L.D. IN ANY FORMAL FASHION FOR WHAT WENT DOWN ENTAILS IT ALL GOING PUBLIC.
AND BEFORE YOU LET THAT HAPPEN, YOU NEED TO THINK THROUGH WHAT IT MEANS...
...LIKE THE FACT THAT THE ENTIRE WORLD WILL KNOW THERE'S A SENTIENT COSMIC CUBE OUT THERE PRETENDING TO BE A LITTLE GIRL.
MOST PEOPLE WON'T RESPOND WELL TO THE NEWS THAT A CHILD GOD IS ON THE LOOSE, BUT HEY, MAYBE THE TRAINS WILL STILL RUN ON TIME.
IT WILL, HOWEVER, GET EVERY WANNABE THAT WANTS TO RULE THE WORLD HUNTING AFTER HER. CAN'T WAIT 'TIL DOCTOR DOOM GETS IN ON THE ACTION, THAT'S WHEN YOU KNOW IT'S A PARTY.
BUT EVEN WORSE THAN THE SUPER VILLAINS? THE LAWYERS.

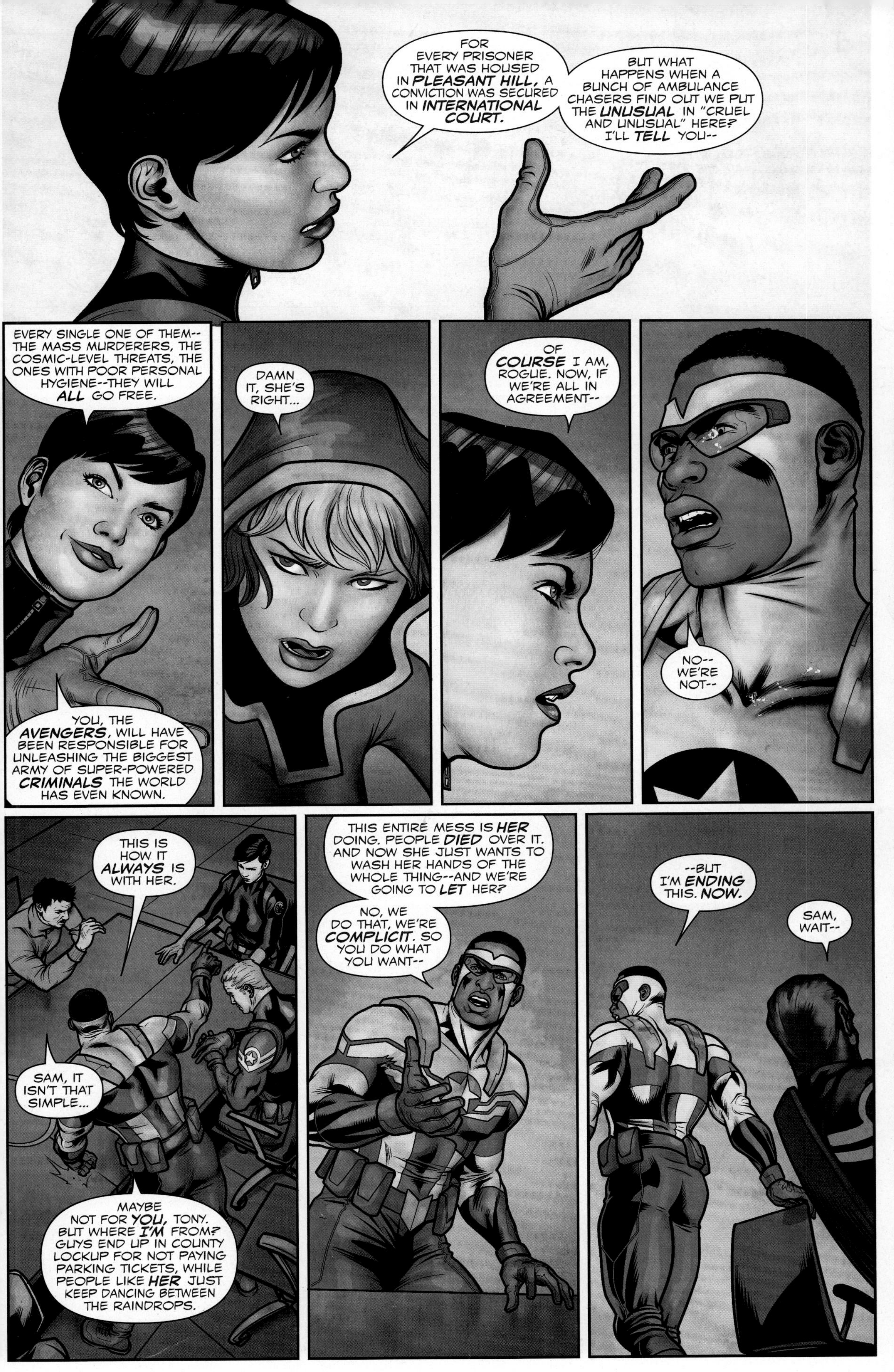
FOR EVERY PRISONER THAT WAS HOUSED IN PLEASANT HILL, A CONVICTION WAS SECURED IN INTERNATIONAL COURT.
BUT WHAT HAPPENS WHEN A BUNCH OF AMBULANCE CHASERS FIND OUT WE PUT THE UNUSUAL IN "CRUEL AND UNUSUAL" HERE? I'LL TELL YOU--
EVERY SINGLE ONE OF THEM--THE MASS MURDERERS, THE COSMIC-LEVEL THREATS, THE ONES WITH POOR PERSONAL HYGIENE--THEY WILL ALL GO FREE.
YOU, THE AVENGERS, WILL HAVE BEEN RESPONSIBLE FOR UNLEASHING THE BIGGEST ARMY OF SUPER-POWERED CRIMINALS THE WORLD HAS EVEN KNOWN.
DAMN IT, SHE'S RIGHT...
OF COURSE I AM, ROGUE. NOW, IF WE'RE ALL IN AGREEMENT--
NO-- WE'RE NOT--
THIS IS HOW IT ALWAYS IS WITH HER.
SAM, IT ISN'T THAT SIMPLE...
MAYBE NOT FOR YOU, TONY. BUT WHERE I'M FROM? GUYS END UP IN COUNTY LOCKUP FOR NOT PAYING PARKING TICKETS, WHILE PEOPLE LIKE HER JUST KEEP DANCING BETWEEN THE RAINDROPS.
THIS ENTIRE MESS IS HER DOING. PEOPLE DIED OVER IT. AND NOW SHE JUST WANTS TO WASH HER HANDS OF THE WHOLE THING--AND WE'RE GOING TO LET HER?
NO, WE DO THAT, WE'RE COMPLICIT. SO YOU DO WHAT YOU WANT--
--BUT I'M ENDING THIS. NOW.
SAM, WAIT--

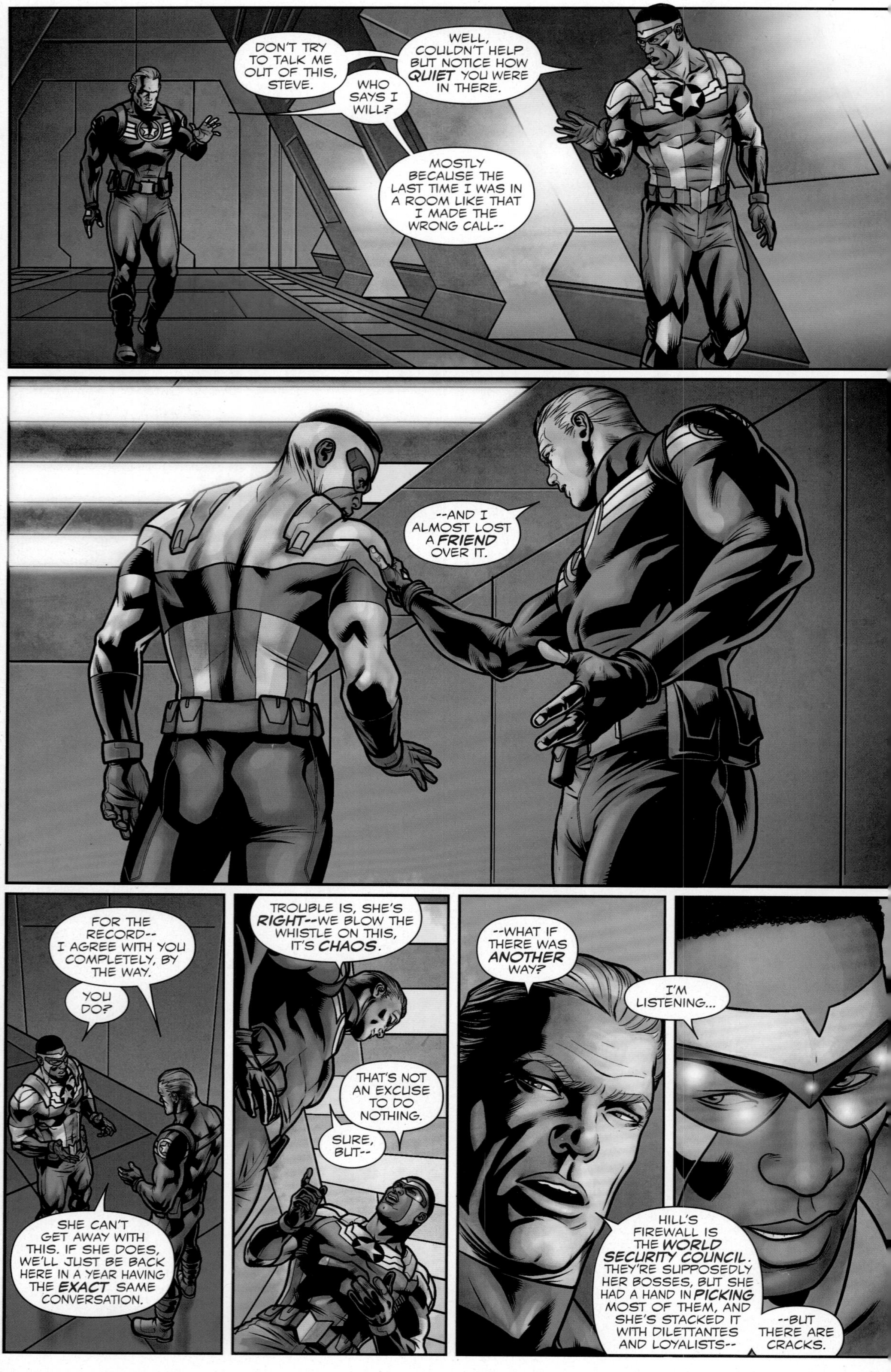
DON'T TRY TO TALK ME OUT OF THIS, STEVE.
WHO SAYS I WILL?
WELL, COULDN'T HELP BUT NOTICE HOW QUIET YOU WERE IN THERE.
MOSTLY BECAUSE THE LAST TIME I WAS IN A ROOM LIKE THAT I MADE THE WRONG CALL--
--AND I ALMOST LOST A FRIEND OVER IT.
FOR THE RECORD-- I AGREE WITH YOU COMPLETELY, BY THE WAY.
YOU DO?
SHE CAN'T GET AWAY WITH THIS. IF SHE DOES, WE'LL JUST BE BACK HERE IN A YEAR HAVING THE EXACT SAME CONVERSATION.
TROUBLE IS, SHE'S RIGHT--WE BLOW THE WHISTLE ON THIS, IT'S CHAOS.
THAT'S NOT AN EXCUSE TO DO NOTHING.
SURE, BUT--
--WHAT IF THERE WAS ANOTHER WAY?
I'M LISTENING...
HILL'S FIREWALL IS THE WORLD SECURITY COUNCIL. THEY'RE SUPPOSEDLY HER BOSSES, BUT SHE HAD A HAND IN PICKING MOST OF THEM, AND SHE'S STACKED IT WITH DILETTANTES AND LOYALISTS--
--BUT THERE ARE CRACKS.

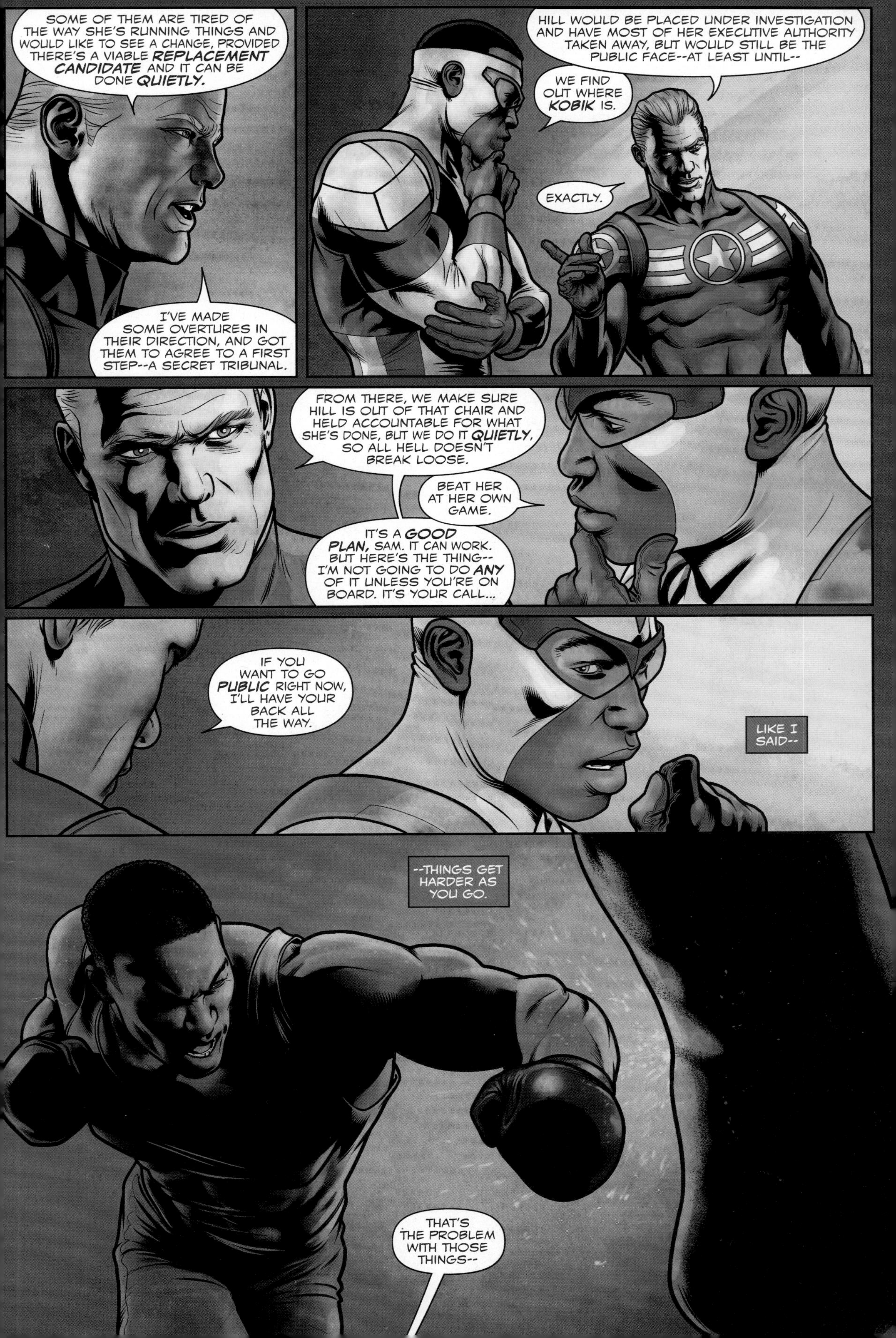
SOME OF THEM ARE TIRED OF THE WAY SHE'S RUNNING THINGS AND WOULD LIKE TO SEE A CHANGE, PROVIDED THERE'S A VIABLE REPLACEMENT CANDIDATE AND IT CAN BE DONE QUIETLY.
I'VE MADE SOME OVERTURES IN THEIR DIRECTION, AND GOT THEM TO AGREE TO A FIRST STEP--A SECRET TRIBUNAL.
HILL WOULD BE PLACED UNDER INVESTIGATION AND HAVE MOST OF HER EXECUTIVE AUTHORITY TAKEN AWAY, BUT WOULD STILL BE THE PUBLIC FACE--AT LEAST UNTIL--
WE FIND OUT WHERE KOBIK IS.
EXACTLY.
FROM THERE, WE MAKE SURE HILL IS OUT OF THAT CHAIR AND HELD ACCOUNTABLE FOR WHAT SHE'S DONE, BUT WE DO IT QUIETLY, SO ALL HELL DOESN'T BREAK LOOSE.
BEAT HER AT HER OWN GAME.
IT'S A GOOD PLAN, SAM. IT CAN WORK. BUT HERE'S THE THING-- I'M NOT GOING TO DO ANY OF IT UNLESS YOU'RE ON BOARD. IT'S YOUR CALL...
IF YOU WANT TO GO PUBLIC RIGHT NOW, I'LL HAVE YOUR BACK ALL THE WAY.
LIKE I SAID--
--THINGS GET HARDER AS YOU GO.
THAT'S THE PROBLEM WITH THOSE THINGS--

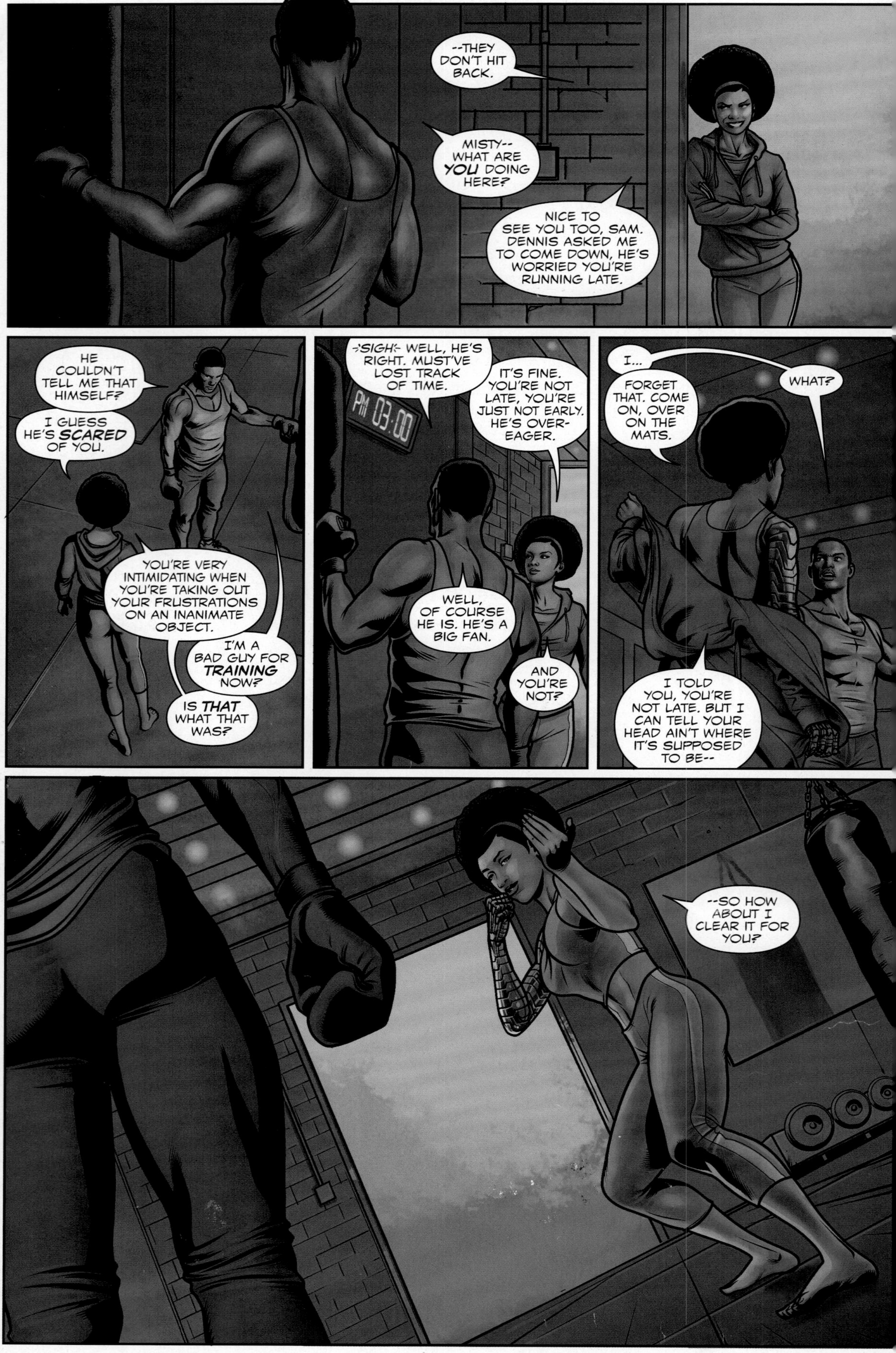
--THEY DON'T HIT BACK.
MISTY-- WHAT ARE YOU DOING HERE?
NICE TO SEE YOU TOO, SAM. DENNIS ASKED ME TO COME DOWN, HE'S WORRIED YOU'RE RUNNING LATE.
HE COULDN'T TELL ME THAT HIMSELF?
I GUESS HE'S SCARED OF YOU.
YOU'RE VERY INTIMIDATING WHEN YOU'RE TAKING OUT YOUR FRUSTRATIONS ON AN INANIMATE OBJECT.
I'M A BAD GUY FOR TRAINING NOW?
IS THAT WHAT THAT WAS?
-SIGH- WELL, HE'S RIGHT. MUST'VE LOST TRACK OF TIME.
PM 03:00
IT'S FINE. YOU'RE NOT LATE, YOU'RE JUST NOT EARLY. HE'S OVER-EAGER.
WELL, OF COURSE HE IS. HE'S A BIG FAN.
AND YOU'RE NOT?
I...
WHAT?
FORGET THAT. COME ON, OVER ON THE MATS.
I TOLD YOU, YOU'RE NOT LATE. BUT I CAN TELL YOUR HEAD AIN'T WHERE IT'S SUPPOSED TO BE--
--SO HOW ABOUT I CLEAR IT FOR YOU?

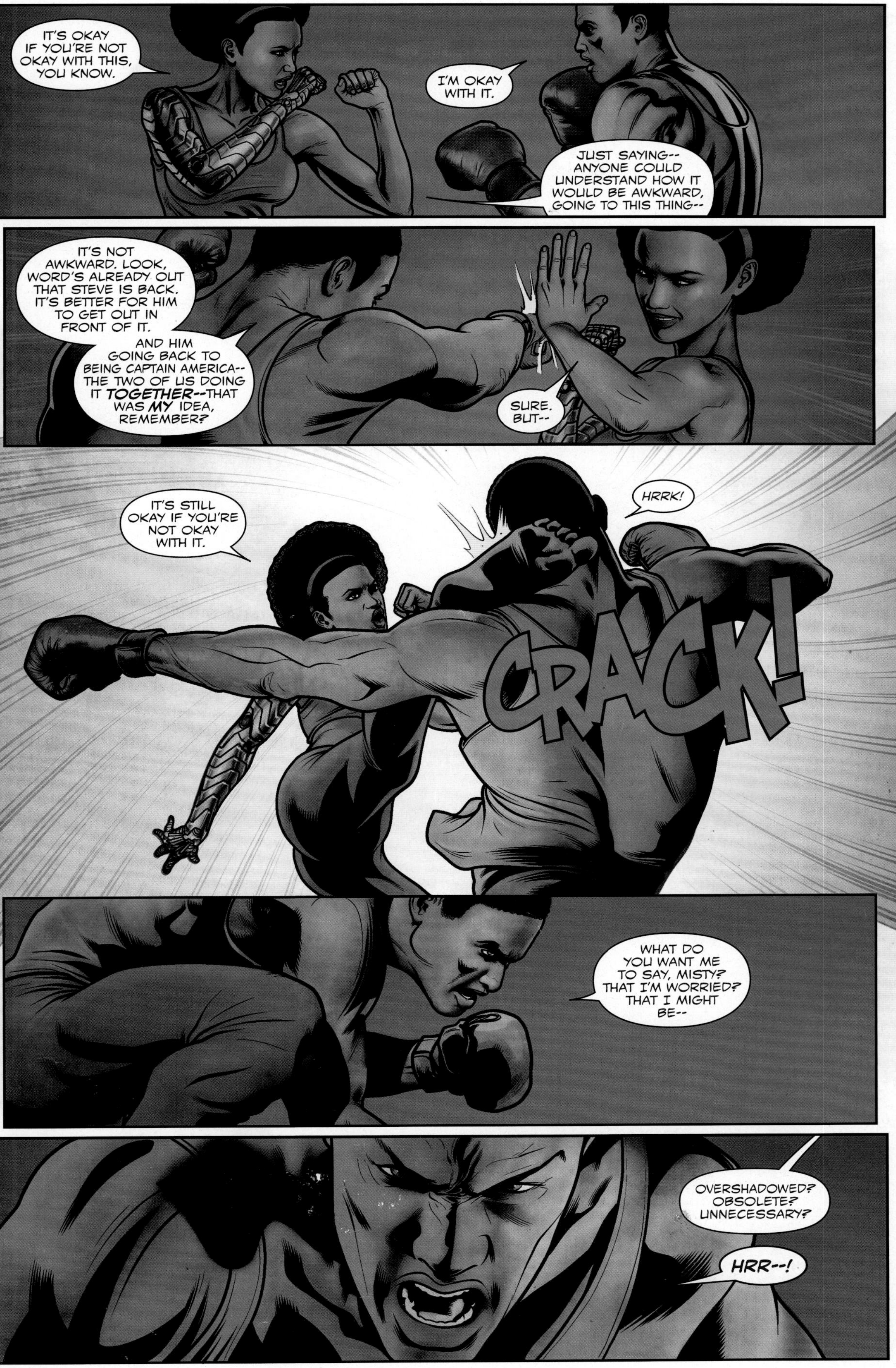
IT'S OKAY IF YOU'RE NOT OKAY WITH THIS, YOU KNOW.
I'M OKAY WITH IT.
JUST SAYING-- ANYONE COULD UNDERSTAND HOW IT WOULD BE AWKWARD, GOING TO THIS THING--
IT'S NOT AWKWARD. LOOK, WORD'S ALREADY OUT THAT STEVE IS BACK. IT'S BETTER FOR HIM TO GET OUT IN FRONT OF IT.
AND HIM GOING BACK TO BEING CAPTAIN AMERICA-- THE TWO OF US DOING IT TOGETHER--THAT WAS MY IDEA, REMEMBER?
SURE. BUT--
IT'S STILL OKAY IF YOU'RE NOT OKAY WITH IT.
HRRK!
CRACK!
WHAT DO YOU WANT ME TO SAY, MISTY? THAT I'M WORRIED? THAT I MIGHT BE--
OVERSHADOWED? OBSOLETE? UNNECESSARY?
HRR--!

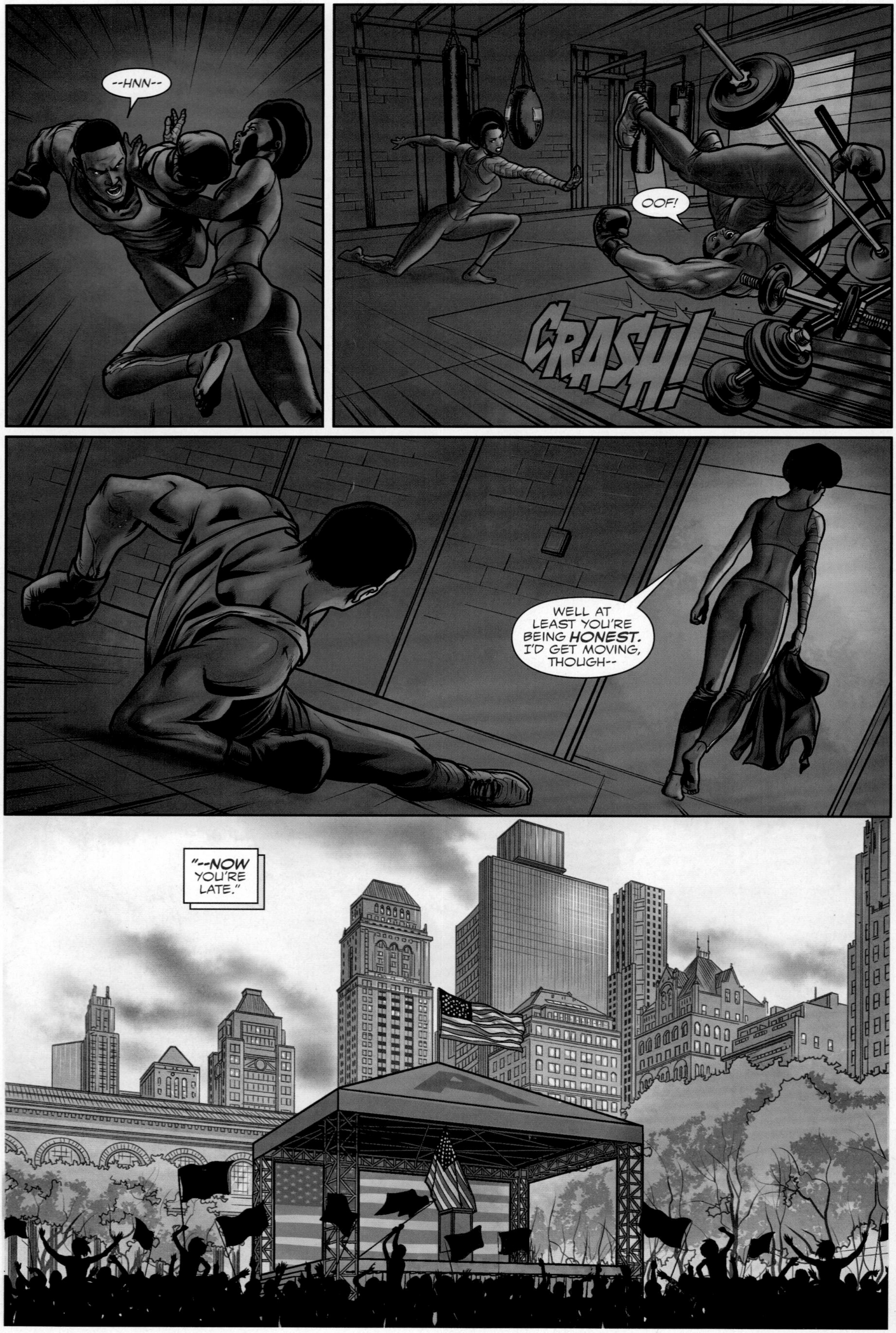
--HNN--
OOF!
CRASH!
WELL AT LEAST YOU'RE BEING HONEST. I'D GET MOVING, THOUGH--
"--NOW YOU'RE LATE."

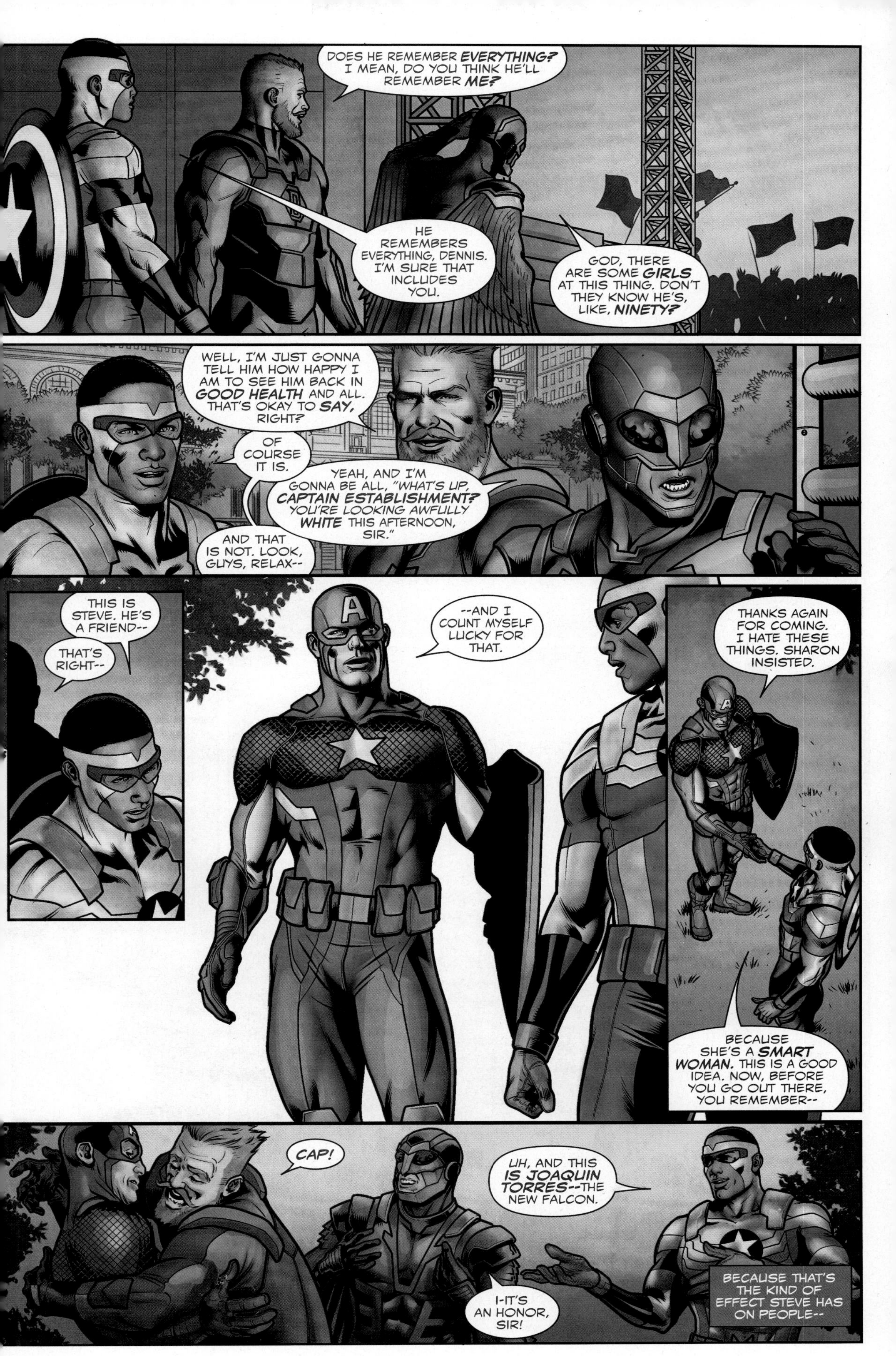

DOES HE REMEMBER EVERYTHING? I MEAN, DO YOU THINK HE'LL REMEMBER ME?
HE REMEMBERS EVERYTHING, DENNIS. I'M SURE THAT INCLUDES YOU.
GOD, THERE ARE SOME GIRLS AT THIS THING. DON'T THEY KNOW HE'S, LIKE, NINETY?
WELL, I'M JUST GONNA TELL HIM HOW HAPPY I AM TO SEE HIM BACK IN GOOD HEALTH AND ALL. THAT'S OKAY TO SAY, RIGHT?
OF COURSE IT IS.
YEAH, AND I'M GONNA BE ALL, "WHAT'S UP, CAPTAIN ESTABLISHMENT? YOU'RE LOOKING AWFULLY WHITE THIS AFTERNOON, SIR."
AND THAT IS NOT. LOOK, GUYS, RELAX--
THIS IS STEVE. HE'S A FRIEND--
THAT'S RIGHT--
--AND I COUNT MYSELF LUCKY FOR THAT.
THANKS AGAIN FOR COMING. I HATE THESE THINGS. SHARON INSISTED.
BECAUSE SHE'S A SMART WOMAN. THIS IS A GOOD IDEA. NOW, BEFORE YOU GO OUT THERE, YOU REMEMBER--
CAP!
UH, AND THIS IS JOAQUIN TORRES--THE NEW FALCON.
I-IT'S AN HONOR, SIR!
BECAUSE THAT'S THE KIND OF EFFECT STEVE HAS ON PEOPLE--

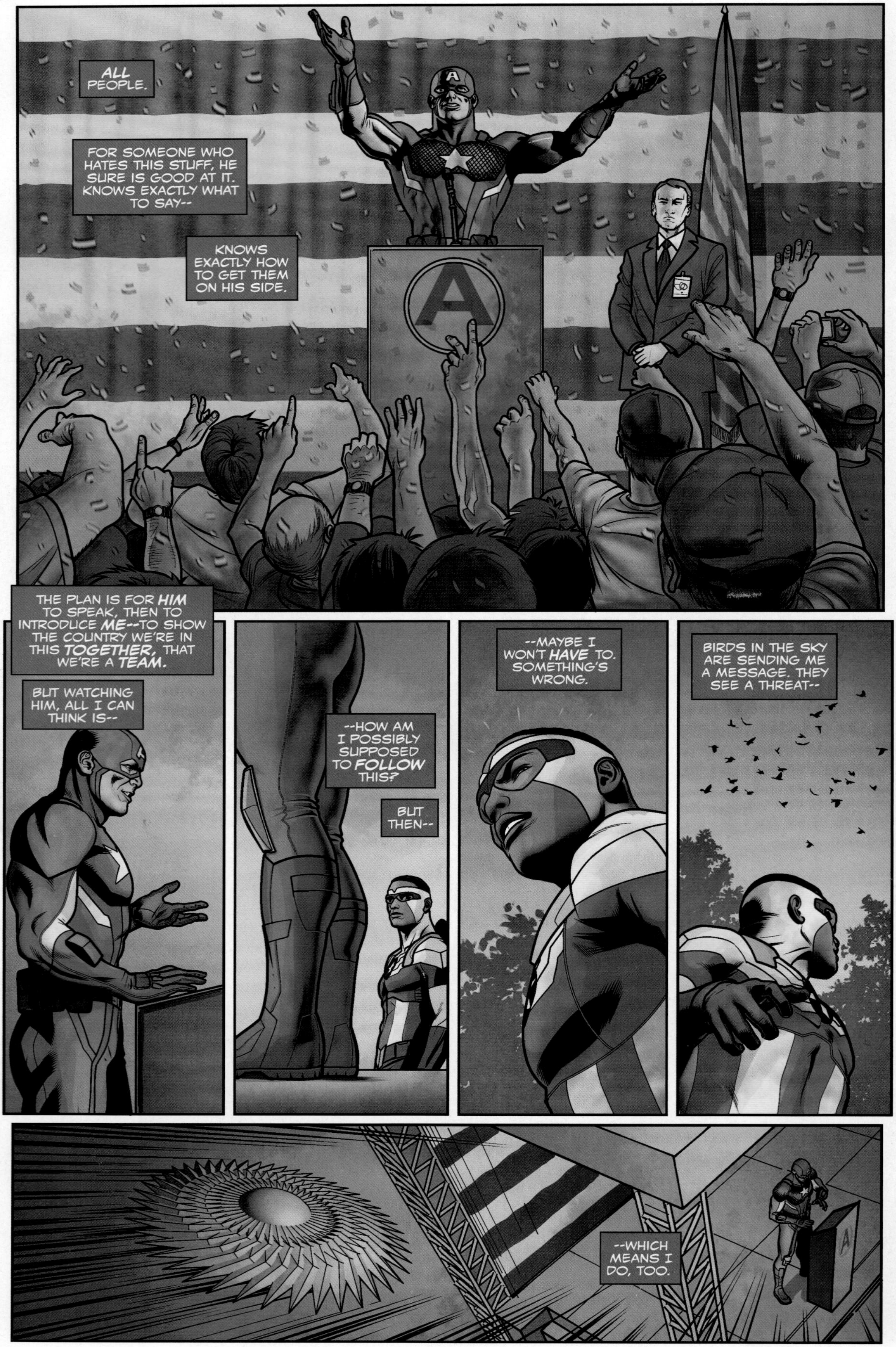
ALL PEOPLE.
FOR SOMEONE WHO HATES THIS STUFF, HE SURE IS GOOD AT IT. KNOWS EXACTLY WHAT TO SAY--
KNOWS EXACTLY HOW TO GET THEM ON HIS SIDE.
THE PLAN IS FOR HIM TO SPEAK, THEN TO INTRODUCE ME--TO SHOW THE COUNTRY WE'RE IN THIS TOGETHER, THAT WE'RE A TEAM.
BUT WATCHING HIM, ALL I CAN THINK IS--
--HOW AM I POSSIBLY SUPPOSED TO FOLLOW THIS?
BUT THEN--
--MAYBE I WON'T HAVE TO. SOMETHING'S WRONG.
BIRDS IN THE SKY ARE SENDING ME A MESSAGE. THEY SEE A THREAT--
--WHICH MEANS I DO, TOO.

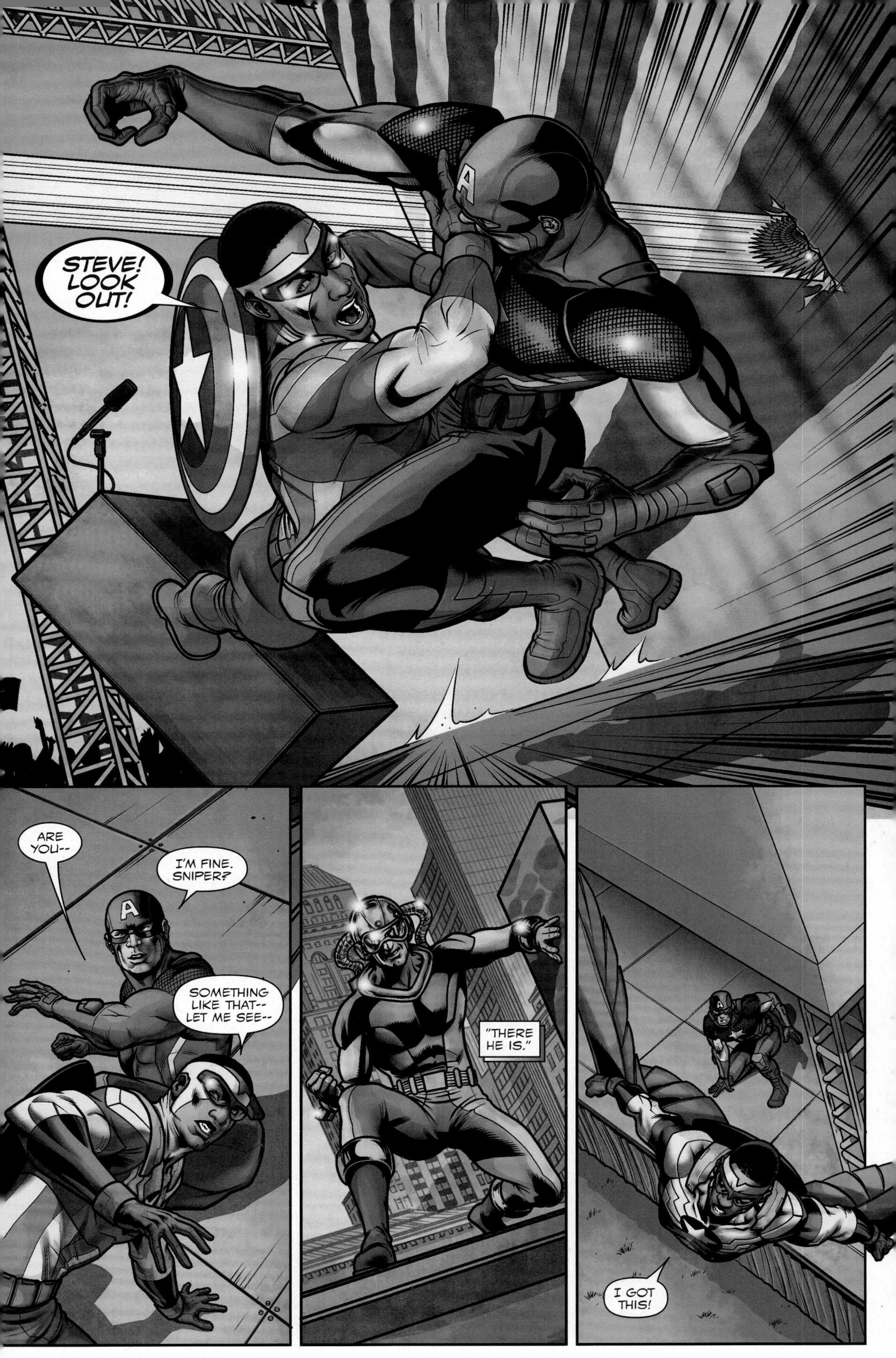
STEVE! LOOK OUT!
ARE YOU--
I'M FINE. SNIPER?
SOMETHING LIKE THAT-- LET ME SEE--
"THERE HE IS."
I GOT THIS!

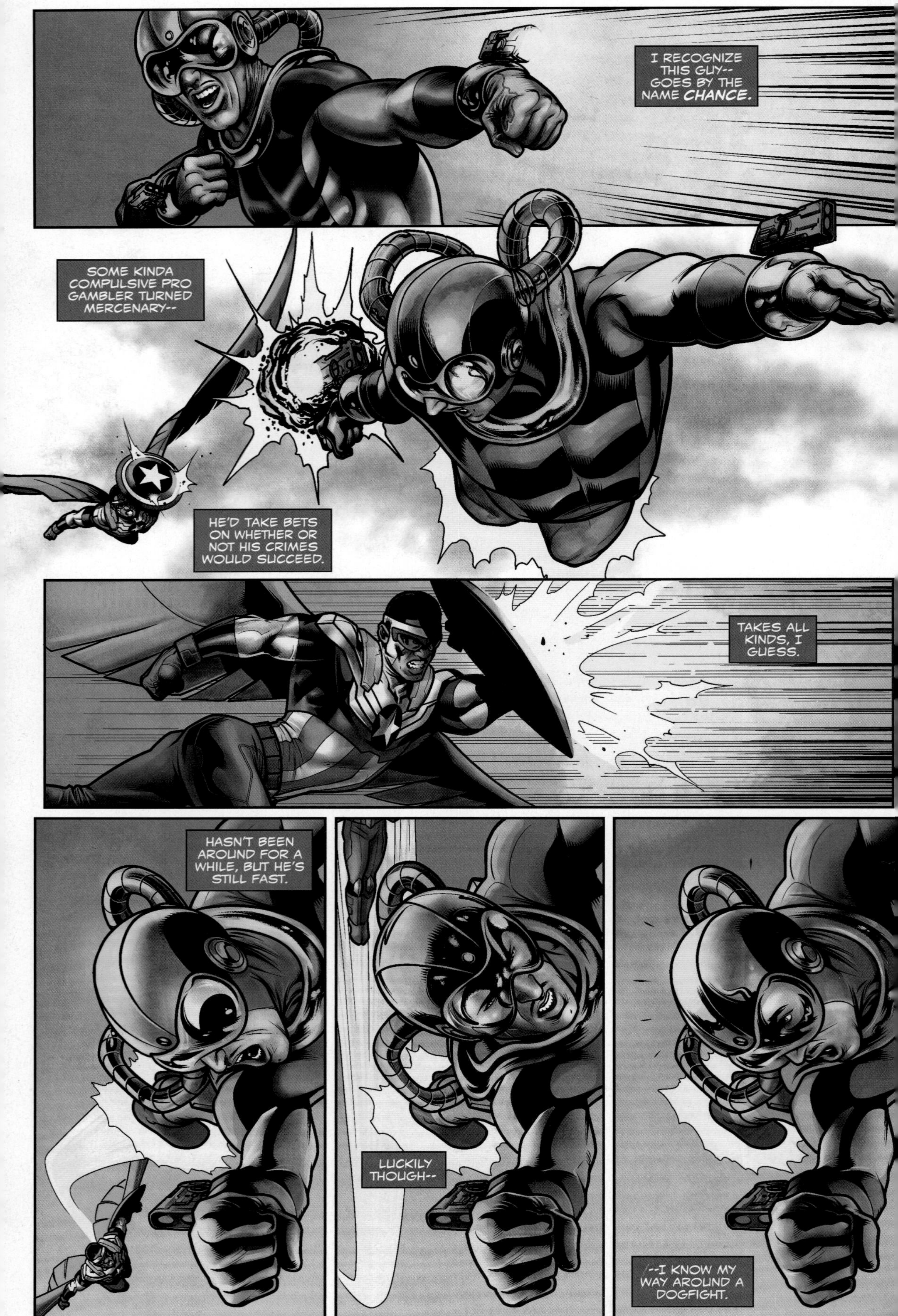
I RECOGNIZE THIS GUY-- GOES BY THE NAME CHANCE.
SOME KINDA COMPULSIVE PRO GAMBLER TURNED MERCENARY--
HE'D TAKE BETS ON WHETHER OR NOT HIS CRIMES WOULD SUCCEED.
TAKES ALL KINDS, I GUESS.
HASN'T BEEN AROUND FOR A WHILE, BUT HE'S STILL FAST.
LUCKILY THOUGH--
--I KNOW MY WAY AROUND A DOGFIGHT.

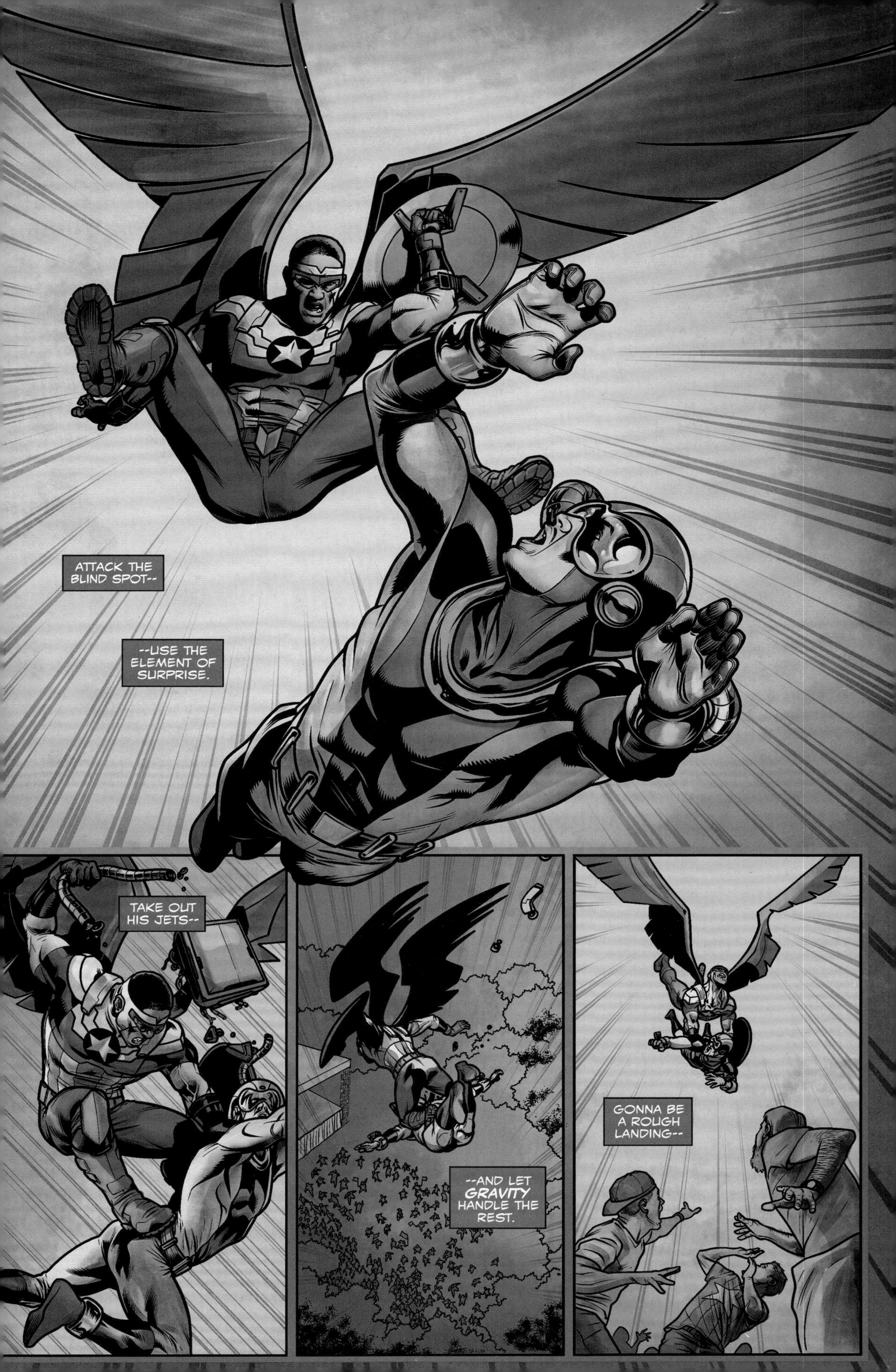
ATTACK THE BLIND SPOT--
--USE THE ELEMENT OF SURPRISE.
TAKE OUT HIS JETS--
--AND LET *GRAVITY* HANDLE THE REST.
GONNA BE A ROUGH LANDING--

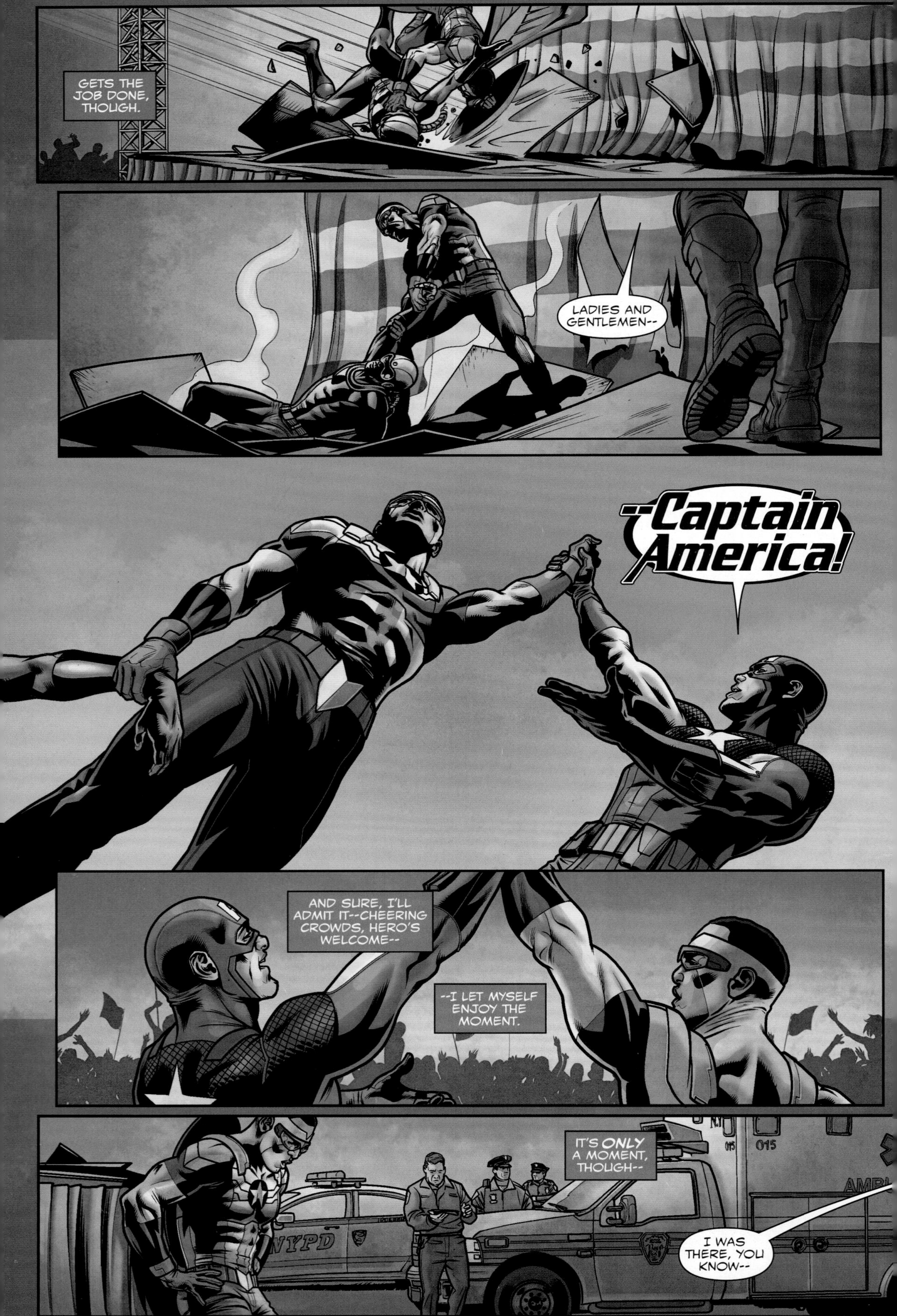
GETS THE JOB DONE, THOUGH.
LADIES AND GENTLEMEN--
--Captain America!
AND SURE, I'LL ADMIT IT--CHEERING CROWDS, HERO'S WELCOME--
--I LET MYSELF ENJOY THE MOMENT.
IT'S ONLY A MOMENT, THOUGH--
I WAS THERE, YOU KNOW--

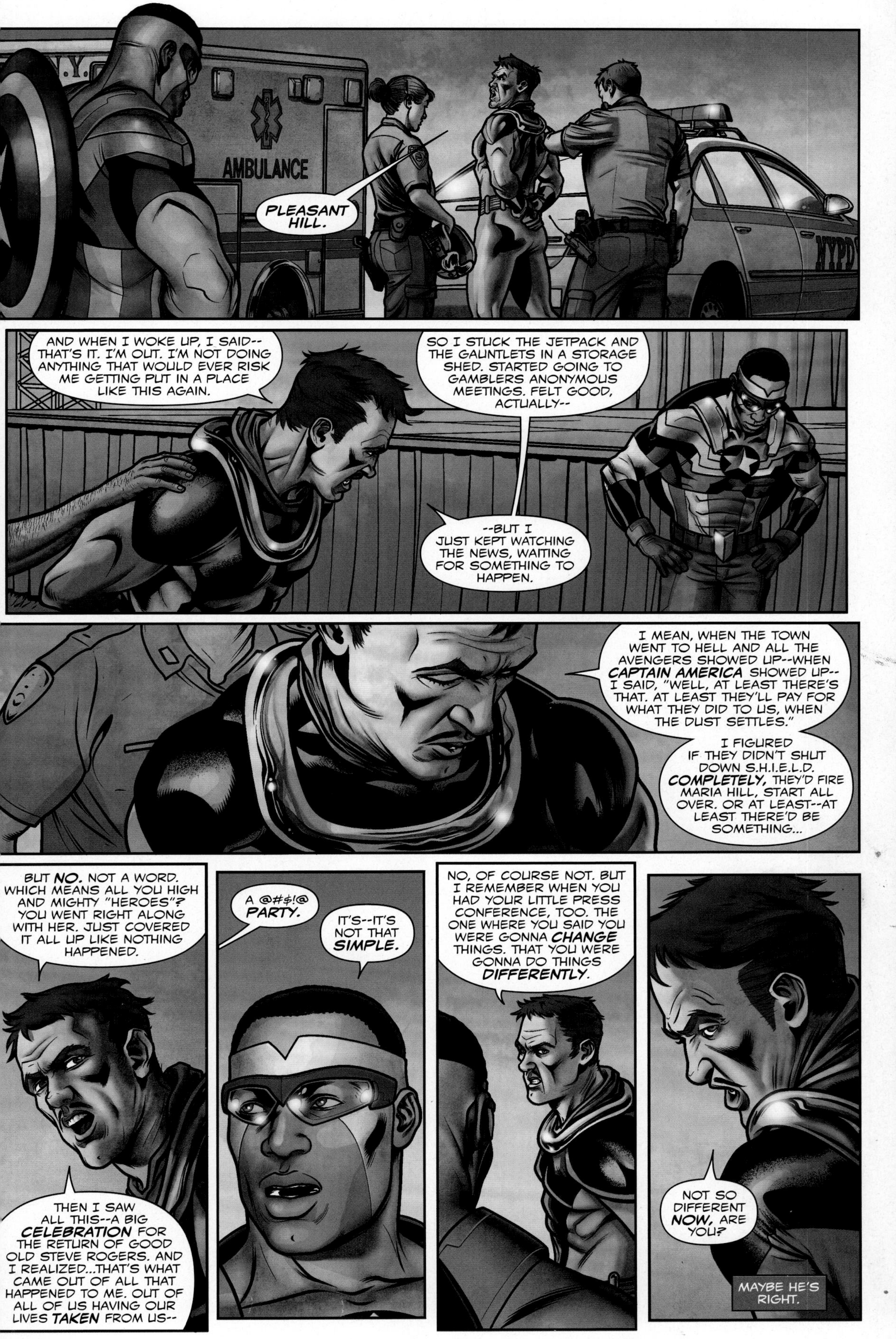
PLEASANT HILL.
AND WHEN I WOKE UP, I SAID-- THAT'S IT. I'M OUT. I'M NOT DOING ANYTHING THAT WOULD EVER RISK ME GETTING PUT IN A PLACE LIKE THIS AGAIN.
SO I STUCK THE JETPACK AND THE GAUNTLETS IN A STORAGE SHED. STARTED GOING TO GAMBLERS ANONYMOUS MEETINGS. FELT GOOD, ACTUALLY--
--BUT I JUST KEPT WATCHING THE NEWS, WAITING FOR SOMETHING TO HAPPEN.
I MEAN, WHEN THE TOWN WENT TO HELL AND ALL THE AVENGERS SHOWED UP--WHEN CAPTAIN AMERICA SHOWED UP-- I SAID, "WELL, AT LEAST THERE'S THAT. AT LEAST THEY'LL PAY FOR WHAT THEY DID TO US, WHEN THE DUST SETTLES."
I FIGURED IF THEY DIDN'T SHUT DOWN S.H.I.E.L.D. COMPLETELY, THEY'D FIRE MARIA HILL, START ALL OVER. OR AT LEAST--AT LEAST THERE'D BE SOMETHING...
BUT NO. NOT A WORD. WHICH MEANS ALL YOU HIGH AND MIGHTY "HEROES"? YOU WENT RIGHT ALONG WITH HER. JUST COVERED IT ALL UP LIKE NOTHING HAPPENED.
THEN I SAW ALL THIS--A BIG CELEBRATION FOR THE RETURN OF GOOD OLD STEVE ROGERS. AND I REALIZED...THAT'S WHAT CAME OUT OF ALL THAT HAPPENED TO ME. OUT OF ALL OF US HAVING OUR LIVES TAKEN FROM US--
A @#$!@ PARTY.
IT'S--IT'S NOT THAT SIMPLE.
NO, OF COURSE NOT. BUT I REMEMBER WHEN YOU HAD YOUR LITTLE PRESS CONFERENCE, TOO. THE ONE WHERE YOU SAID YOU WERE GONNA CHANGE THINGS. THAT YOU WERE GONNA DO THINGS DIFFERENTLY.
NOT SO DIFFERENT NOW, ARE YOU?
MAYBE HE'S RIGHT.

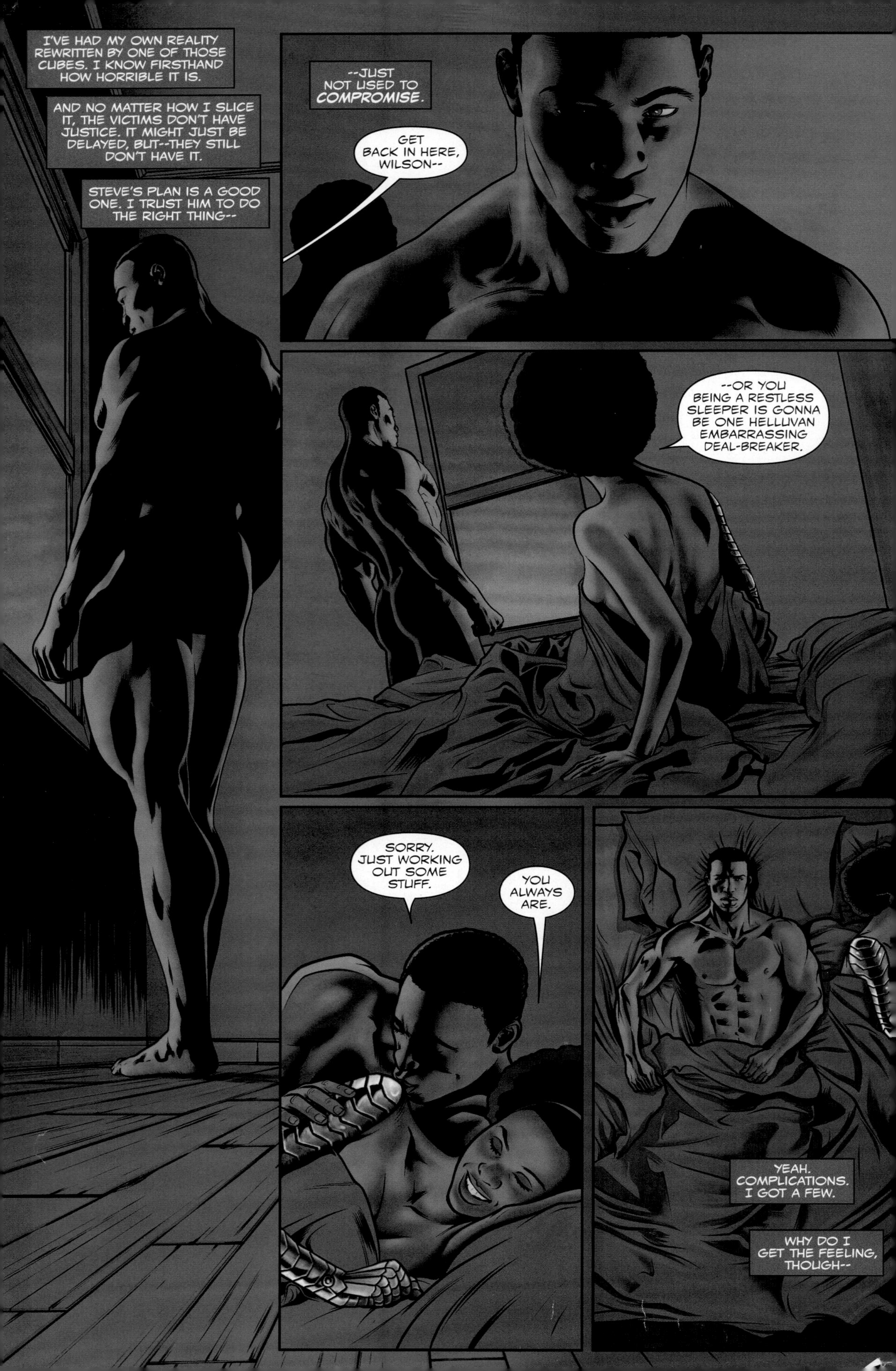
I'VE HAD MY OWN REALITY REWRITTEN BY ONE OF THOSE CUBES. I KNOW FIRSTHAND HOW HORRIBLE IT IS.
AND NO MATTER HOW I SLICE IT, THE VICTIMS DON'T HAVE JUSTICE. IT MIGHT JUST BE DELAYED, BUT--THEY STILL DON'T HAVE IT.
STEVE'S PLAN IS A GOOD ONE. I TRUST HIM TO DO THE RIGHT THING--
--JUST NOT USED TO *COMPROMISE*.
GET BACK IN HERE, WILSON--
--OR YOU BEING A RESTLESS SLEEPER IS GONNA BE ONE HELLUVAN EMBARRASSING DEAL-BREAKER.
SORRY. JUST WORKING OUT SOME STUFF.
YOU ALWAYS ARE.
YEAH. COMPLICATIONS. I GOT A FEW.
WHY DO I GET THE FEELING, THOUGH--

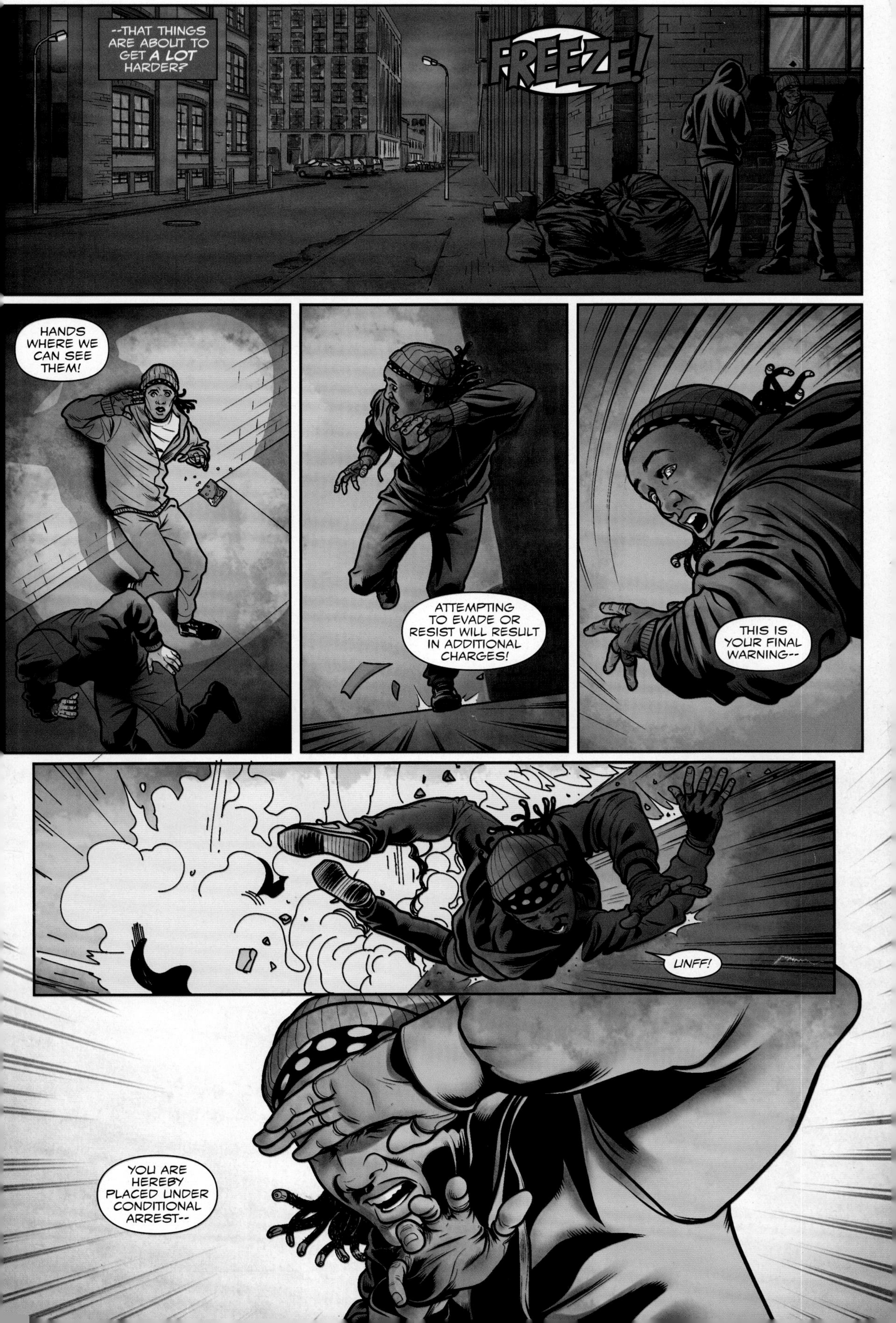
--THAT THINGS ARE ABOUT TO GET A LOT HARDER?
FREEZE!
HANDS WHERE WE CAN SEE THEM!
ATTEMPTING TO EVADE OR RESIST WILL RESULT IN ADDITIONAL CHARGES!
THIS IS YOUR FINAL WARNING--
UNFF!
YOU ARE HEREBY PLACED UNDER CONDITIONAL ARREST--

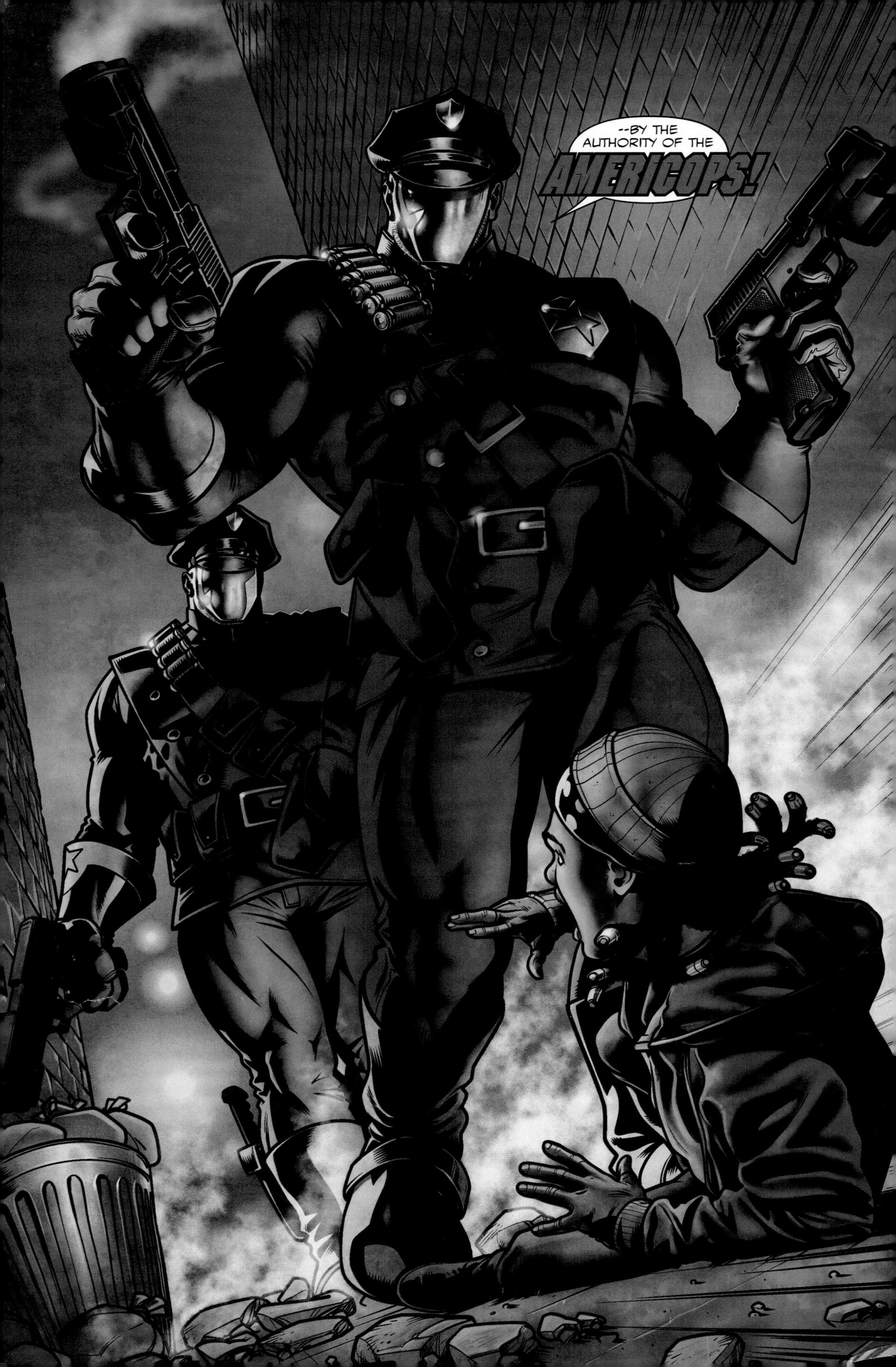
--BY THE AUTHORITY OF THE AMERICOPS!

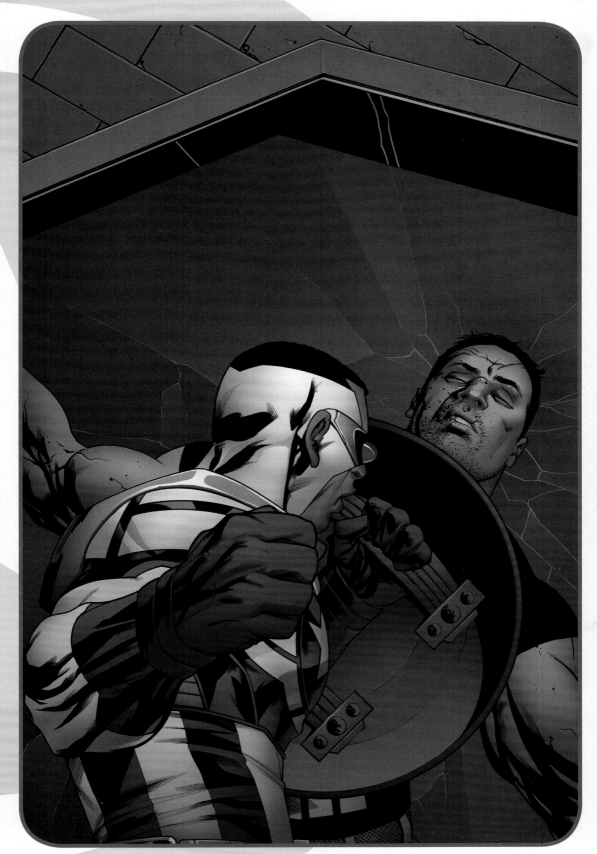

#10 Civil War Reenactment variant by
MIKE MCKONE & FRANK D'ARMATA

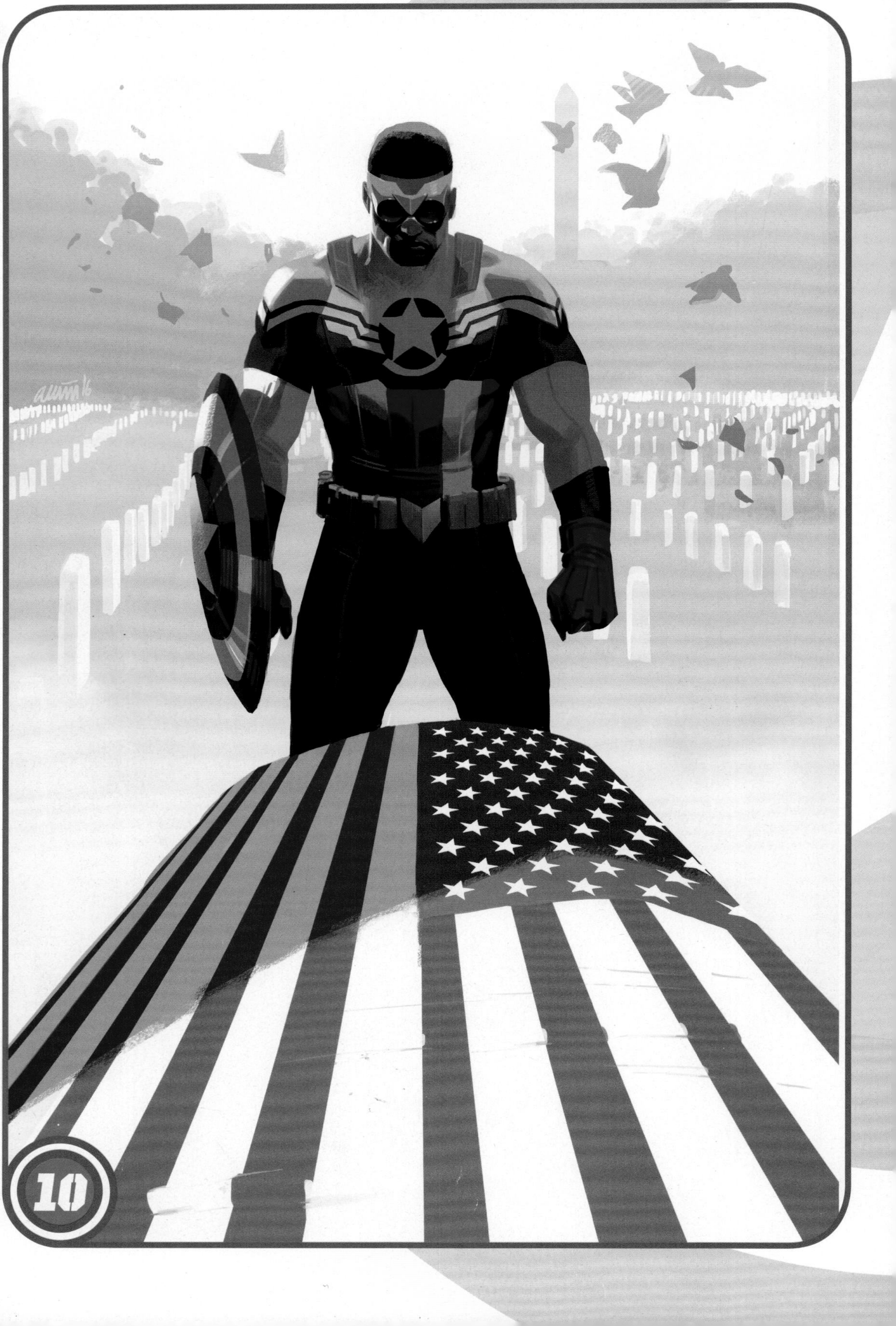
10

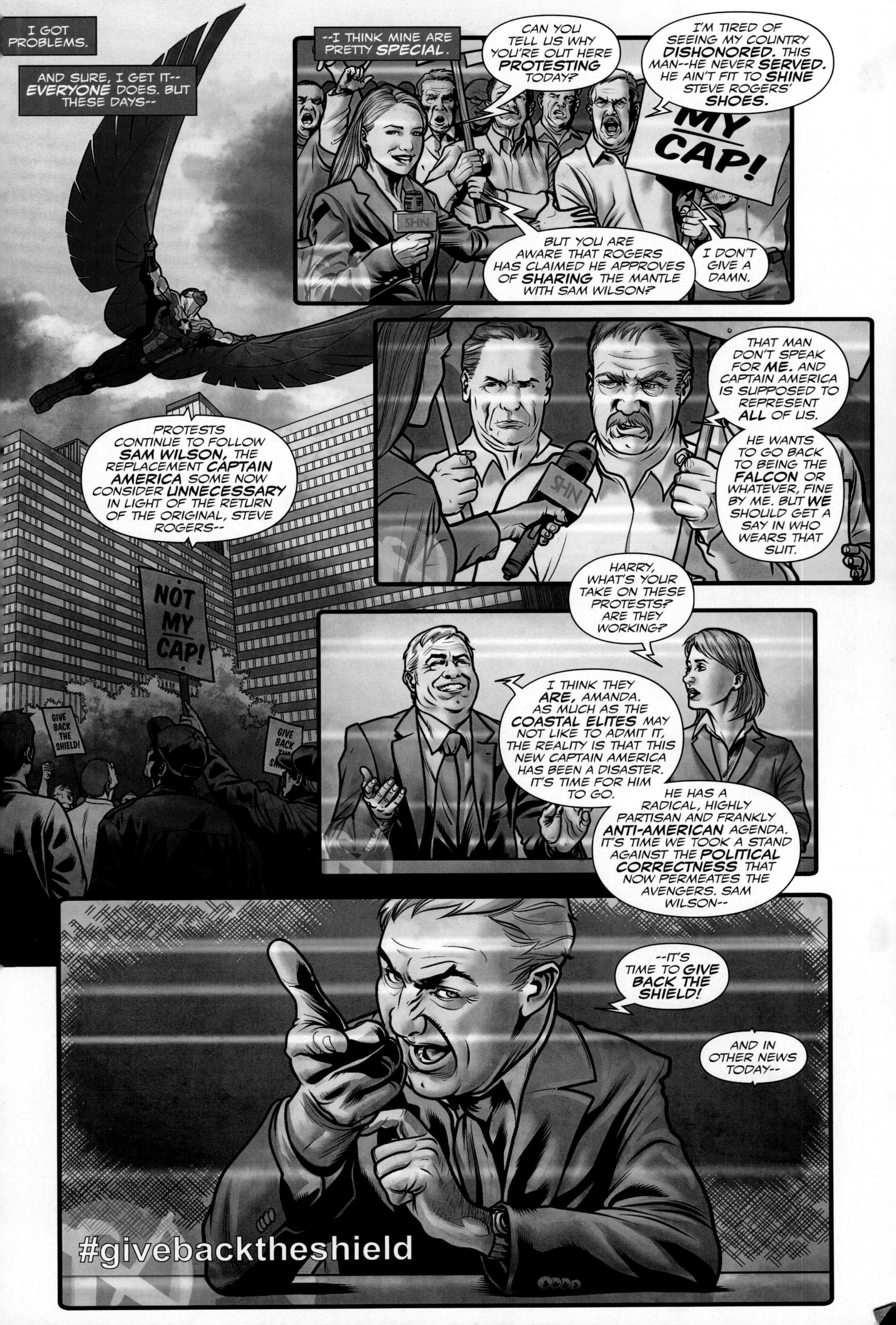
I GOT PROBLEMS.
AND SURE, I GET IT--EVERYONE DOES. BUT THESE DAYS--
--I THINK MINE ARE PRETTY SPECIAL.
CAN YOU TELL US WHY YOU'RE OUT HERE PROTESTING TODAY?
I'M TIRED OF SEEING MY COUNTRY DISHONORED. THIS MAN--HE NEVER SERVED. HE AIN'T FIT TO SHINE STEVE ROGERS' SHOES.
MY CAP!
BUT YOU ARE AWARE THAT ROGERS HAS CLAIMED HE APPROVES OF SHARING THE MANTLE WITH SAM WILSON?
I DON'T GIVE A DAMN.
SHN
PROTESTS CONTINUE TO FOLLOW SAM WILSON, THE REPLACEMENT CAPTAIN AMERICA SOME NOW CONSIDER UNNECESSARY IN LIGHT OF THE RETURN OF THE ORIGINAL, STEVE ROGERS--
THAT MAN DON'T SPEAK FOR ME. AND CAPTAIN AMERICA IS SUPPOSED TO REPRESENT ALL OF US.
HE WANTS TO GO BACK TO BEING THE FALCON OR WHATEVER, FINE BY ME. BUT WE SHOULD GET A SAY IN WHO WEARS THAT SUIT.
NOT MY CAP!
GIVE BACK THE SHIELD!
HARRY, WHAT'S YOUR TAKE ON THESE PROTESTS? ARE THEY WORKING?
I THINK THEY ARE, AMANDA. AS MUCH AS THE COASTAL ELITES MAY NOT LIKE TO ADMIT IT, THE REALITY IS THAT THIS NEW CAPTAIN AMERICA HAS BEEN A DISASTER. IT'S TIME FOR HIM TO GO.
HE HAS A RADICAL, HIGHLY PARTISAN AND FRANKLY ANTI-AMERICAN AGENDA. IT'S TIME WE TOOK A STAND AGAINST THE POLITICAL CORRECTNESS THAT NOW PERMEATES THE AVENGERS. SAM WILSON--
--IT'S TIME TO GIVE BACK THE SHIELD!
AND IN OTHER NEWS TODAY--
#givebacktheshield

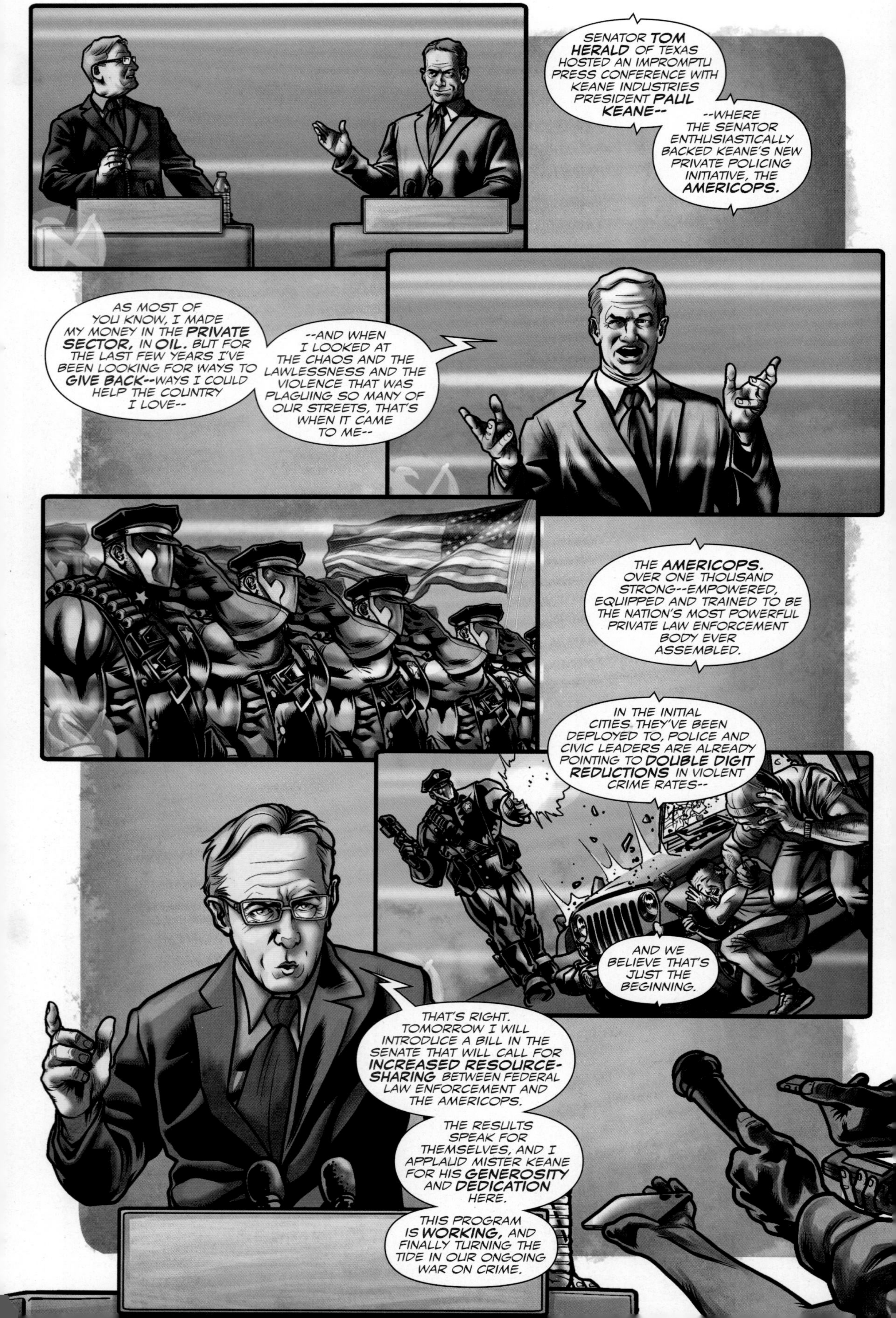
SENATOR TOM HERALD OF TEXAS HOSTED AN IMPROMPTU PRESS CONFERENCE WITH KEANE INDUSTRIES PRESIDENT PAUL KEANE--
--WHERE THE SENATOR ENTHUSIASTICALLY BACKED KEANE'S NEW PRIVATE POLICING INITIATIVE, THE AMERICOPS.
AS MOST OF YOU KNOW, I MADE MY MONEY IN THE PRIVATE SECTOR, IN OIL. BUT FOR THE LAST FEW YEARS I'VE BEEN LOOKING FOR WAYS TO GIVE BACK--WAYS I COULD HELP THE COUNTRY I LOVE--
--AND WHEN I LOOKED AT THE CHAOS AND THE LAWLESSNESS AND THE VIOLENCE THAT WAS PLAGUING SO MANY OF OUR STREETS, THAT'S WHEN IT CAME TO ME--
THE AMERICOPS. OVER ONE THOUSAND STRONG--EMPOWERED, EQUIPPED AND TRAINED TO BE THE NATION'S MOST POWERFUL PRIVATE LAW ENFORCEMENT BODY EVER ASSEMBLED.
IN THE INITIAL CITIES THEY'VE BEEN DEPLOYED TO, POLICE AND CIVIC LEADERS ARE ALREADY POINTING TO DOUBLE DIGIT REDUCTIONS IN VIOLENT CRIME RATES--
AND WE BELIEVE THAT'S JUST THE BEGINNING.
THAT'S RIGHT. TOMORROW I WILL INTRODUCE A BILL IN THE SENATE THAT WILL CALL FOR INCREASED RESOURCE-SHARING BETWEEN FEDERAL LAW ENFORCEMENT AND THE AMERICOPS.
THE RESULTS SPEAK FOR THEMSELVES, AND I APPLAUD MISTER KEANE FOR HIS GENEROSITY AND DEDICATION HERE.
THIS PROGRAM IS WORKING, AND FINALLY TURNING THE TIDE IN OUR ONGOING WAR ON CRIME.

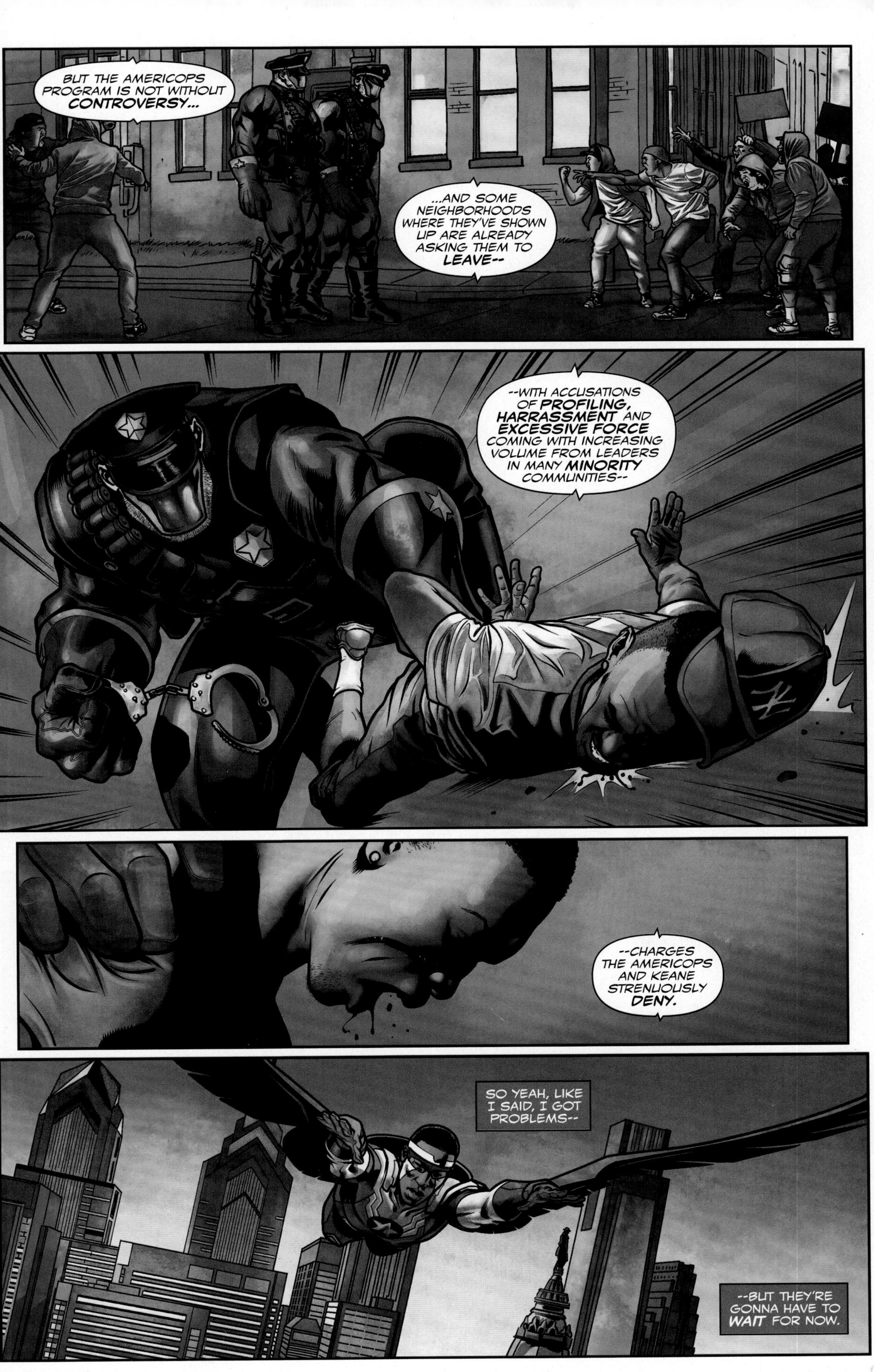
BUT THE AMERICOPS PROGRAM IS NOT WITHOUT **CONTROVERSY...**
...AND SOME NEIGHBORHOODS WHERE THEY'VE SHOWN UP ARE ALREADY ASKING THEM TO **LEAVE--**
--WITH ACCUSATIONS OF **PROFILING, HARRASSMENT** AND **EXCESSIVE FORCE** COMING WITH INCREASING VOLUME FROM LEADERS IN MANY **MINORITY** COMMUNITIES--
--CHARGES THE AMERICOPS AND KEANE STRENUOUSLY **DENY.**
SO YEAH, LIKE I SAID, I GOT PROBLEMS--
--BUT THEY'RE GONNA HAVE TO ***WAIT*** FOR NOW.

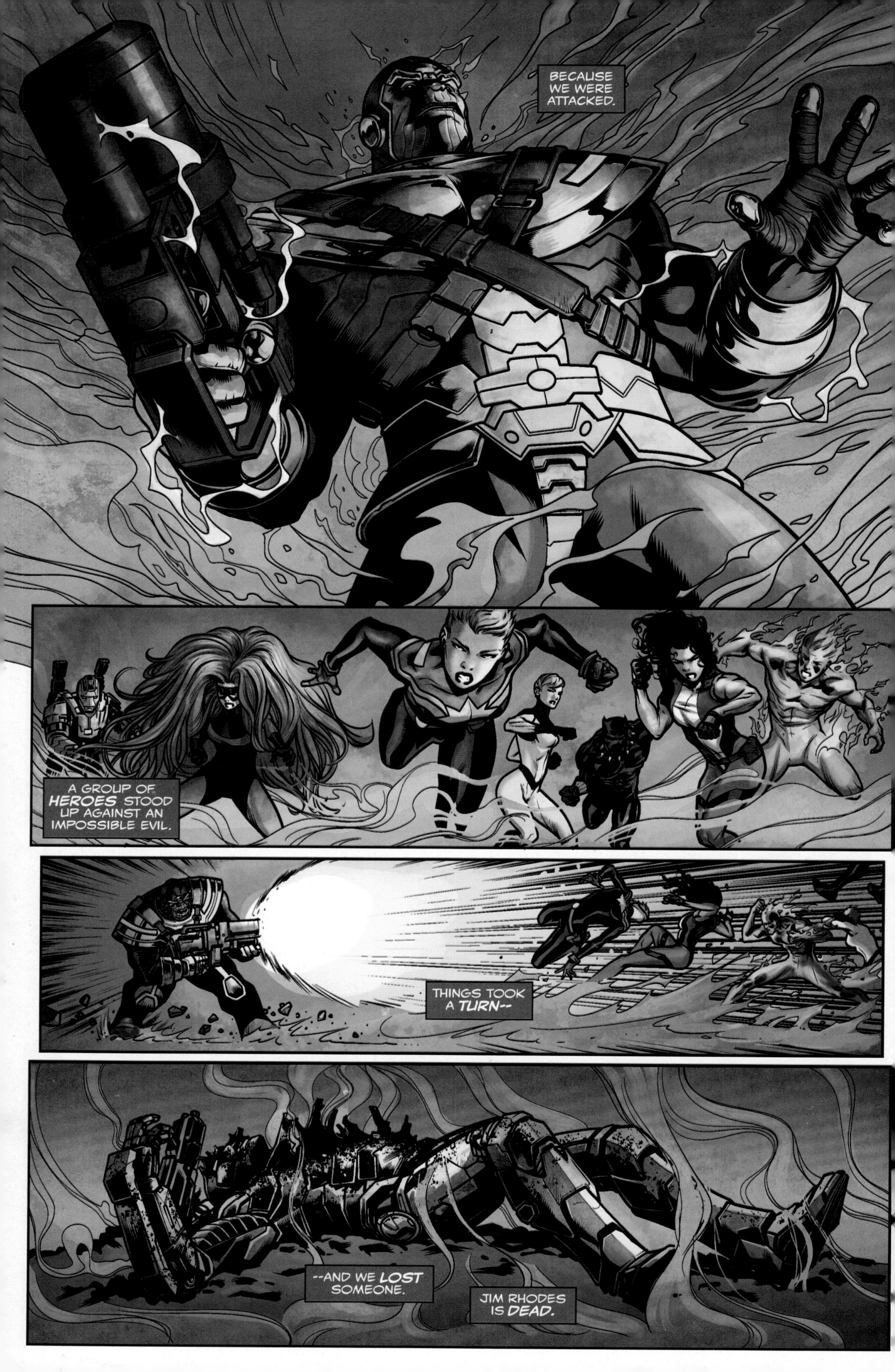
BECAUSE WE WERE ATTACKED.
A GROUP OF HEROES STOOD UP AGAINST AN IMPOSSIBLE EVIL.
THINGS TOOK A TURN--
--AND WE LOST SOMEONE.
JIM RHODES IS DEAD.

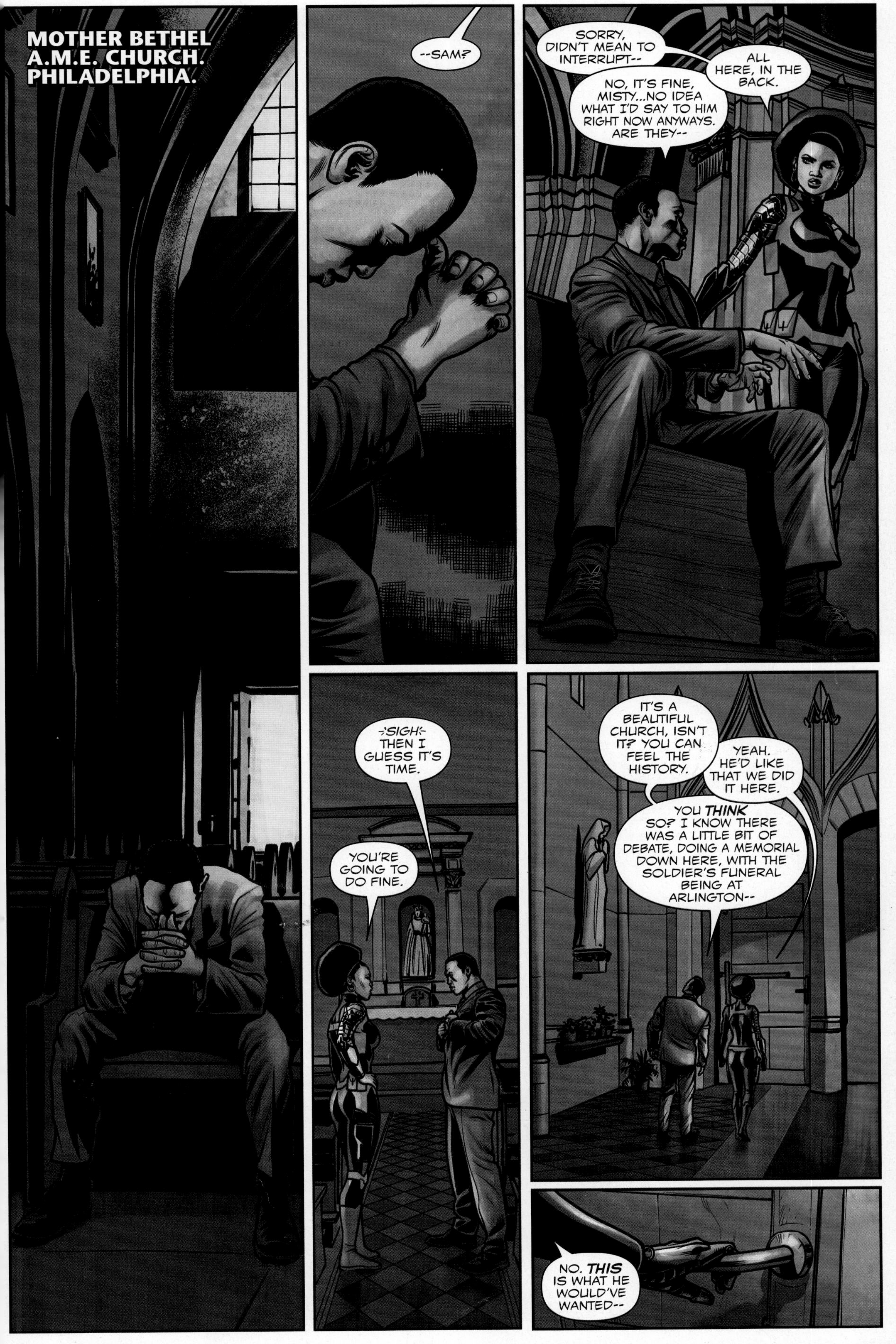
MOTHER BETHEL A.M.E. CHURCH. PHILADELPHIA.
--SAM?
SORRY, DIDN'T MEAN TO INTERRUPT--
NO, IT'S FINE, MISTY...NO IDEA WHAT I'D SAY TO HIM RIGHT NOW ANYWAYS. ARE THEY--
ALL HERE, IN THE BACK.
-SIGH- THEN I GUESS IT'S TIME.
YOU'RE GOING TO DO FINE.
IT'S A BEAUTIFUL CHURCH, ISN'T IT? YOU CAN FEEL THE HISTORY.
YEAH. HE'D LIKE THAT WE DID IT HERE.
YOU THINK SO? I KNOW THERE WAS A LITTLE BIT OF DEBATE, DOING A MEMORIAL DOWN HERE, WITH THE SOLDIER'S FUNERAL BEING AT ARLINGTON--
NO. THIS IS WHAT HE WOULD'VE WANTED--

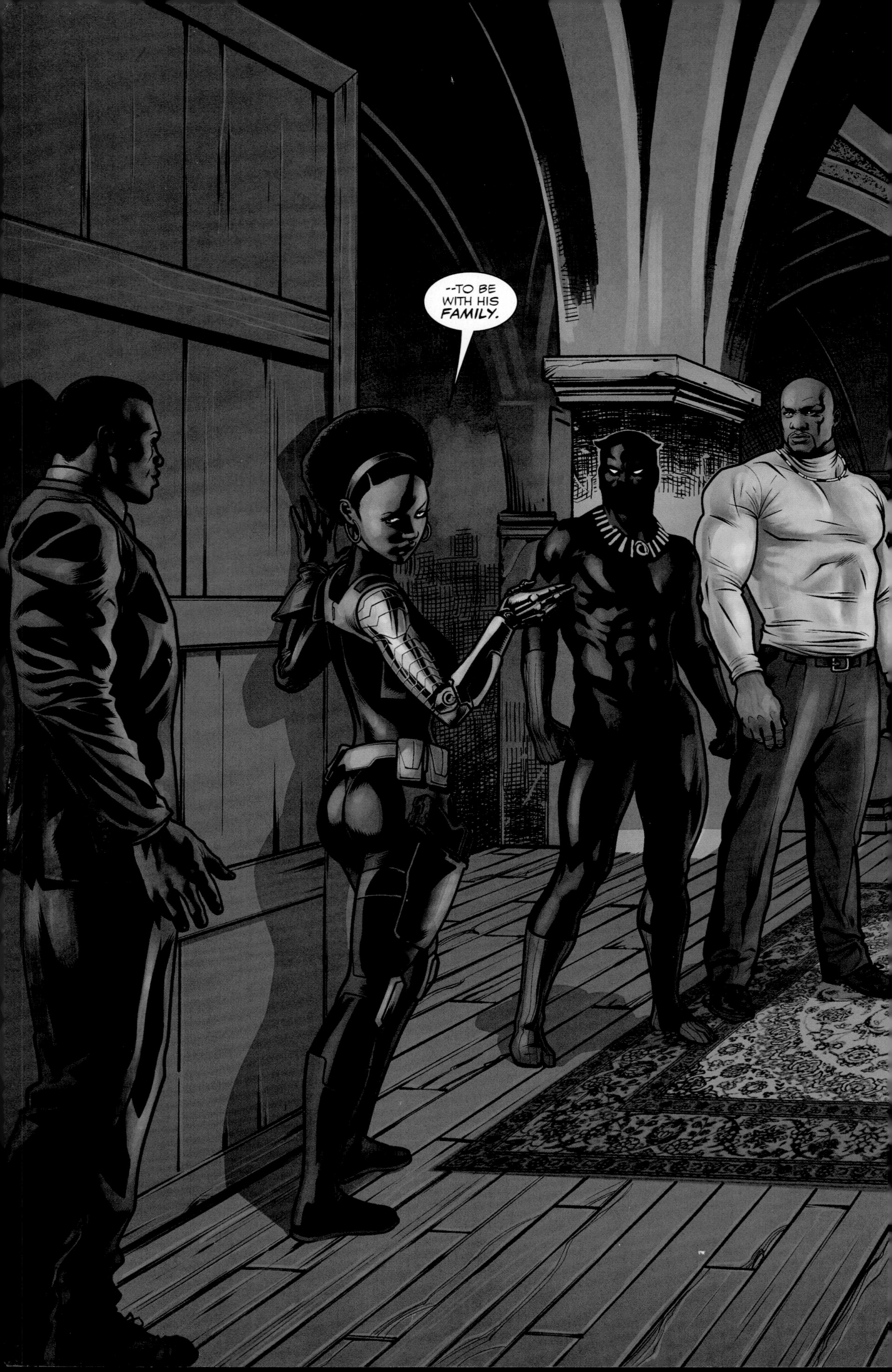
--TO BE WITH HIS FAMILY.

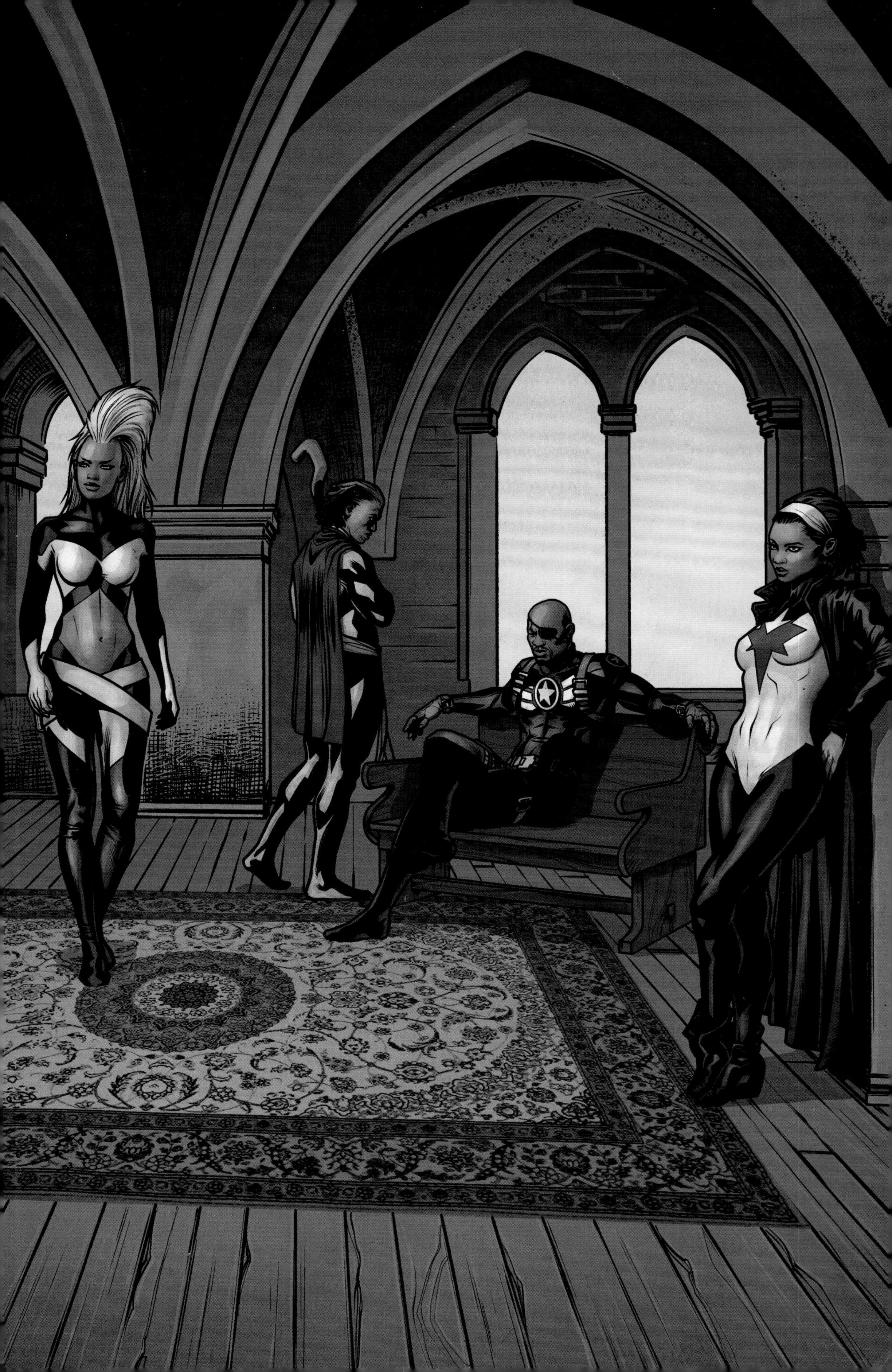

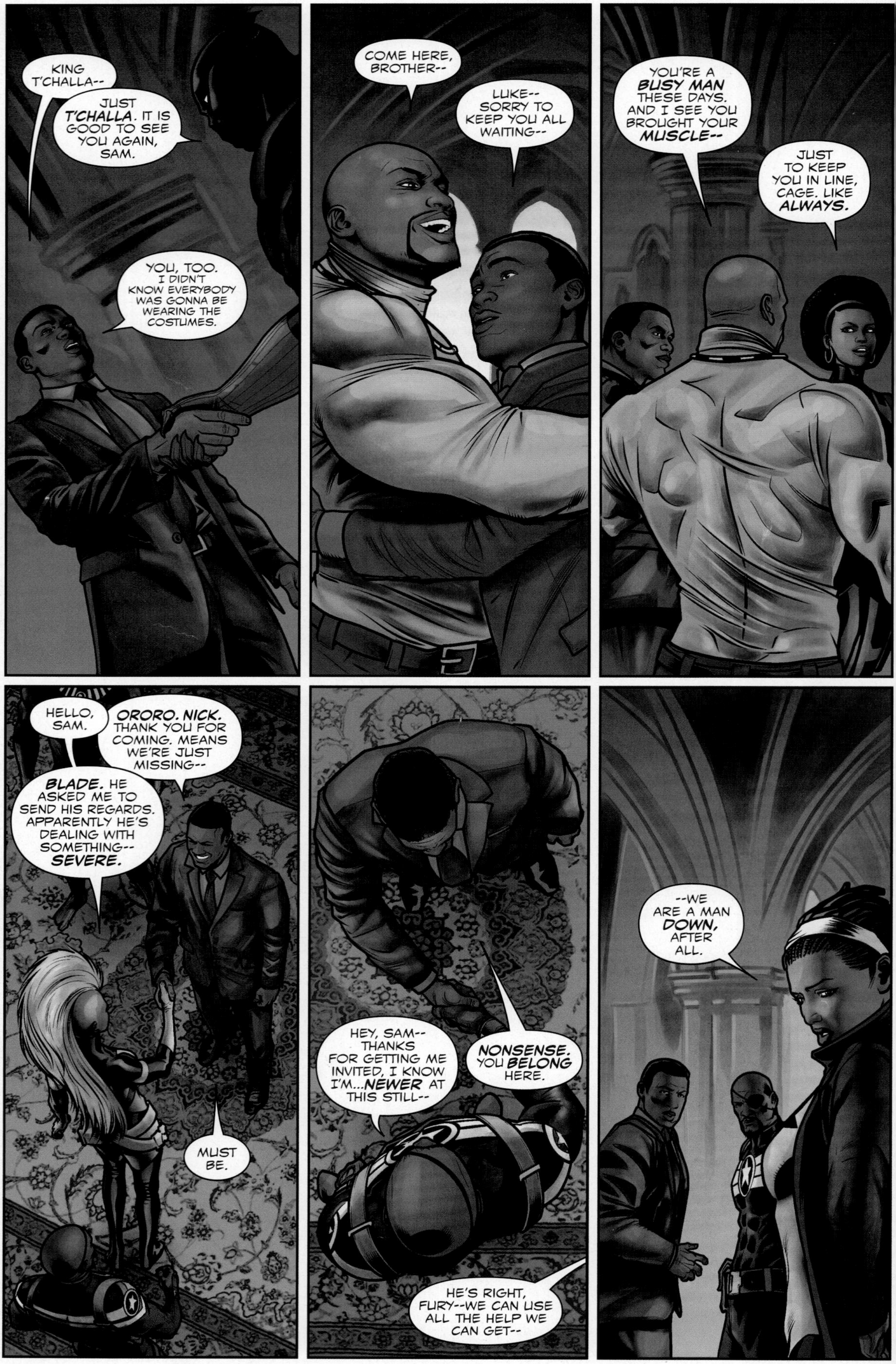

KING T'CHALLA--
JUST T'CHALLA. IT IS GOOD TO SEE YOU AGAIN, SAM.
YOU, TOO. I DIDN'T KNOW EVERYBODY WAS GONNA BE WEARING THE COSTUMES.
COME HERE, BROTHER--
LUKE-- SORRY TO KEEP YOU ALL WAITING--
YOU'RE A BUSY MAN THESE DAYS. AND I SEE YOU BROUGHT YOUR MUSCLE--
JUST TO KEEP YOU IN LINE, CAGE. LIKE ALWAYS.
HELLO, SAM.
ORORO. NICK. THANK YOU FOR COMING. MEANS WE'RE JUST MISSING--
BLADE. HE ASKED ME TO SEND HIS REGARDS. APPARENTLY HE'S DEALING WITH SOMETHING-- SEVERE.
MUST BE.
HEY, SAM-- THANKS FOR GETTING ME INVITED, I KNOW I'M...NEWER AT THIS STILL--
NONSENSE. YOU BELONG HERE.
HE'S RIGHT, FURY--WE CAN USE ALL THE HELP WE CAN GET--
--WE ARE A MAN DOWN, AFTER ALL.

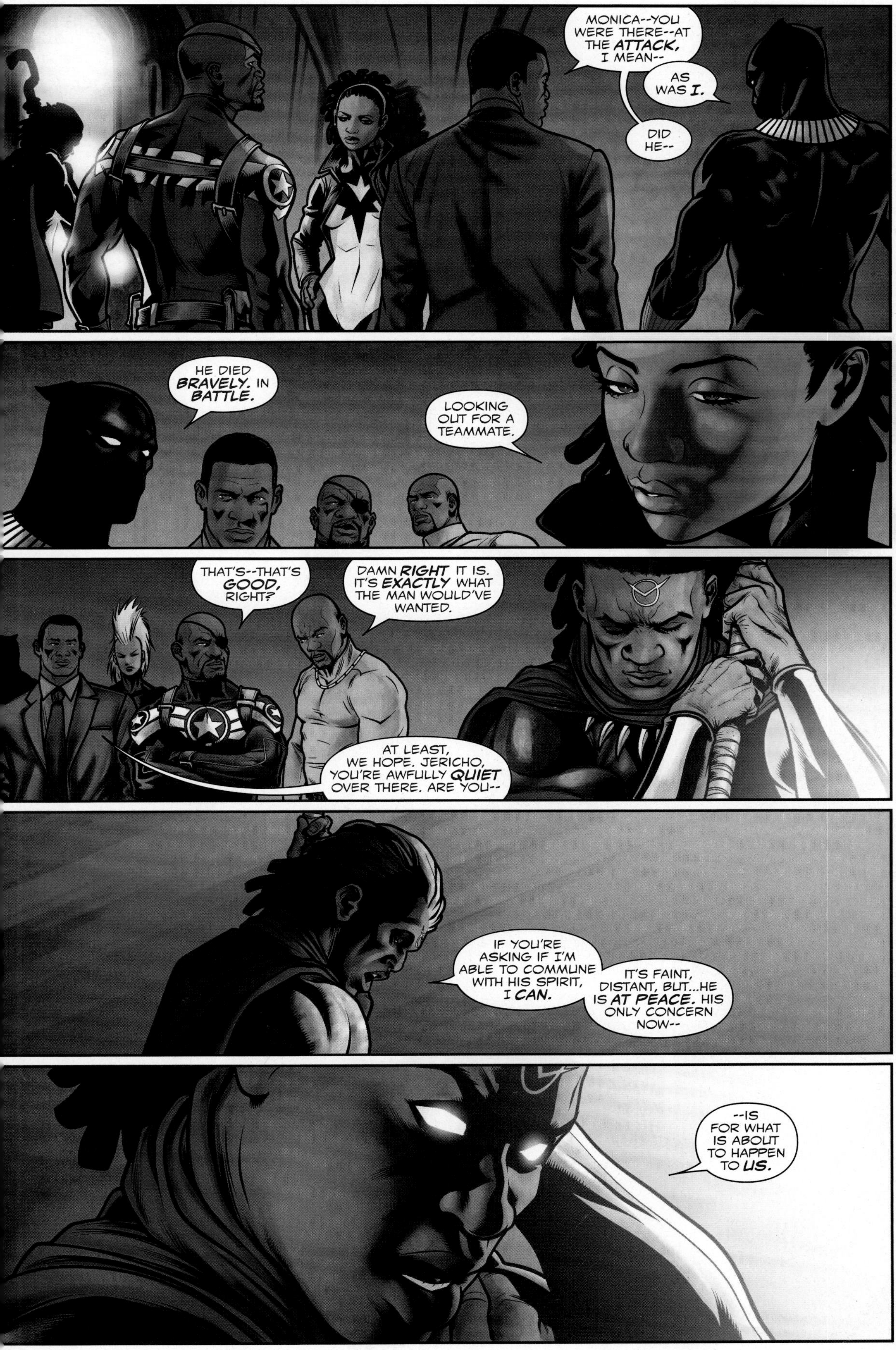
MONICA--YOU WERE THERE--AT THE ATTACK, I MEAN--
AS WAS I.
DID HE--
HE DIED BRAVELY. IN BATTLE.
LOOKING OUT FOR A TEAMMATE.
THAT'S--THAT'S GOOD, RIGHT?
DAMN RIGHT IT IS. IT'S EXACTLY WHAT THE MAN WOULD'VE WANTED.
AT LEAST, WE HOPE. JERICHO, YOU'RE AWFULLY QUIET OVER THERE. ARE YOU--
IF YOU'RE ASKING IF I'M ABLE TO COMMUNE WITH HIS SPIRIT, I CAN.
IT'S FAINT, DISTANT, BUT...HE IS AT PEACE. HIS ONLY CONCERN NOW--
--IS FOR WHAT IS ABOUT TO HAPPEN TO US.

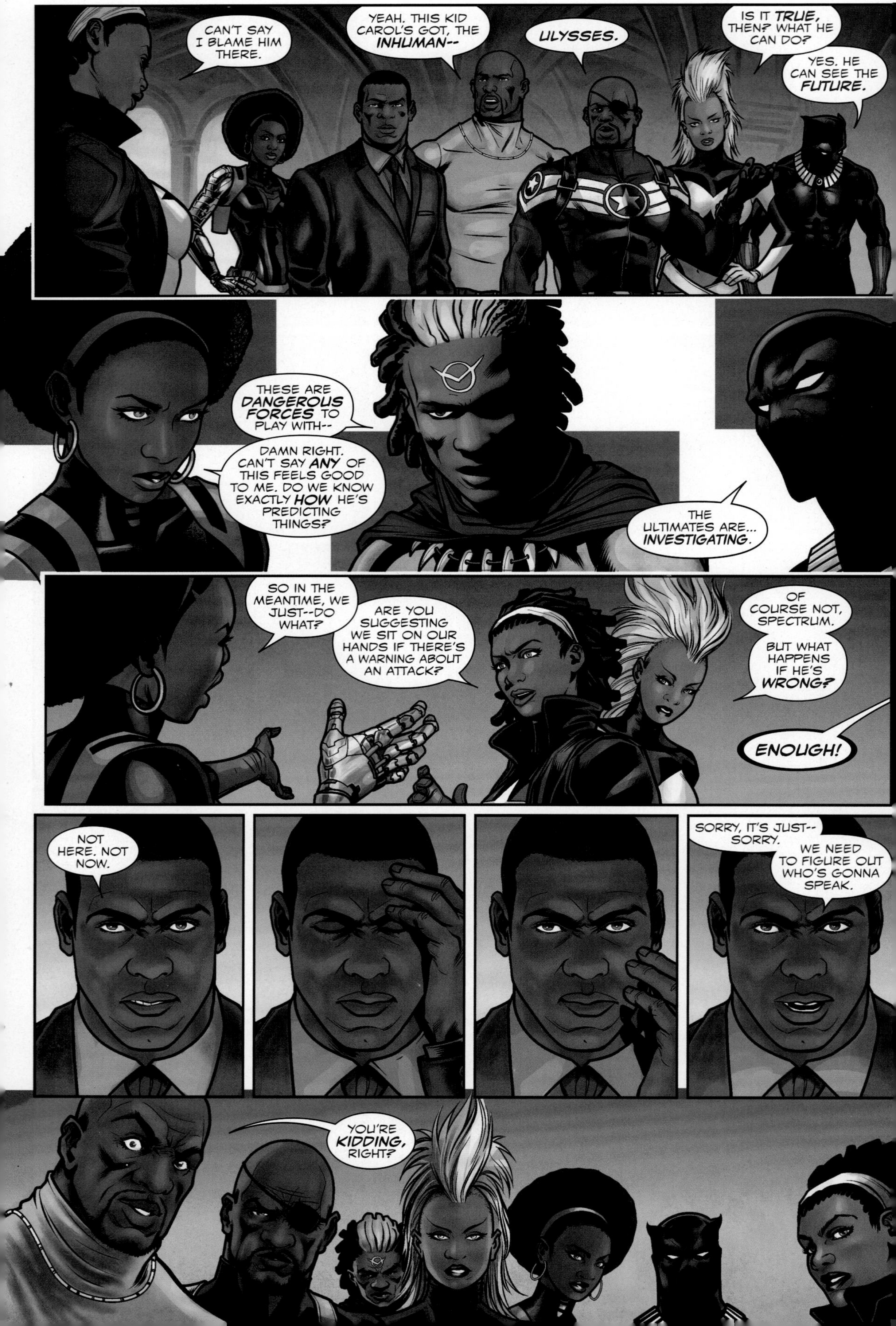

CAN'T SAY I BLAME HIM THERE.
YEAH. THIS KID CAROL'S GOT, THE INHUMAN--
ULYSSES.
IS IT TRUE, THEN? WHAT HE CAN DO?
YES. HE CAN SEE THE FUTURE.
THESE ARE DANGEROUS FORCES TO PLAY WITH--
DAMN RIGHT. CAN'T SAY ANY OF THIS FEELS GOOD TO ME. DO WE KNOW EXACTLY HOW HE'S PREDICTING THINGS?
THE ULTIMATES ARE... INVESTIGATING.
SO IN THE MEANTIME, WE JUST--DO WHAT?
ARE YOU SUGGESTING WE SIT ON OUR HANDS IF THERE'S A WARNING ABOUT AN ATTACK?
OF COURSE NOT, SPECTRUM.
BUT WHAT HAPPENS IF HE'S WRONG?
ENOUGH!
NOT HERE. NOT NOW.
SORRY, IT'S JUST-- SORRY.
WE NEED TO FIGURE OUT WHO'S GONNA SPEAK.
YOU'RE KIDDING, RIGHT?

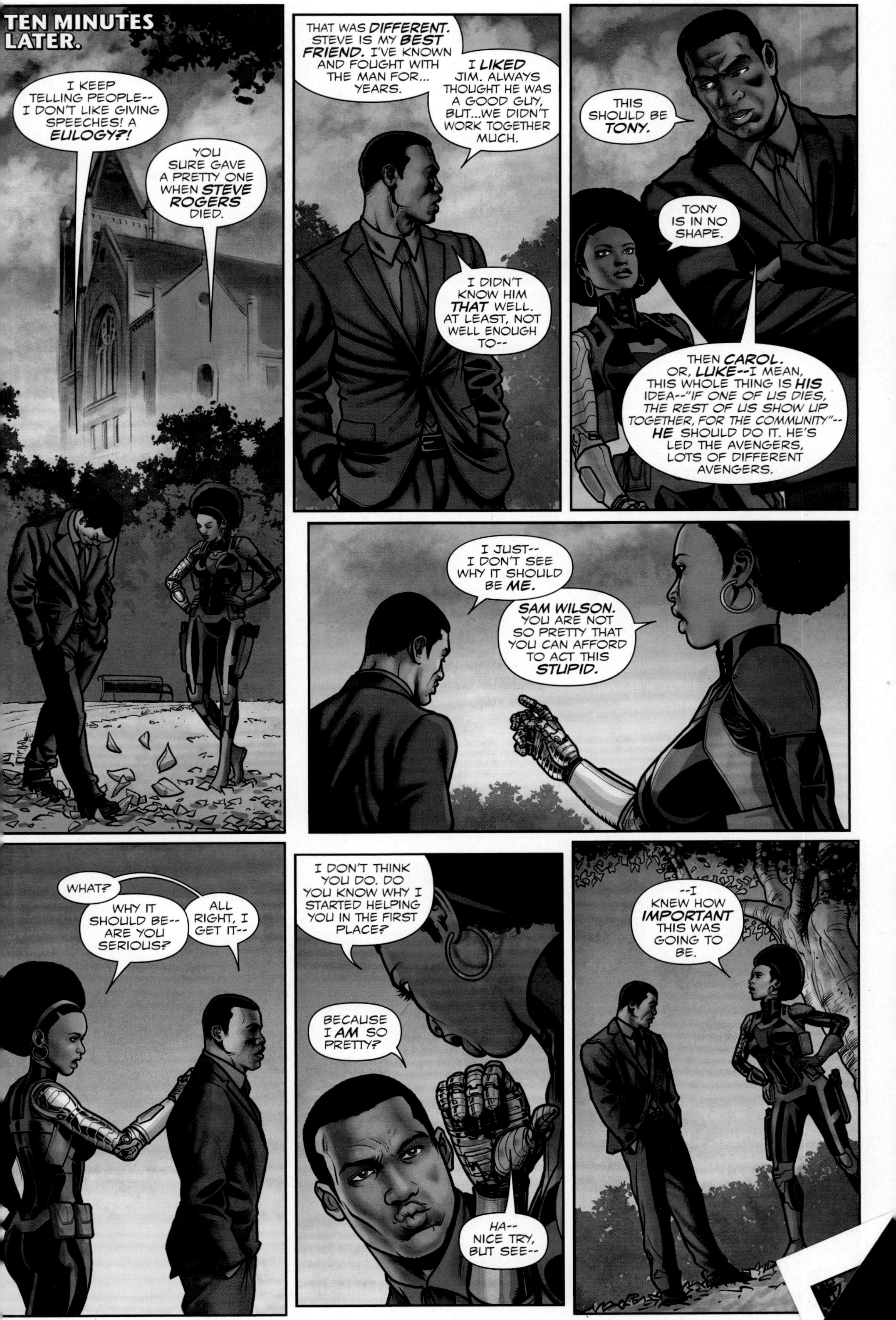
TEN MINUTES LATER.
I KEEP TELLING PEOPLE-- I DON'T LIKE GIVING SPEECHES! A EULOGY?!
YOU SURE GAVE A PRETTY ONE WHEN STEVE ROGERS DIED.
THAT WAS DIFFERENT. STEVE IS MY BEST FRIEND. I'VE KNOWN AND FOUGHT WITH THE MAN FOR... YEARS.
I LIKED JIM. ALWAYS THOUGHT HE WAS A GOOD GUY, BUT...WE DIDN'T WORK TOGETHER MUCH.
I DIDN'T KNOW HIM THAT WELL. AT LEAST, NOT WELL ENOUGH TO--
THIS SHOULD BE TONY.
TONY IS IN NO SHAPE.
THEN CAROL. OR, LUKE--I MEAN, THIS WHOLE THING IS HIS IDEA--"IF ONE OF US DIES, THE REST OF US SHOW UP TOGETHER, FOR THE COMMUNITY"--HE SHOULD DO IT. HE'S LED THE AVENGERS, LOTS OF DIFFERENT AVENGERS.
I JUST-- I DON'T SEE WHY IT SHOULD BE ME.
SAM WILSON. YOU ARE NOT SO PRETTY THAT YOU CAN AFFORD TO ACT THIS STUPID.
WHAT?
WHY IT SHOULD BE-- ARE YOU SERIOUS?
ALL RIGHT, I GET IT--
I DON'T THINK YOU DO. DO YOU KNOW WHY I STARTED HELPING YOU IN THE FIRST PLACE?
BECAUSE I AM SO PRETTY?
HA-- NICE TRY, BUT SEE--
--I KNEW HOW IMPORTANT THIS WAS GOING TO BE.

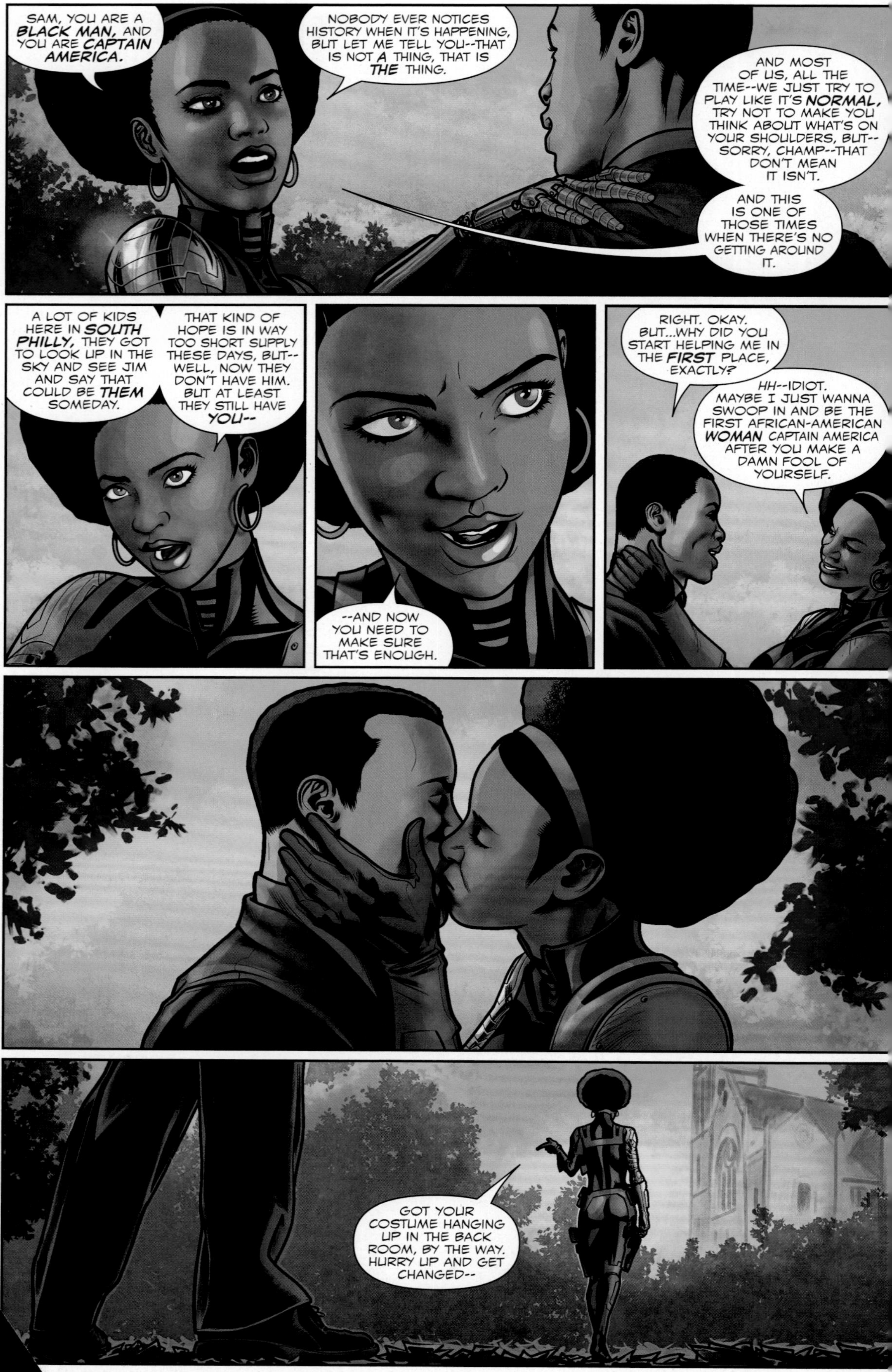
SAM, YOU ARE A BLACK MAN, AND YOU ARE CAPTAIN AMERICA.
NOBODY EVER NOTICES HISTORY WHEN IT'S HAPPENING, BUT LET ME TELL YOU--THAT IS NOT A THING, THAT IS THE THING.
AND MOST OF US, ALL THE TIME--WE JUST TRY TO PLAY LIKE IT'S NORMAL, TRY NOT TO MAKE YOU THINK ABOUT WHAT'S ON YOUR SHOULDERS, BUT--SORRY, CHAMP--THAT DON'T MEAN IT ISN'T.
AND THIS IS ONE OF THOSE TIMES WHEN THERE'S NO GETTING AROUND IT.
A LOT OF KIDS HERE IN SOUTH PHILLY, THEY GOT TO LOOK UP IN THE SKY AND SEE JIM AND SAY THAT COULD BE THEM SOMEDAY.
THAT KIND OF HOPE IS IN WAY TOO SHORT SUPPLY THESE DAYS, BUT--WELL, NOW THEY DON'T HAVE HIM. BUT AT LEAST THEY STILL HAVE YOU--
--AND NOW YOU NEED TO MAKE SURE THAT'S ENOUGH.
RIGHT. OKAY. BUT...WHY DID YOU START HELPING ME IN THE FIRST PLACE, EXACTLY?
HH--IDIOT. MAYBE I JUST WANNA SWOOP IN AND BE THE FIRST AFRICAN-AMERICAN WOMAN CAPTAIN AMERICA AFTER YOU MAKE A DAMN FOOL OF YOURSELF.
GOT YOUR COSTUME HANGING UP IN THE BACK ROOM, BY THE WAY. HURRY UP AND GET CHANGED--

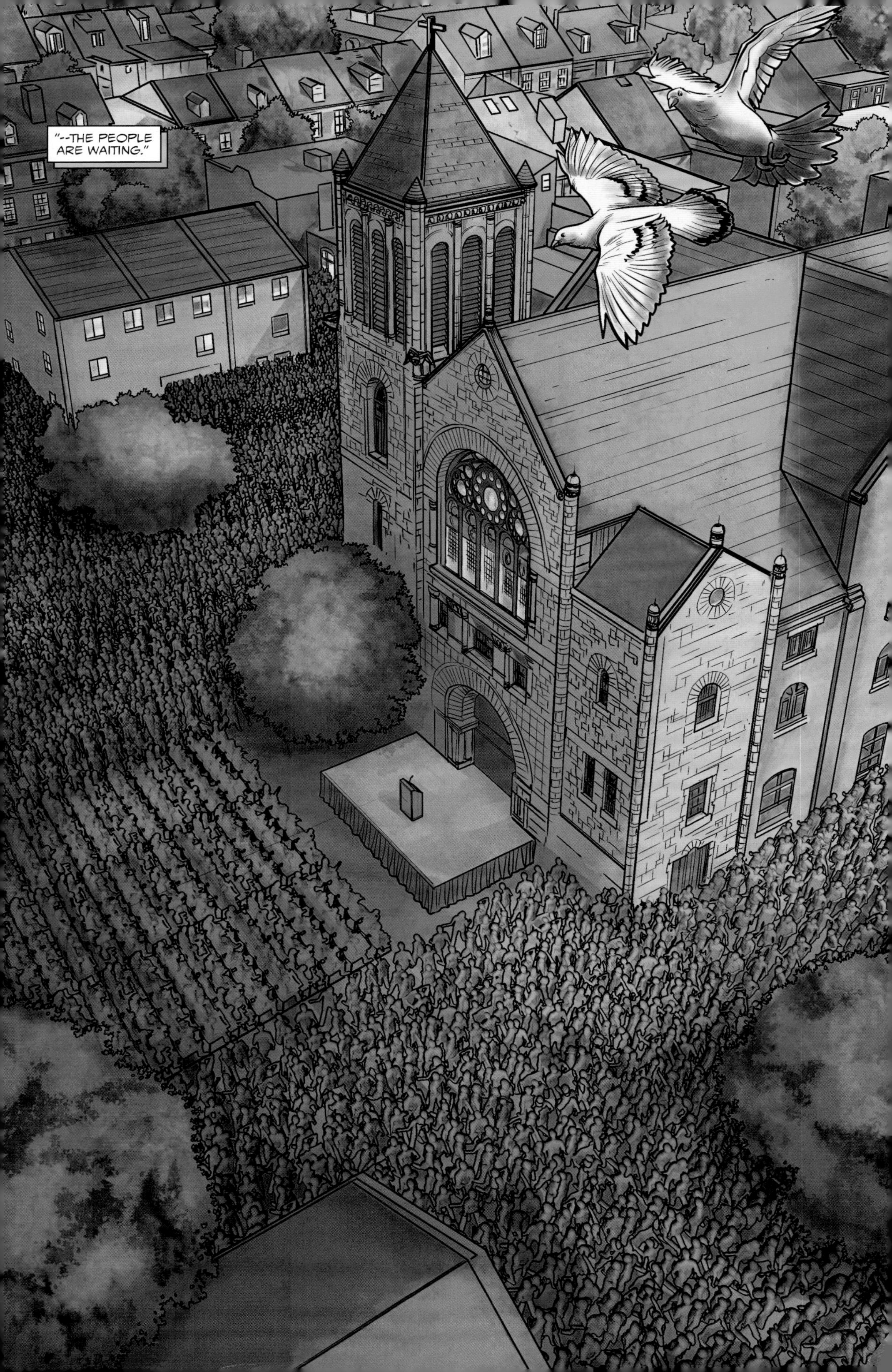
"--THE PEOPLE ARE WAITING."

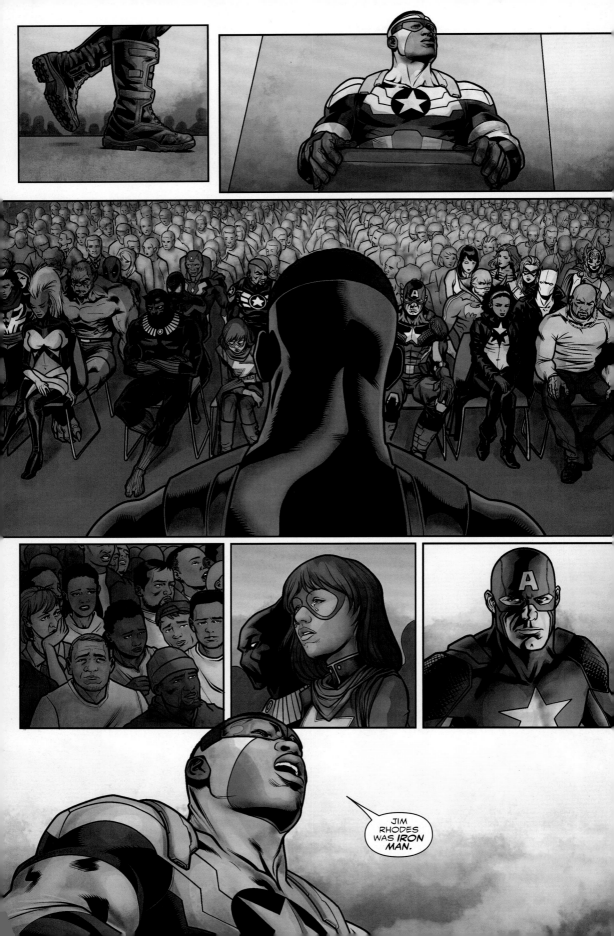

JIM RHODES WAS *IRON MAN.*

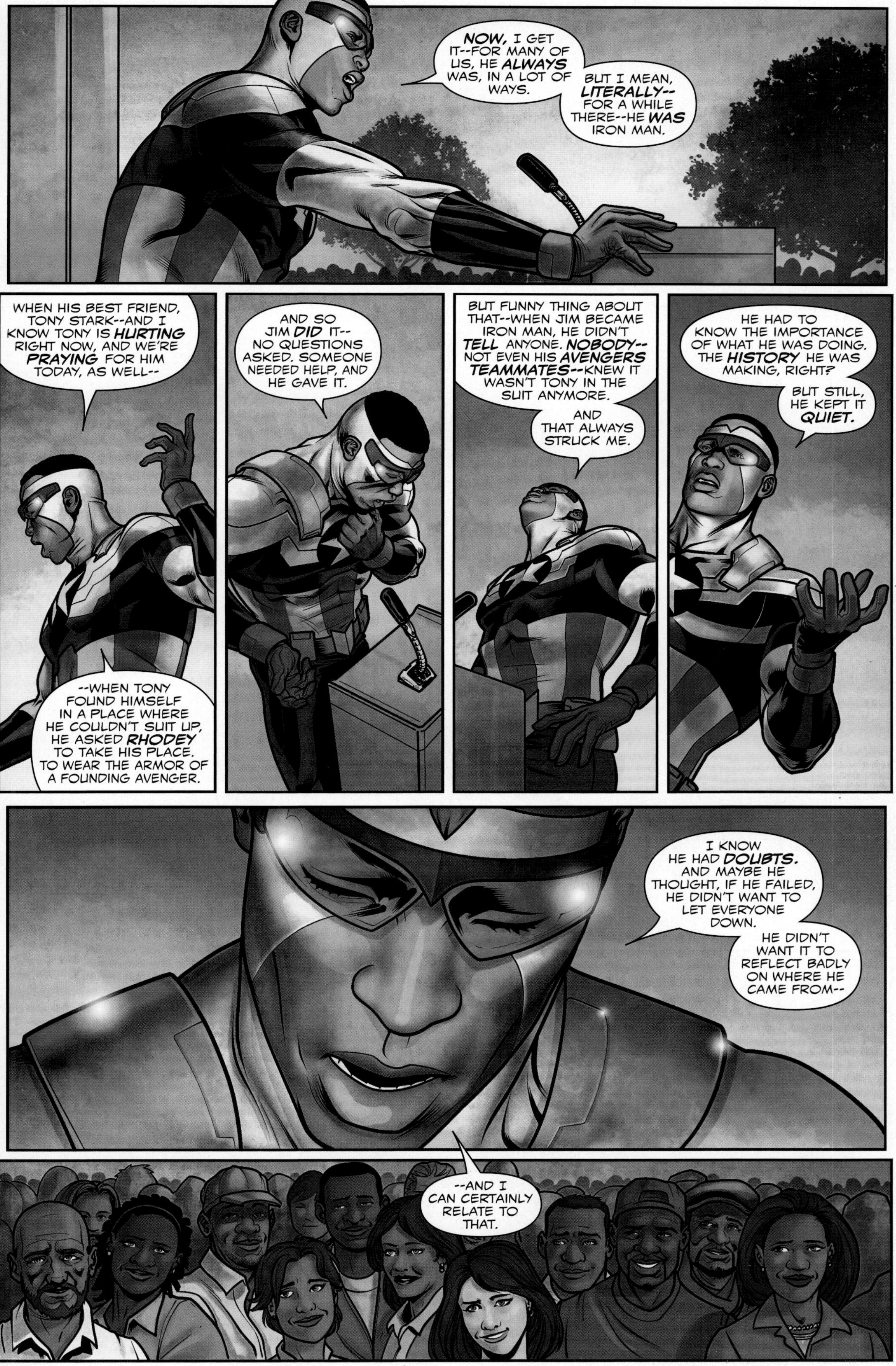
NOW, I GET IT--FOR MANY OF US, HE ALWAYS WAS, IN A LOT OF WAYS.
BUT I MEAN, LITERALLY--FOR A WHILE THERE--HE WAS IRON MAN.
WHEN HIS BEST FRIEND, TONY STARK--AND I KNOW TONY IS HURTING RIGHT NOW, AND WE'RE PRAYING FOR HIM TODAY, AS WELL--
--WHEN TONY FOUND HIMSELF IN A PLACE WHERE HE COULDN'T SUIT UP, HE ASKED RHODEY TO TAKE HIS PLACE. TO WEAR THE ARMOR OF A FOUNDING AVENGER.
AND SO JIM DID IT--NO QUESTIONS ASKED. SOMEONE NEEDED HELP, AND HE GAVE IT.
BUT FUNNY THING ABOUT THAT--WHEN JIM BECAME IRON MAN, HE DIDN'T TELL ANYONE. NOBODY--NOT EVEN HIS AVENGERS TEAMMATES--KNEW IT WASN'T TONY IN THE SUIT ANYMORE.
AND THAT ALWAYS STRUCK ME.
HE HAD TO KNOW THE IMPORTANCE OF WHAT HE WAS DOING. THE HISTORY HE WAS MAKING, RIGHT?
BUT STILL, HE KEPT IT QUIET.
I KNOW HE HAD DOUBTS. AND MAYBE HE THOUGHT, IF HE FAILED, HE DIDN'T WANT TO LET EVERYONE DOWN.
HE DIDN'T WANT IT TO REFLECT BADLY ON WHERE HE CAME FROM--
--AND I CAN CERTAINLY RELATE TO THAT.

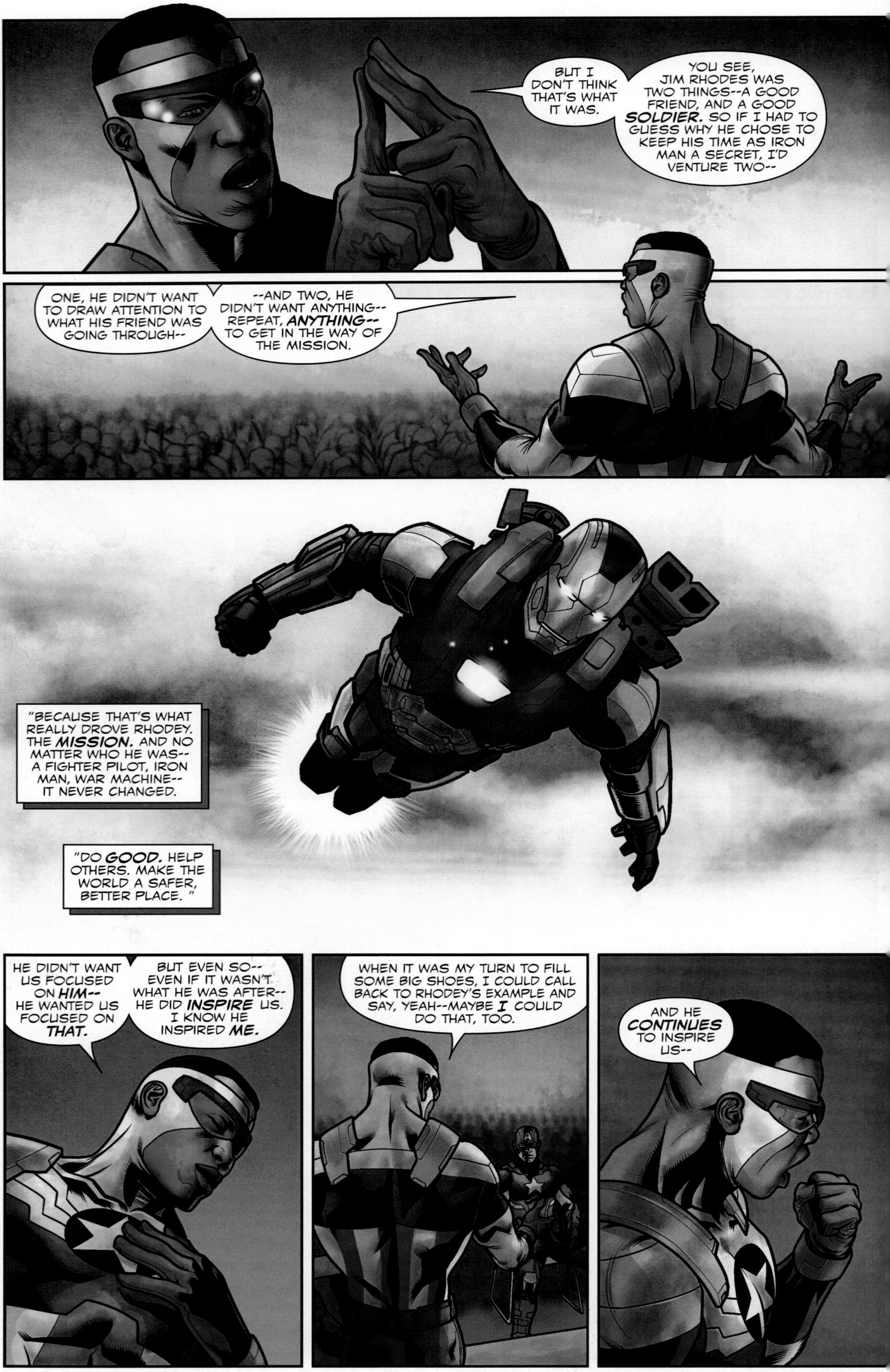

BUT I DON'T THINK THAT'S WHAT IT WAS.
YOU SEE, JIM RHODES WAS TWO THINGS--A GOOD FRIEND, AND A GOOD SOLDIER. SO IF I HAD TO GUESS WHY HE CHOSE TO KEEP HIS TIME AS IRON MAN A SECRET, I'D VENTURE TWO--
ONE, HE DIDN'T WANT TO DRAW ATTENTION TO WHAT HIS FRIEND WAS GOING THROUGH--
--AND TWO, HE DIDN'T WANT ANYTHING--REPEAT, ANYTHING--TO GET IN THE WAY OF THE MISSION.
"BECAUSE THAT'S WHAT REALLY DROVE RHODEY. THE MISSION. AND NO MATTER WHO HE WAS--A FIGHTER PILOT, IRON MAN, WAR MACHINE--IT NEVER CHANGED.
"DO GOOD. HELP OTHERS. MAKE THE WORLD A SAFER, BETTER PLACE."
HE DIDN'T WANT US FOCUSED ON HIM--HE WANTED US FOCUSED ON THAT.
BUT EVEN SO--EVEN IF IT WASN'T WHAT HE WAS AFTER--HE DID INSPIRE US. I KNOW HE INSPIRED ME.
WHEN IT WAS MY TURN TO FILL SOME BIG SHOES, I COULD CALL BACK TO RHODEY'S EXAMPLE AND SAY, YEAH--MAYBE I COULD DO THAT, TOO.
AND HE CONTINUES TO INSPIRE US--

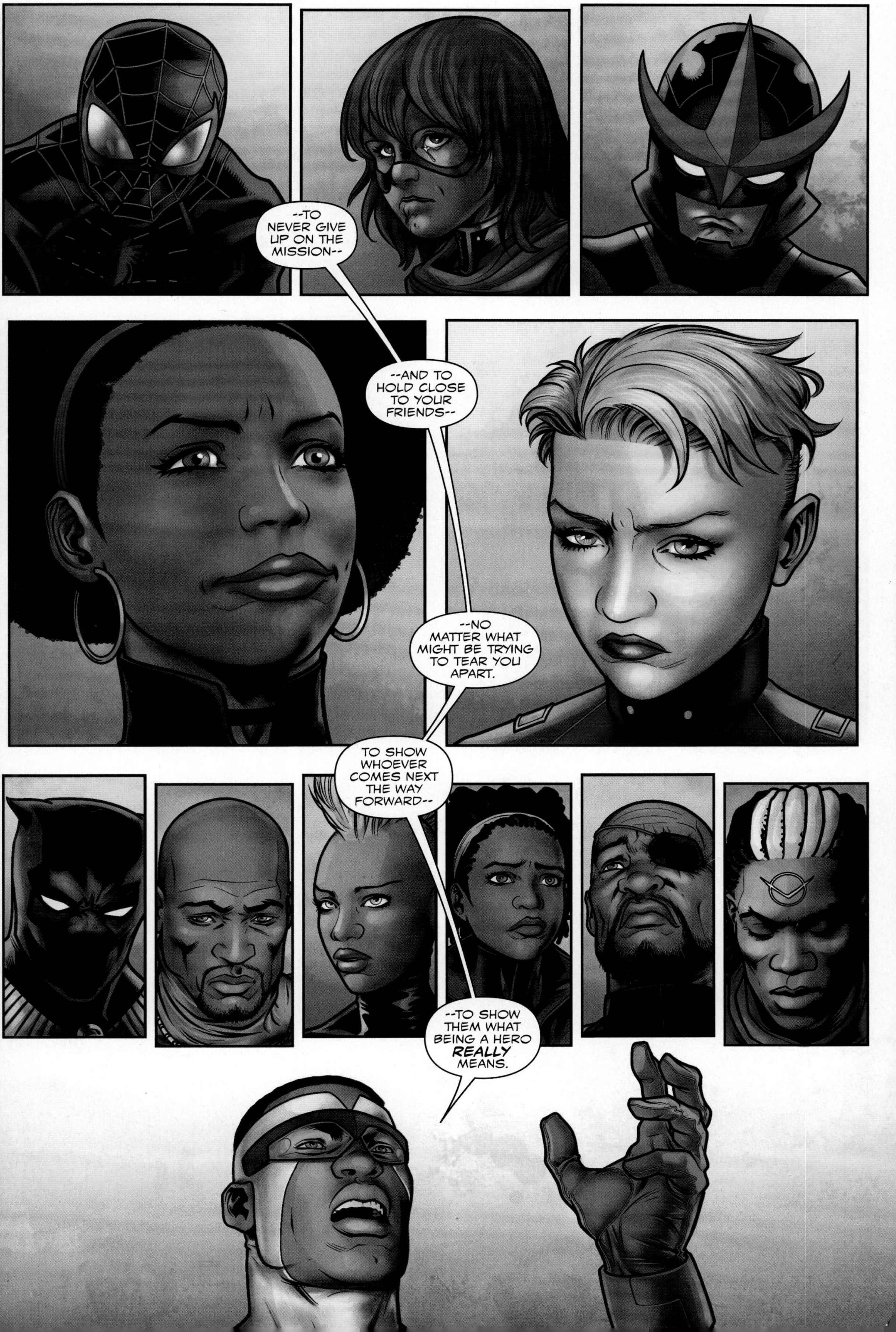
--TO NEVER GIVE UP ON THE MISSION--
--AND TO HOLD CLOSE TO YOUR FRIENDS--
--NO MATTER WHAT MIGHT BE TRYING TO TEAR YOU APART.
TO SHOW WHOEVER COMES NEXT THE WAY FORWARD--
--TO SHOW THEM WHAT BEING A HERO *REALLY* MEANS.

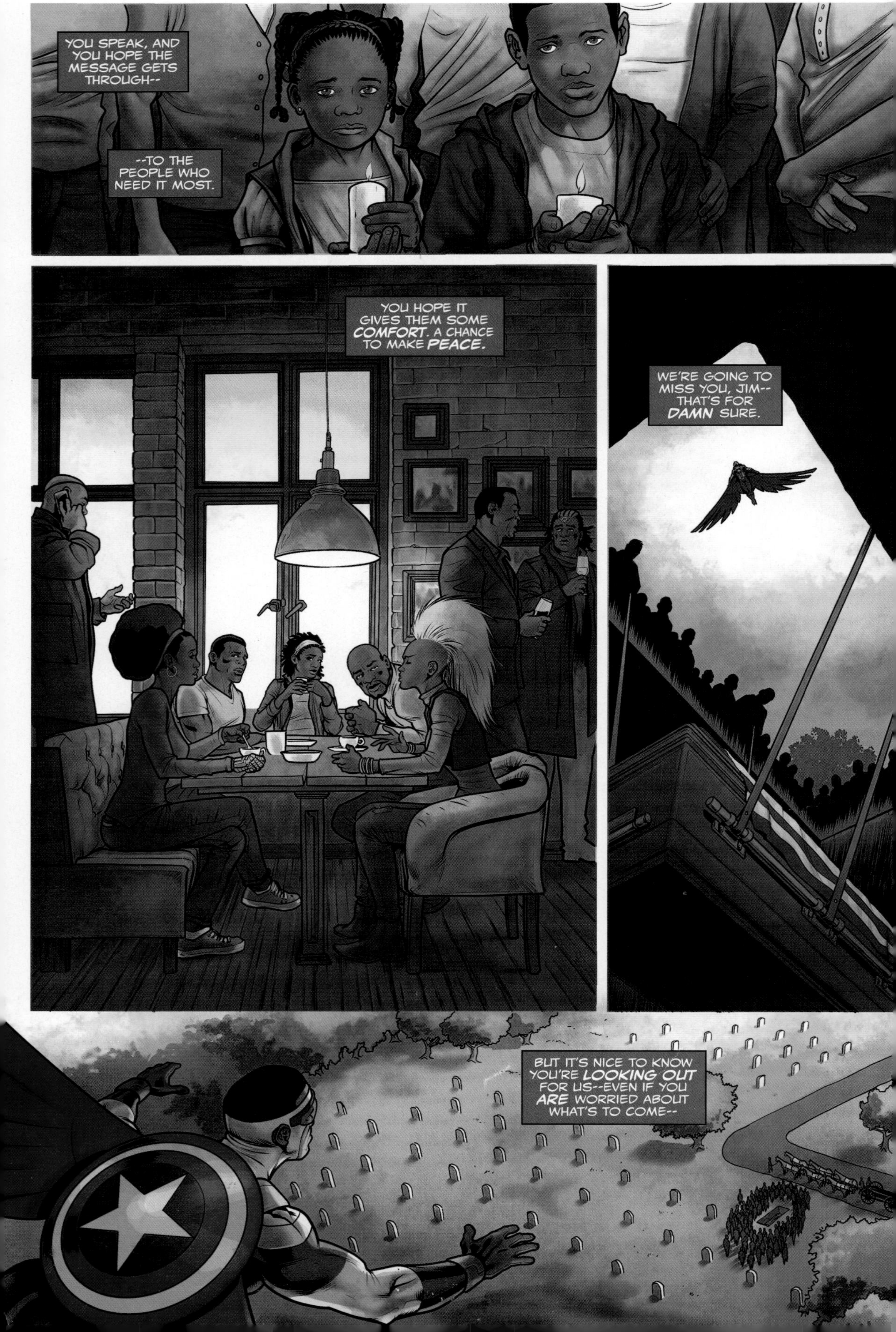
YOU SPEAK, AND YOU HOPE THE MESSAGE GETS THROUGH--
--TO THE PEOPLE WHO NEED IT MOST.
YOU HOPE IT GIVES THEM SOME COMFORT. A CHANCE TO MAKE PEACE.
WE'RE GOING TO MISS YOU, JIM-- THAT'S FOR DAMN SURE.
BUT IT'S NICE TO KNOW YOU'RE LOOKING OUT FOR US--EVEN IF YOU ARE WORRIED ABOUT WHAT'S TO COME--

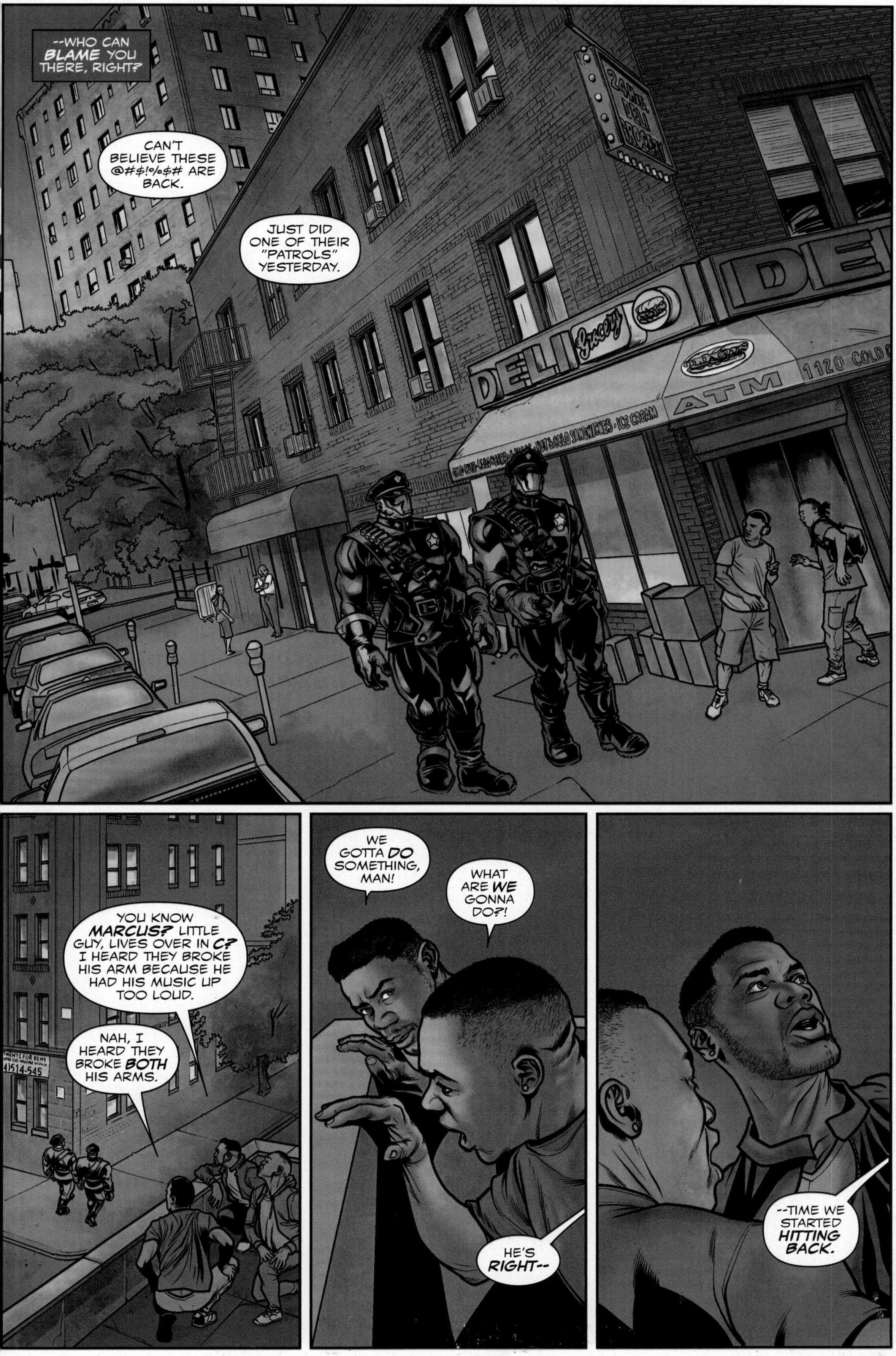
--WHO CAN BLAME YOU THERE, RIGHT?
CAN'T BELIEVE THESE @#$!%$# ARE BACK.
JUST DID ONE OF THEIR "PATROLS" YESTERDAY.
DELI
DELI
ATM
YOU KNOW MARCUS? LITTLE GUY, LIVES OVER IN C? I HEARD THEY BROKE HIS ARM BECAUSE HE HAD HIS MUSIC UP TOO LOUD.
NAH, I HEARD THEY BROKE BOTH HIS ARMS.
WE GOTTA DO SOMETHING, MAN!
WHAT ARE WE GONNA DO?!
HE'S RIGHT--
--TIME WE STARTED HITTING BACK.

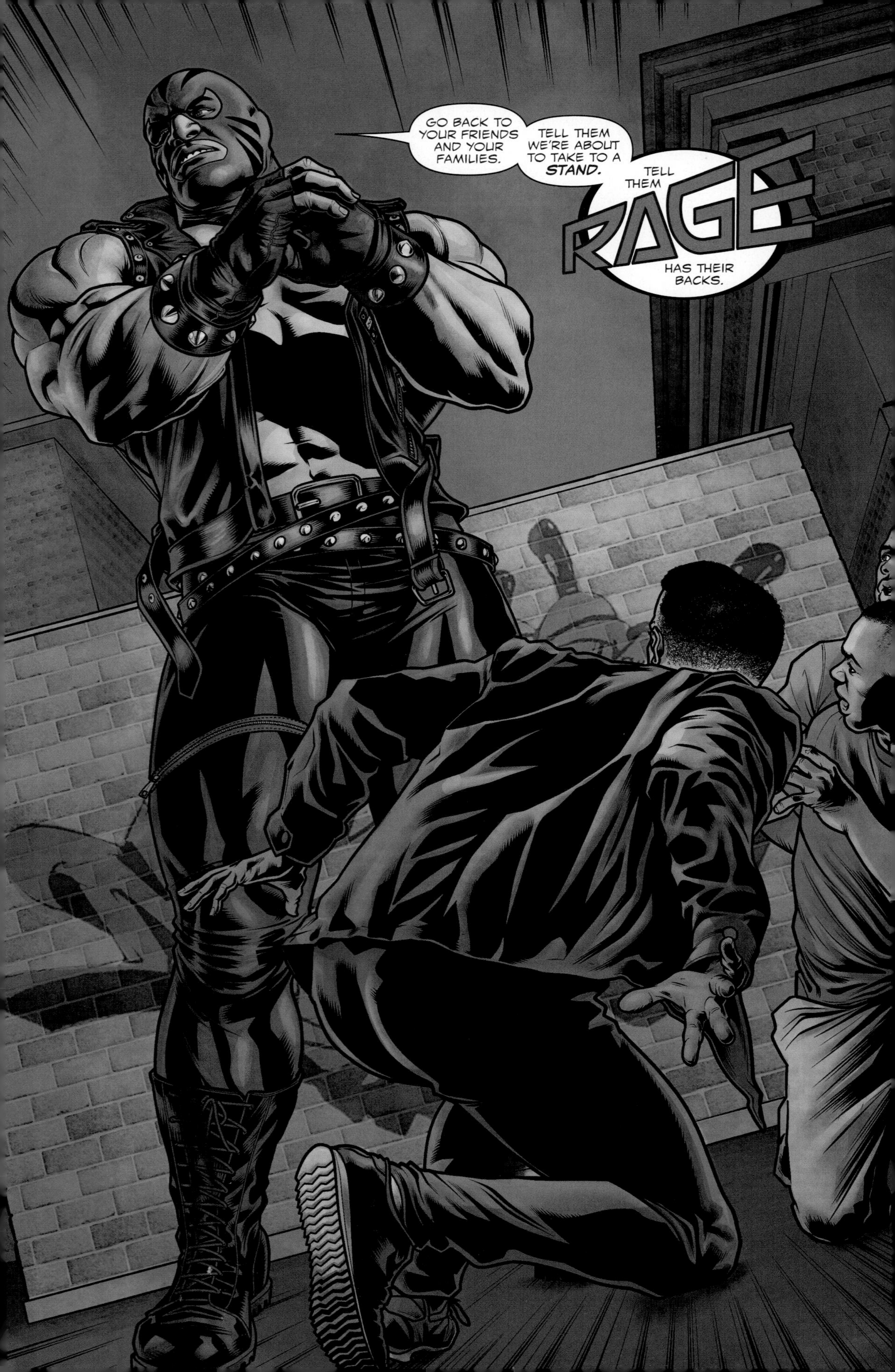
GO BACK TO YOUR FRIENDS AND YOUR FAMILIES.
TELL THEM WE'RE ABOUT TO TAKE TO A STAND.
TELL THEM
RAGE
HAS THEIR BACKS.

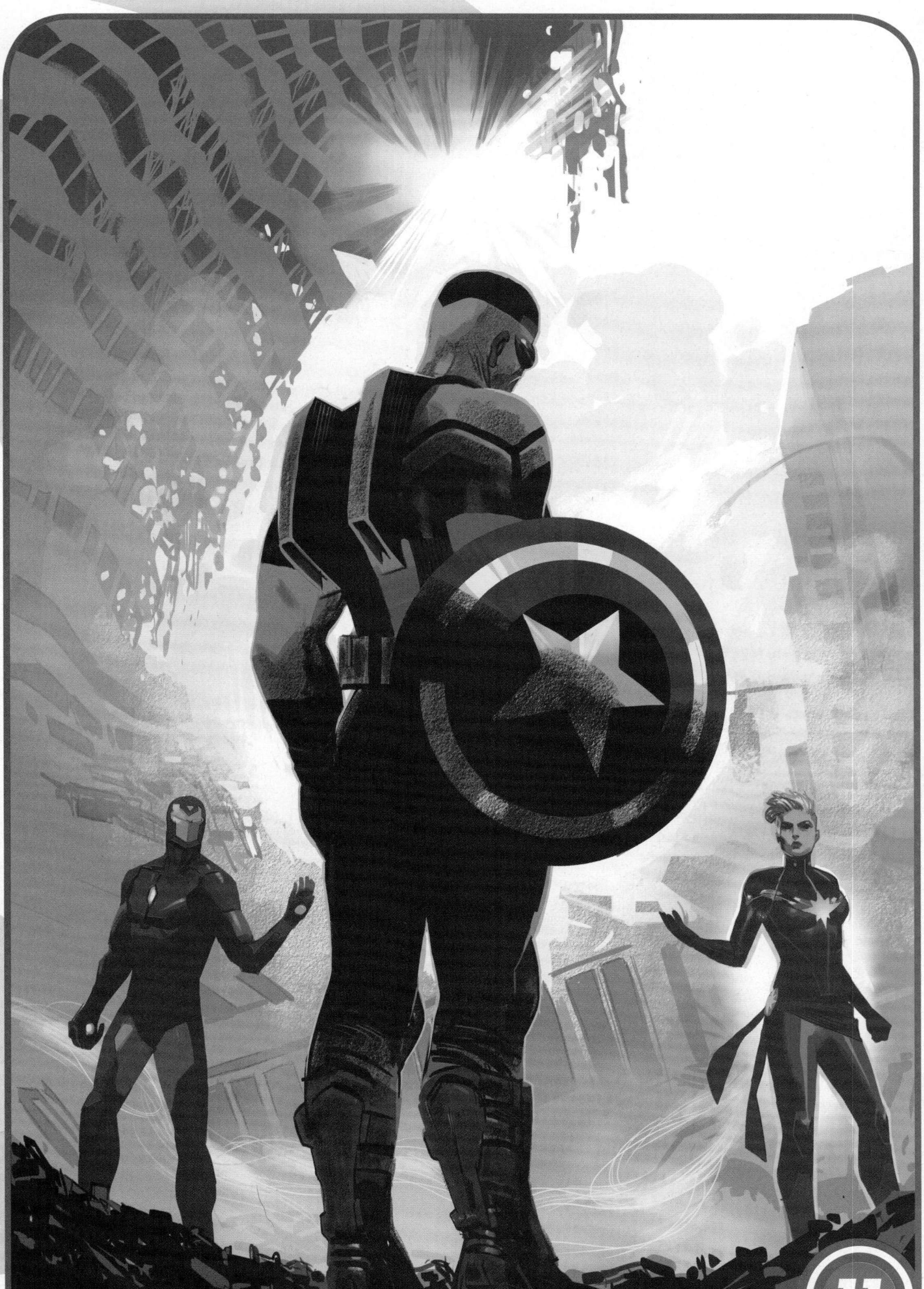
11

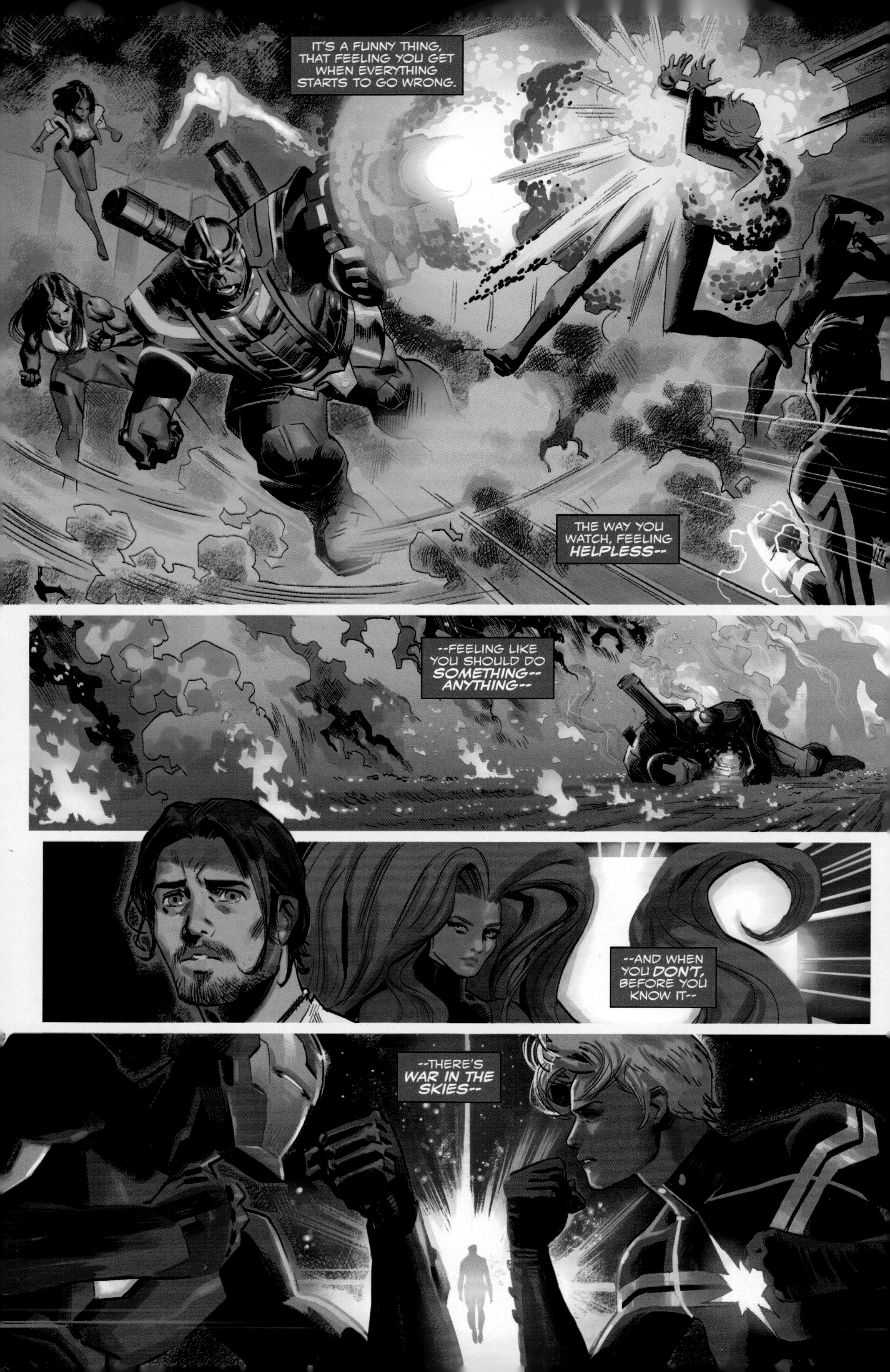
IT'S A FUNNY THING, THAT FEELING YOU GET WHEN EVERYTHING STARTS TO GO WRONG.
THE WAY YOU WATCH, FEELING HELPLESS--
--FEELING LIKE YOU SHOULD DO SOMETHING-- ANYTHING--
--AND WHEN YOU DON'T, BEFORE YOU KNOW IT--
--THERE'S WAR IN THE SKIES--

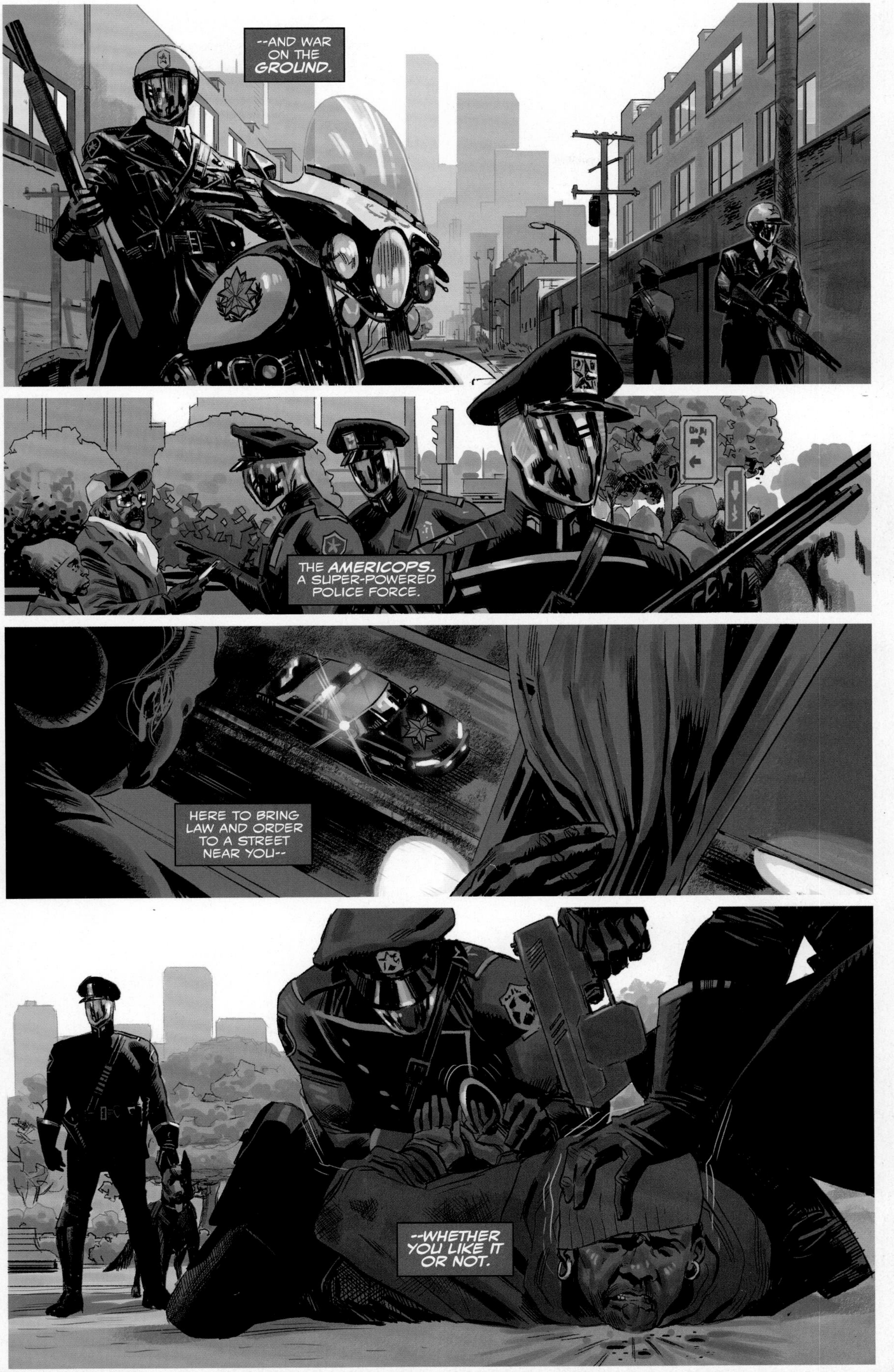

--AND WAR ON THE GROUND.
THE AMERICOPS. A SUPER-POWERED POLICE FORCE.
HERE TO BRING LAW AND ORDER TO A STREET NEAR YOU--
--WHETHER YOU LIKE IT OR NOT.

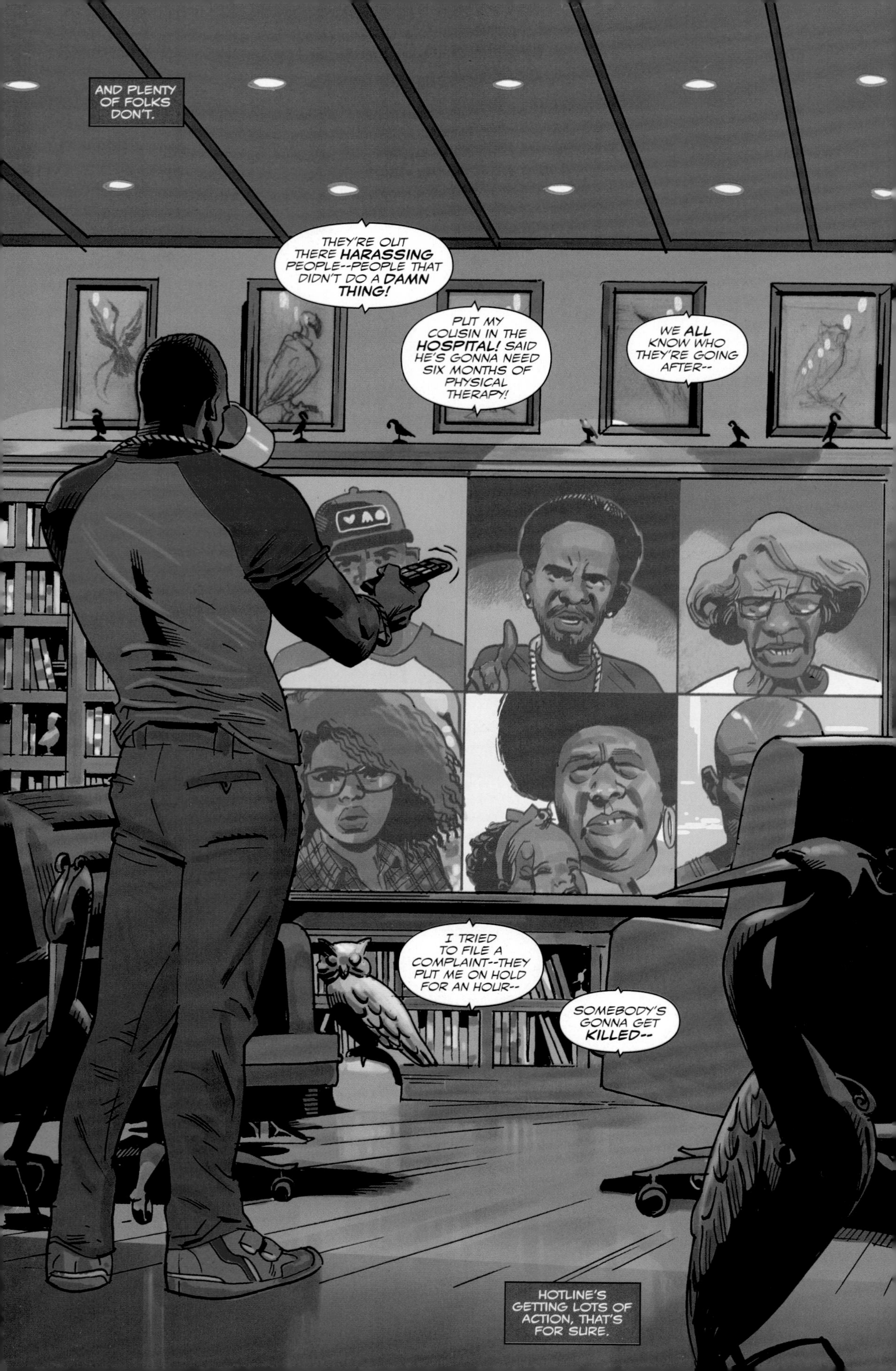
AND PLENTY OF FOLKS DON'T.
THEY'RE OUT THERE HARASSING PEOPLE--PEOPLE THAT DIDN'T DO A DAMN THING!
PUT MY COUSIN IN THE HOSPITAL! SAID HE'S GONNA NEED SIX MONTHS OF PHYSICAL THERAPY!
WE ALL KNOW WHO THEY'RE GOING AFTER--
I TRIED TO FILE A COMPLAINT--THEY PUT ME ON HOLD FOR AN HOUR--
SOMEBODY'S GONNA GET KILLED--
HOTLINE'S GETTING LOTS OF ACTION, THAT'S FOR SURE.

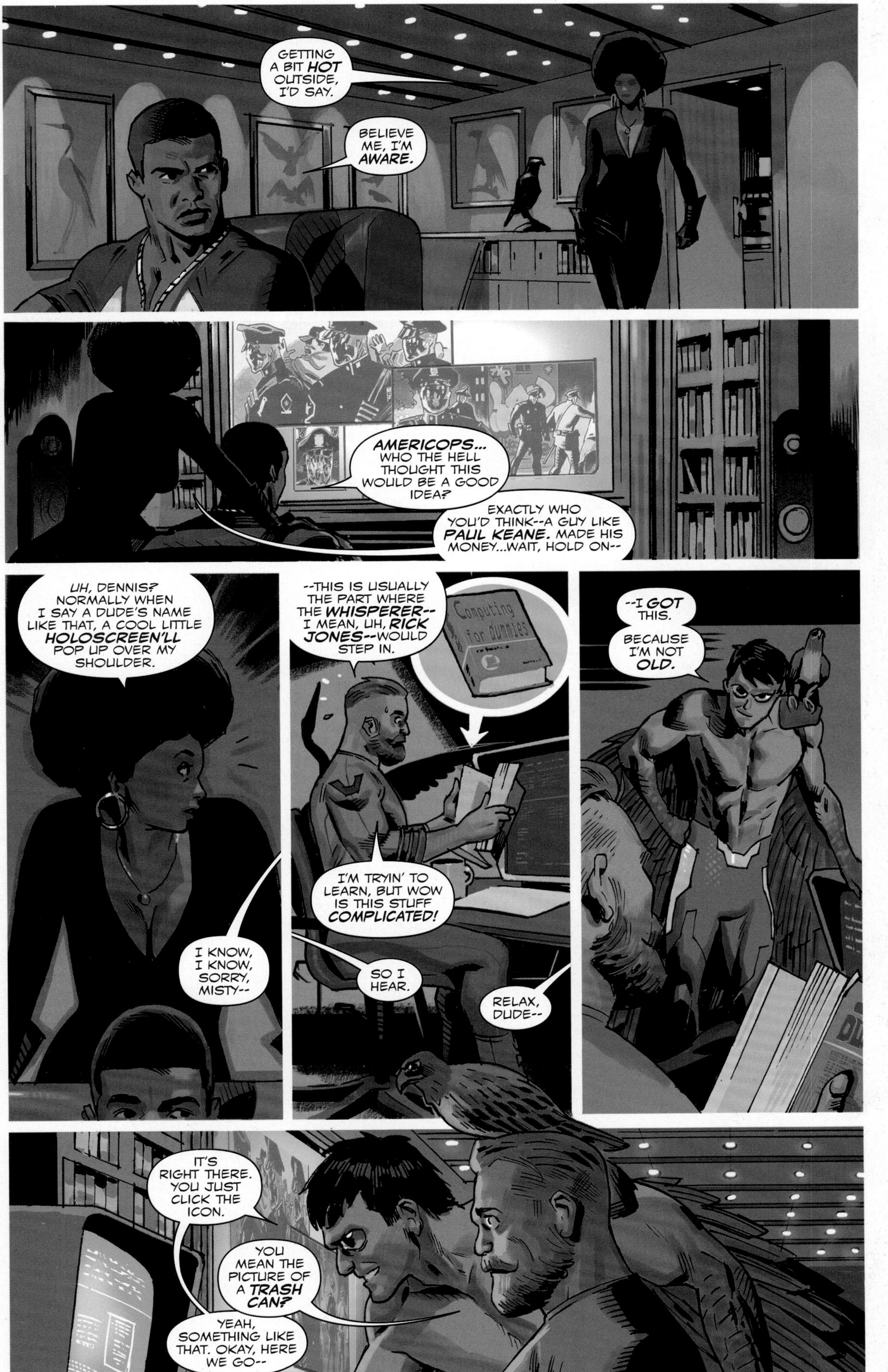

GETTING A BIT HOT OUTSIDE, I'D SAY.
BELIEVE ME, I'M AWARE.
AMERICOPS... WHO THE HELL THOUGHT THIS WOULD BE A GOOD IDEA?
EXACTLY WHO YOU'D THINK--A GUY LIKE PAUL KEANE. MADE HIS MONEY...WAIT, HOLD ON--
UH, DENNIS? NORMALLY WHEN I SAY A DUDE'S NAME LIKE THAT, A COOL LITTLE HOLOSCREEN'LL POP UP OVER MY SHOULDER.
I KNOW, I KNOW, SORRY, MISTY--
--THIS IS USUALLY THE PART WHERE THE WHISPERER--I MEAN, UH, RICK JONES--WOULD STEP IN.
Computing for dummies
I'M TRYIN' TO LEARN, BUT WOW IS THIS STUFF COMPLICATED!
SO I HEAR.
RELAX, DUDE--
--I GOT THIS.
BECAUSE I'M NOT OLD.
IT'S RIGHT THERE. YOU JUST CLICK THE ICON.
YOU MEAN THE PICTURE OF A TRASH CAN?
YEAH, SOMETHING LIKE THAT. OKAY, HERE WE GO--

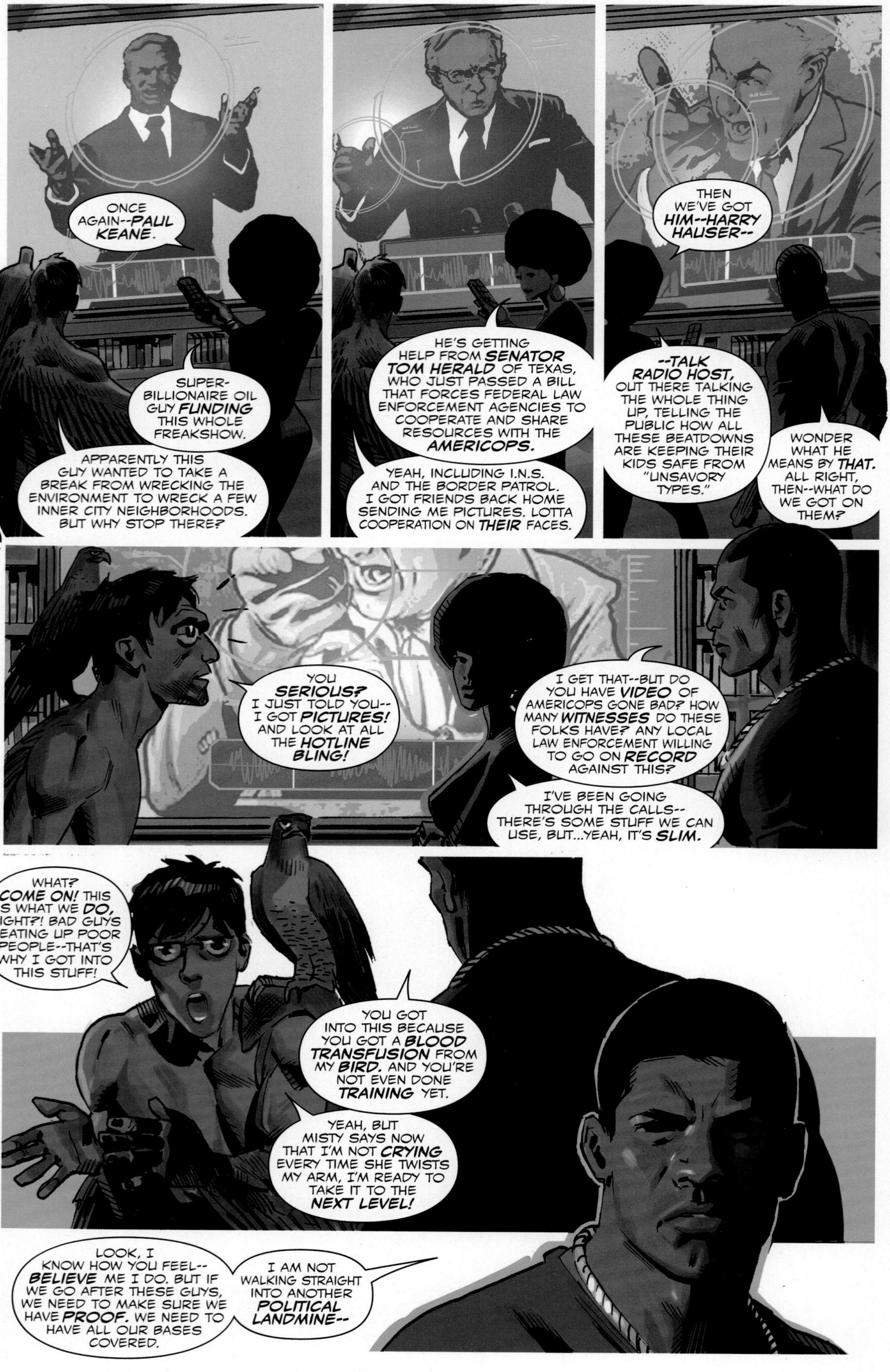
ONCE AGAIN--PAUL KEANE.
SUPER-BILLIONAIRE OIL GUY FUNDING THIS WHOLE FREAKSHOW.
APPARENTLY THIS GUY WANTED TO TAKE A BREAK FROM WRECKING THE ENVIRONMENT TO WRECK A FEW INNER CITY NEIGHBORHOODS. BUT WHY STOP THERE?
HE'S GETTING HELP FROM SENATOR TOM HERALD OF TEXAS, WHO JUST PASSED A BILL THAT FORCES FEDERAL LAW ENFORCEMENT AGENCIES TO COOPERATE AND SHARE RESOURCES WITH THE AMERICOPS.
YEAH, INCLUDING I.N.S. AND THE BORDER PATROL. I GOT FRIENDS BACK HOME SENDING ME PICTURES. LOTTA COOPERATION ON THEIR FACES.
THEN WE'VE GOT HIM--HARRY HAUSER--
--TALK RADIO HOST, OUT THERE TALKING THE WHOLE THING UP, TELLING THE PUBLIC HOW ALL THESE BEATDOWNS ARE KEEPING THEIR KIDS SAFE FROM "UNSAVORY TYPES."
WONDER WHAT HE MEANS BY THAT. ALL RIGHT, THEN--WHAT DO WE GOT ON THEM?
YOU SERIOUS? I JUST TOLD YOU--I GOT PICTURES! AND LOOK AT ALL THE HOTLINE BLING!
I GET THAT--BUT DO YOU HAVE VIDEO OF AMERICOPS GONE BAD? HOW MANY WITNESSES DO THESE FOLKS HAVE? ANY LOCAL LAW ENFORCEMENT WILLING TO GO ON RECORD AGAINST THIS?
I'VE BEEN GOING THROUGH THE CALLS--THERE'S SOME STUFF WE CAN USE, BUT...YEAH, IT'S SLIM.
WHAT? COME ON! THIS IS WHAT WE DO, RIGHT?! BAD GUYS BEATING UP POOR PEOPLE--THAT'S WHY I GOT INTO THIS STUFF!
YOU GOT INTO THIS BECAUSE YOU GOT A BLOOD TRANSFUSION FROM MY BIRD. AND YOU'RE NOT EVEN DONE TRAINING YET.
YEAH, BUT MISTY SAYS NOW THAT I'M NOT CRYING EVERY TIME SHE TWISTS MY ARM, I'M READY TO TAKE IT TO THE NEXT LEVEL!
LOOK, I KNOW HOW YOU FEEL--BELIEVE ME I DO. BUT IF WE GO AFTER THESE GUYS, WE NEED TO MAKE SURE WE HAVE PROOF. WE NEED TO HAVE ALL OUR BASES COVERED.
I AM NOT WALKING STRAIGHT INTO ANOTHER POLITICAL LANDMINE--

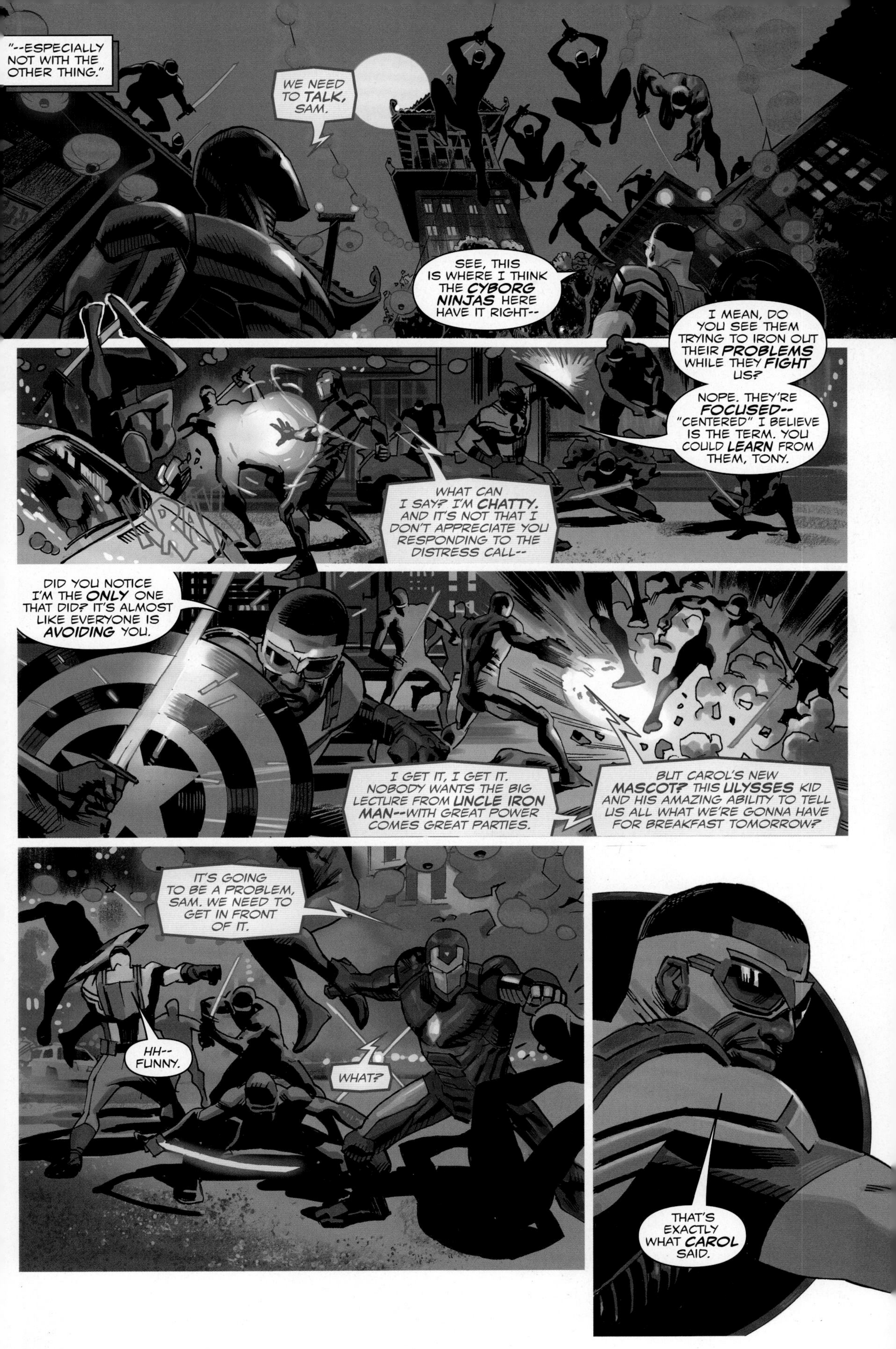
"--ESPECIALLY NOT WITH THE OTHER THING."
WE NEED TO TALK, SAM.
SEE, THIS IS WHERE I THINK THE CYBORG NINJAS HERE HAVE IT RIGHT--
I MEAN, DO YOU SEE THEM TRYING TO IRON OUT THEIR PROBLEMS WHILE THEY FIGHT US?
NOPE. THEY'RE FOCUSED-- "CENTERED" I BELIEVE IS THE TERM. YOU COULD LEARN FROM THEM, TONY.
WHAT CAN I SAY? I'M CHATTY. AND IT'S NOT THAT I DON'T APPRECIATE YOU RESPONDING TO THE DISTRESS CALL--
DID YOU NOTICE I'M THE ONLY ONE THAT DID? IT'S ALMOST LIKE EVERYONE IS AVOIDING YOU.
I GET IT, I GET IT. NOBODY WANTS THE BIG LECTURE FROM UNCLE IRON MAN--WITH GREAT POWER COMES GREAT PARTIES.
BUT CAROL'S NEW MASCOT? THIS ULYSSES KID AND HIS AMAZING ABILITY TO TELL US ALL WHAT WE'RE GONNA HAVE FOR BREAKFAST TOMORROW?
IT'S GOING TO BE A PROBLEM, SAM. WE NEED TO GET IN FRONT OF IT.
HH-- FUNNY.
WHAT?
THAT'S EXACTLY WHAT CAROL SAID.

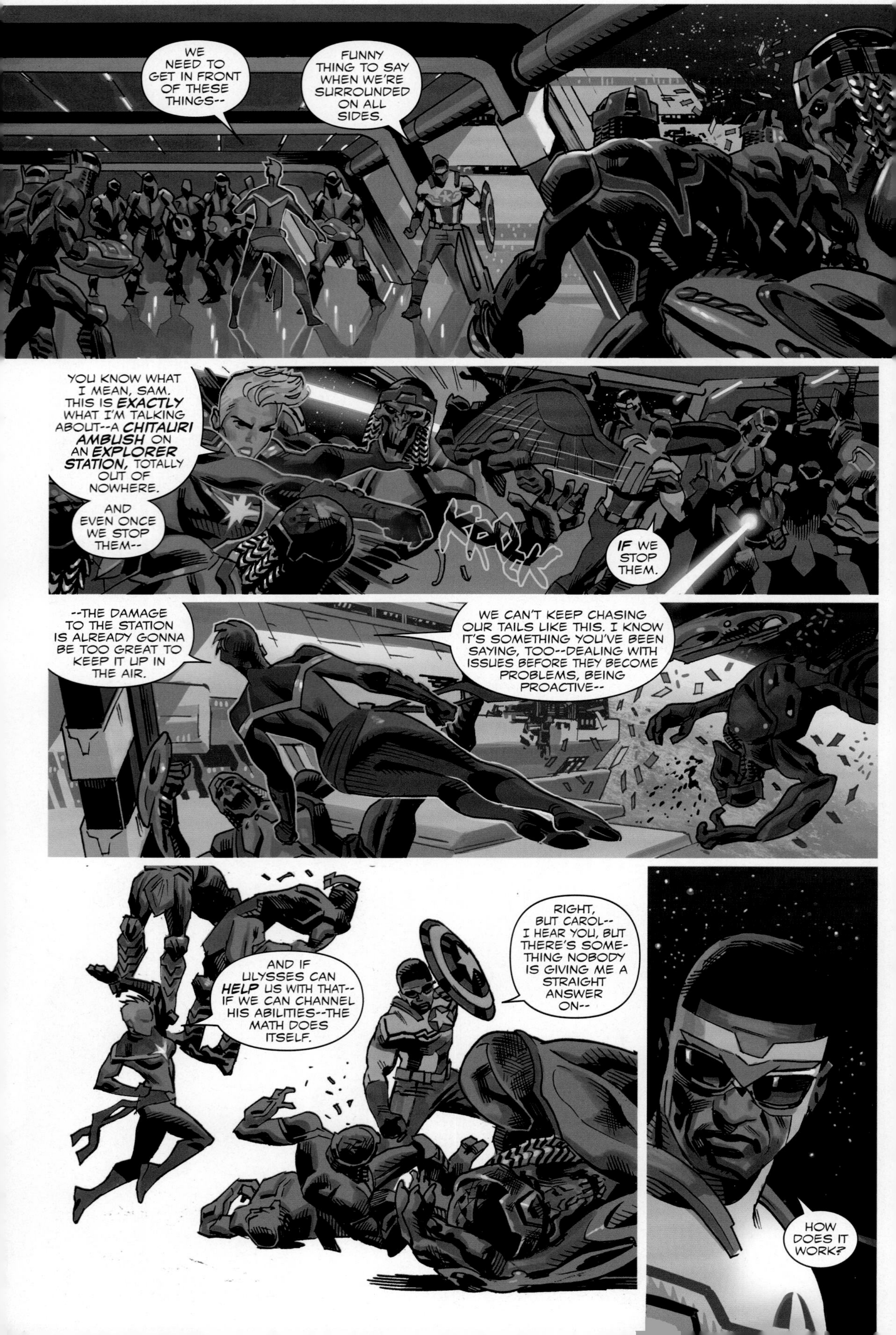
WE NEED TO GET IN FRONT OF THESE THINGS--
FUNNY THING TO SAY WHEN WE'RE SURROUNDED ON ALL SIDES.
YOU KNOW WHAT I MEAN, SAM. THIS IS EXACTLY WHAT I'M TALKING ABOUT--A CHITAURI AMBUSH ON AN EXPLORER STATION, TOTALLY OUT OF NOWHERE.
AND EVEN ONCE WE STOP THEM--
IF WE STOP THEM.
--THE DAMAGE TO THE STATION IS ALREADY GONNA BE TOO GREAT TO KEEP IT UP IN THE AIR.
WE CAN'T KEEP CHASING OUR TAILS LIKE THIS. I KNOW IT'S SOMETHING YOU'VE BEEN SAYING, TOO--DEALING WITH ISSUES BEFORE THEY BECOME PROBLEMS, BEING PROACTIVE--
AND IF ULYSSES CAN HELP US WITH THAT--IF WE CAN CHANNEL HIS ABILITIES--THE MATH DOES ITSELF.
RIGHT, BUT CAROL--I HEAR YOU, BUT THERE'S SOMETHING NOBODY IS GIVING ME A STRAIGHT ANSWER ON--
HOW DOES IT WORK?

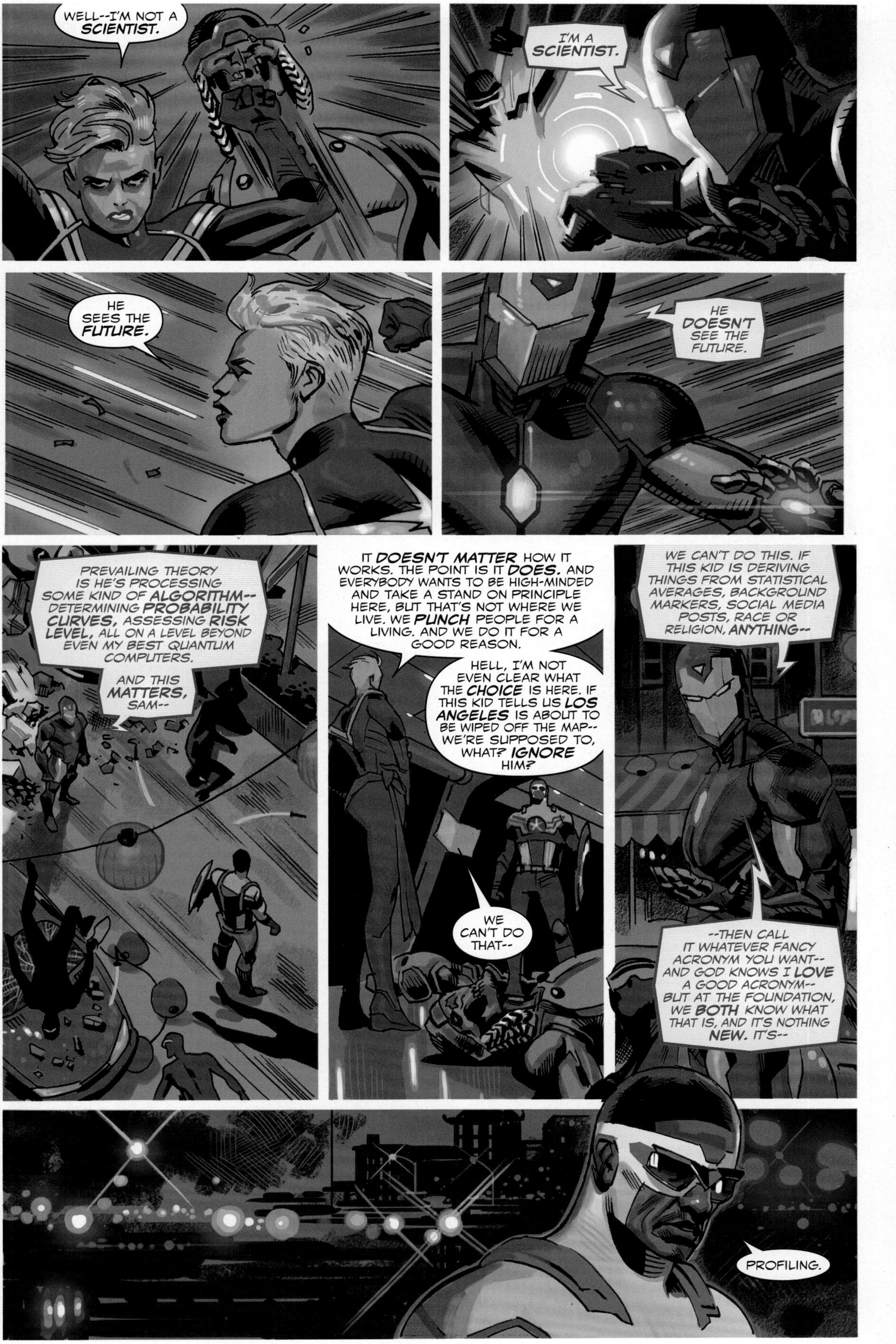

WELL--I'M NOT A SCIENTIST.
I'M A SCIENTIST.
HE SEES THE FUTURE.
HE DOESN'T SEE THE FUTURE.
PREVAILING THEORY IS HE'S PROCESSING SOME KIND OF ALGORITHM-- DETERMINING PROBABILITY CURVES, ASSESSING RISK LEVEL, ALL ON A LEVEL BEYOND EVEN MY BEST QUANTUM COMPUTERS.
AND THIS MATTERS, SAM--
IT DOESN'T MATTER HOW IT WORKS. THE POINT IS IT DOES. AND EVERYBODY WANTS TO BE HIGH-MINDED AND TAKE A STAND ON PRINCIPLE HERE, BUT THAT'S NOT WHERE WE LIVE. WE PUNCH PEOPLE FOR A LIVING. AND WE DO IT FOR A GOOD REASON.
HELL, I'M NOT EVEN CLEAR WHAT THE CHOICE IS HERE. IF THIS KID TELLS US LOS ANGELES IS ABOUT TO BE WIPED OFF THE MAP-- WE'RE SUPPOSED TO, WHAT? IGNORE HIM?
WE CAN'T DO THAT--
WE CAN'T DO THIS. IF THIS KID IS DERIVING THINGS FROM STATISTICAL AVERAGES, BACKGROUND MARKERS, SOCIAL MEDIA POSTS, RACE OR RELIGION, ANYTHING--
--THEN CALL IT WHATEVER FANCY ACRONYM YOU WANT-- AND GOD KNOWS I LOVE A GOOD ACRONYM-- BUT AT THE FOUNDATION, WE BOTH KNOW WHAT THAT IS, AND IT'S NOTHING NEW. IT'S--
PROFILING.

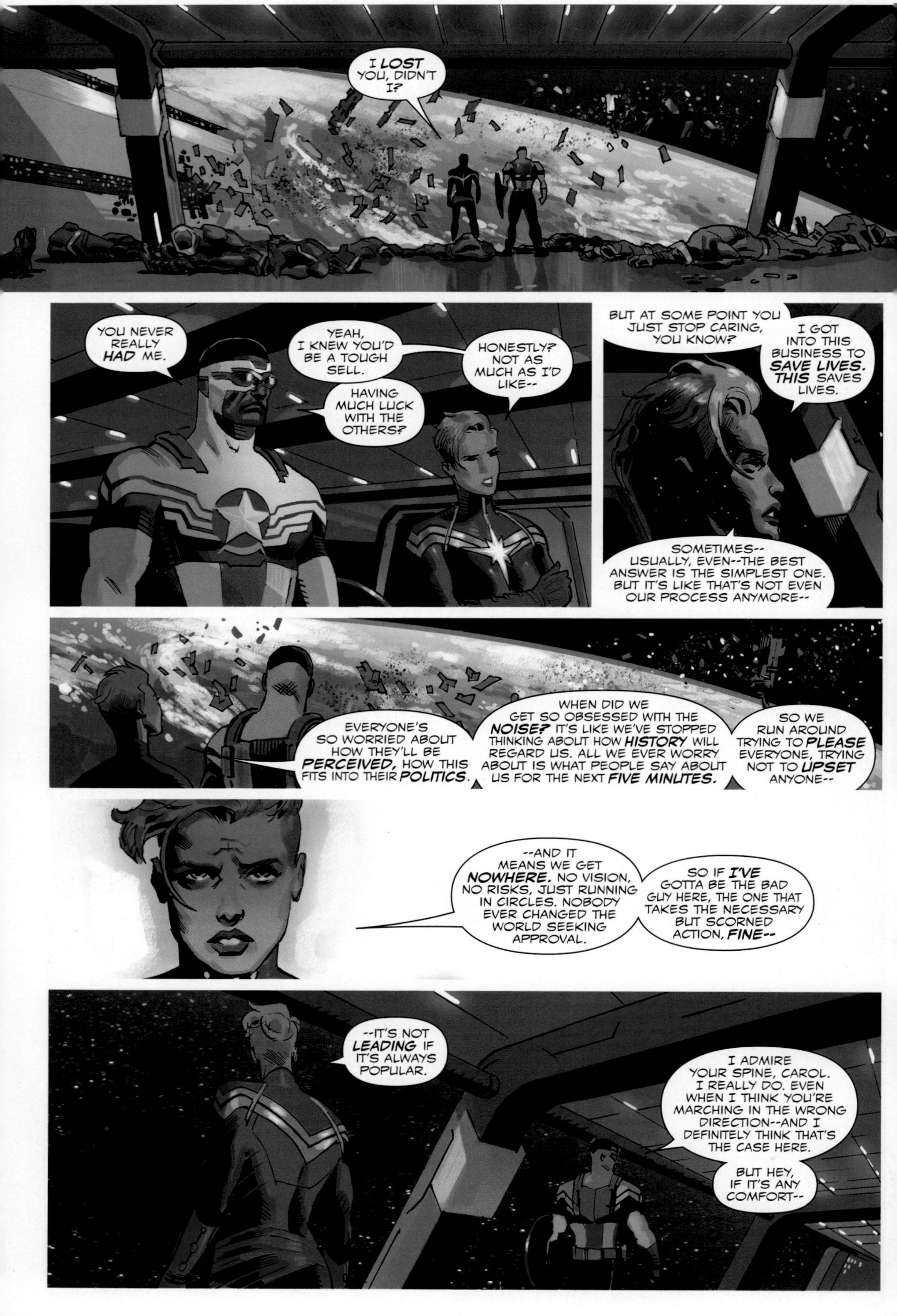
I LOST YOU, DIDN'T I?
YOU NEVER REALLY HAD ME.
YEAH, I KNEW YOU'D BE A TOUGH SELL.
HAVING MUCH LUCK WITH THE OTHERS?
HONESTLY? NOT AS MUCH AS I'D LIKE--
BUT AT SOME POINT YOU JUST STOP CARING, YOU KNOW?
I GOT INTO THIS BUSINESS TO SAVE LIVES. THIS SAVES LIVES.
SOMETIMES--USUALLY, EVEN--THE BEST ANSWER IS THE SIMPLEST ONE. BUT IT'S LIKE THAT'S NOT EVEN OUR PROCESS ANYMORE--
EVERYONE'S SO WORRIED ABOUT HOW THEY'LL BE PERCEIVED, HOW THIS FITS INTO THEIR POLITICS.
WHEN DID WE GET SO OBSESSED WITH THE NOISE? IT'S LIKE WE'VE STOPPED THINKING ABOUT HOW HISTORY WILL REGARD US. ALL WE EVER WORRY ABOUT IS WHAT PEOPLE SAY ABOUT US FOR THE NEXT FIVE MINUTES.
SO WE RUN AROUND TRYING TO PLEASE EVERYONE, TRYING NOT TO UPSET ANYONE--
--AND IT MEANS WE GET NOWHERE. NO VISION, NO RISKS, JUST RUNNING IN CIRCLES. NOBODY EVER CHANGED THE WORLD SEEKING APPROVAL.
SO IF I'VE GOTTA BE THE BAD GUY HERE, THE ONE THAT TAKES THE NECESSARY BUT SCORNED ACTION, FINE--
--IT'S NOT LEADING IF IT'S ALWAYS POPULAR.
I ADMIRE YOUR SPINE, CAROL. I REALLY DO. EVEN WHEN I THINK YOU'RE MARCHING IN THE WRONG DIRECTION--AND I DEFINITELY THINK THAT'S THE CASE HERE.
BUT HEY, IF IT'S ANY COMFORT--

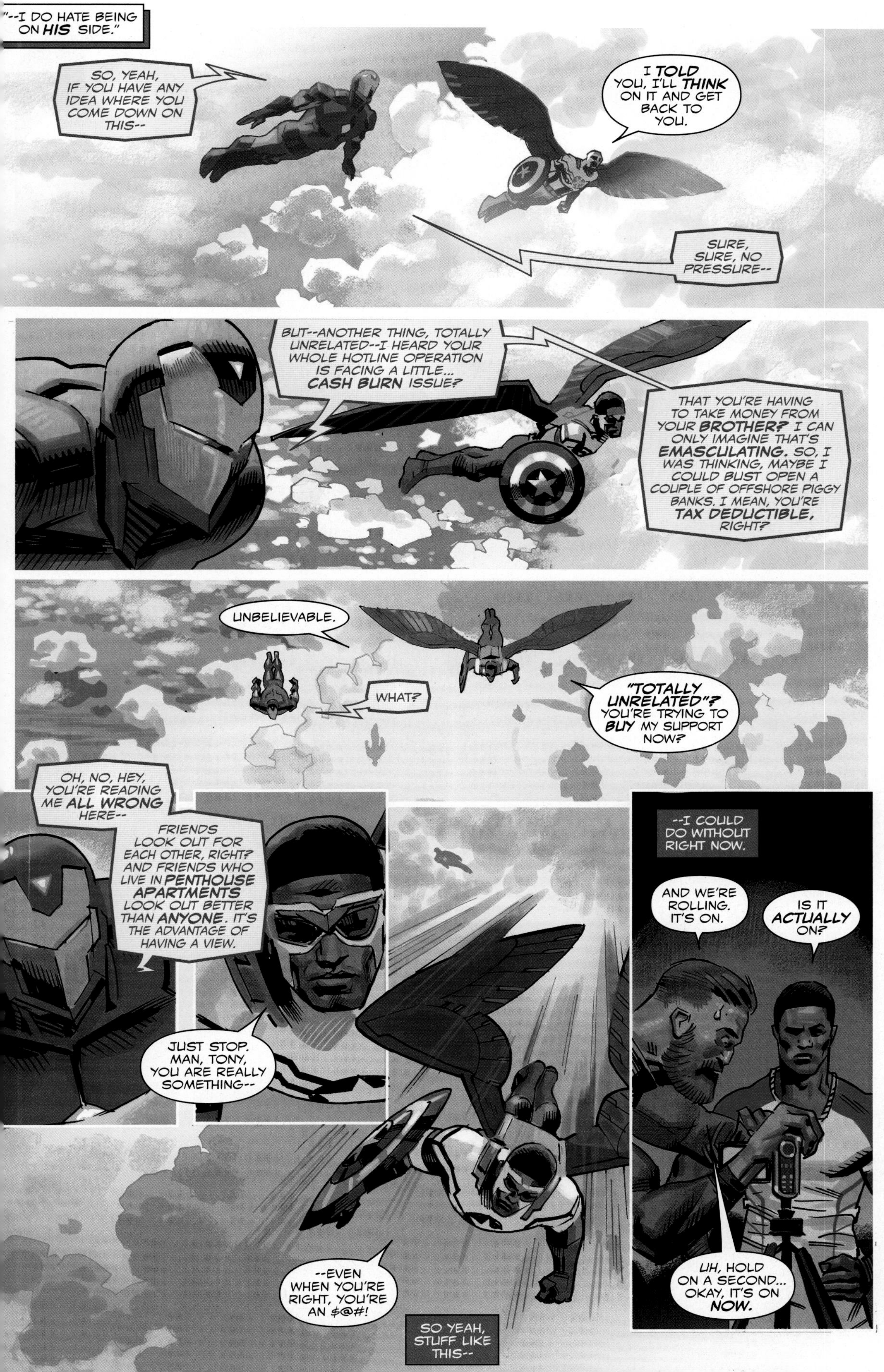
"--I DO HATE BEING ON HIS SIDE."
SO, YEAH, IF YOU HAVE ANY IDEA WHERE YOU COME DOWN ON THIS--
I TOLD YOU, I'LL THINK ON IT AND GET BACK TO YOU.
SURE, SURE, NO PRESSURE--
BUT--ANOTHER THING, TOTALLY UNRELATED--I HEARD YOUR WHOLE HOTLINE OPERATION IS FACING A LITTLE... CASH BURN ISSUE?
THAT YOU'RE HAVING TO TAKE MONEY FROM YOUR BROTHER? I CAN ONLY IMAGINE THAT'S EMASCULATING. SO, I WAS THINKING, MAYBE I COULD BUST OPEN A COUPLE OF OFFSHORE PIGGY BANKS. I MEAN, YOU'RE TAX DEDUCTIBLE, RIGHT?
UNBELIEVABLE.
WHAT?
"TOTALLY UNRELATED"? YOU'RE TRYING TO BUY MY SUPPORT NOW?
OH, NO, HEY, YOU'RE READING ME ALL WRONG HERE--
FRIENDS LOOK OUT FOR EACH OTHER, RIGHT? AND FRIENDS WHO LIVE IN PENTHOUSE APARTMENTS LOOK OUT BETTER THAN ANYONE. IT'S THE ADVANTAGE OF HAVING A VIEW.
JUST STOP. MAN, TONY, YOU ARE REALLY SOMETHING--
--EVEN WHEN YOU'RE RIGHT, YOU'RE AN $@#!
SO YEAH, STUFF LIKE THIS--
--I COULD DO WITHOUT RIGHT NOW.
AND WE'RE ROLLING. IT'S ON.
IS IT ACTUALLY ON?
UH, HOLD ON A SECOND... OKAY, IT'S ON NOW.

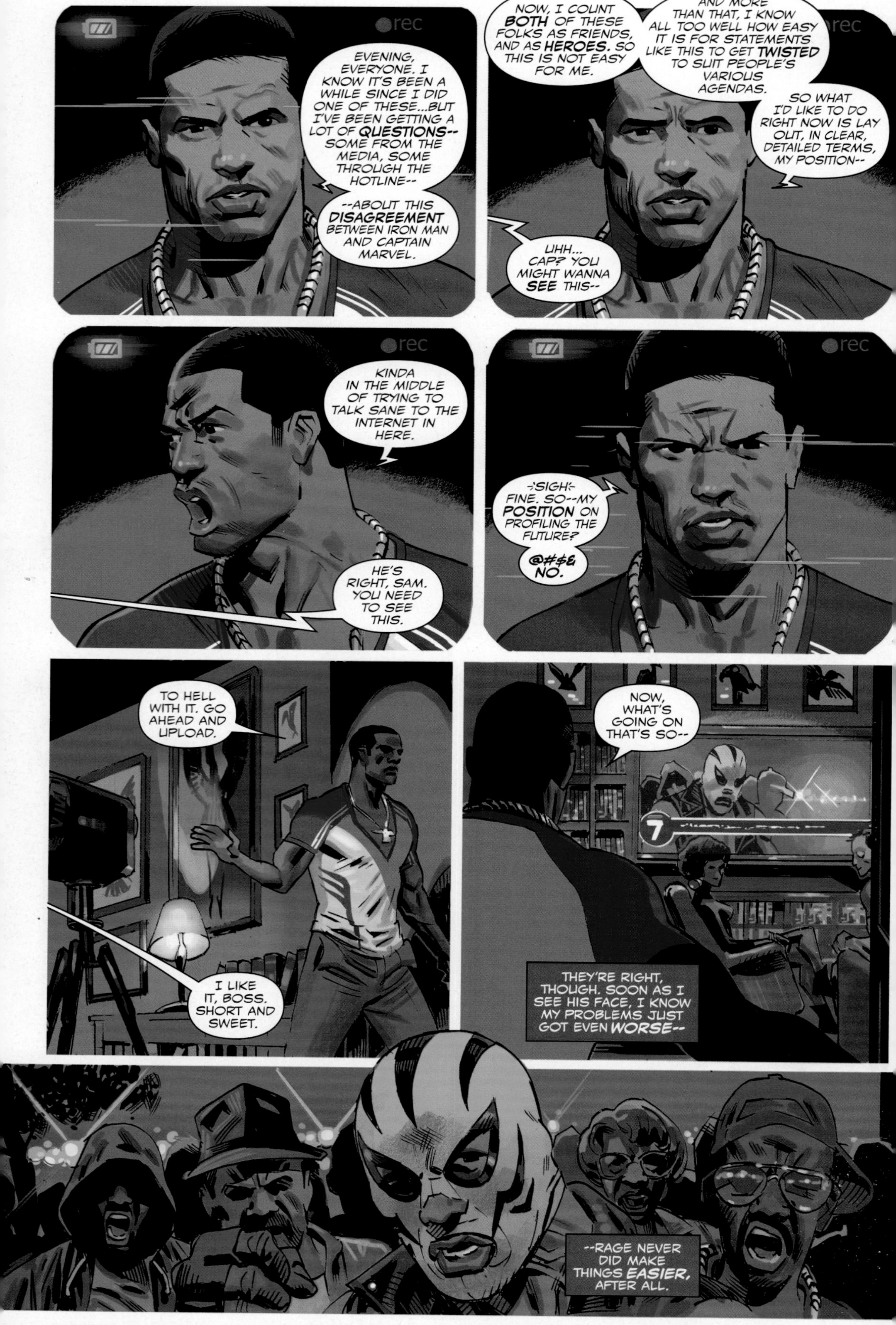

rec
EVENING, EVERYONE. I KNOW IT'S BEEN A WHILE SINCE I DID ONE OF THESE...BUT I'VE BEEN GETTING A LOT OF QUESTIONS--SOME FROM THE MEDIA, SOME THROUGH THE HOTLINE--
--ABOUT THIS DISAGREEMENT BETWEEN IRON MAN AND CAPTAIN MARVEL.
NOW, I COUNT BOTH OF THESE FOLKS AS FRIENDS, AND AS HEROES. SO THIS IS NOT EASY FOR ME.
AND MORE THAN THAT, I KNOW ALL TOO WELL HOW EASY IT IS FOR STATEMENTS LIKE THIS TO GET TWISTED TO SUIT PEOPLE'S VARIOUS AGENDAS.
SO WHAT I'D LIKE TO DO RIGHT NOW IS LAY OUT, IN CLEAR, DETAILED TERMS, MY POSITION--
UHH... CAP? YOU MIGHT WANNA SEE THIS--
KINDA IN THE MIDDLE OF TRYING TO TALK SANE TO THE INTERNET IN HERE.
HE'S RIGHT, SAM. YOU NEED TO SEE THIS.
SIGH FINE. SO--MY POSITION ON PROFILING THE FUTURE?
@#$& NO.
TO HELL WITH IT. GO AHEAD AND UPLOAD.
I LIKE IT, BOSS. SHORT AND SWEET.
NOW, WHAT'S GOING ON THAT'S SO--
7
THEY'RE RIGHT, THOUGH. SOON AS I SEE HIS FACE, I KNOW MY PROBLEMS JUST GOT EVEN WORSE--
--RAGE NEVER DID MAKE THINGS EASIER, AFTER ALL.

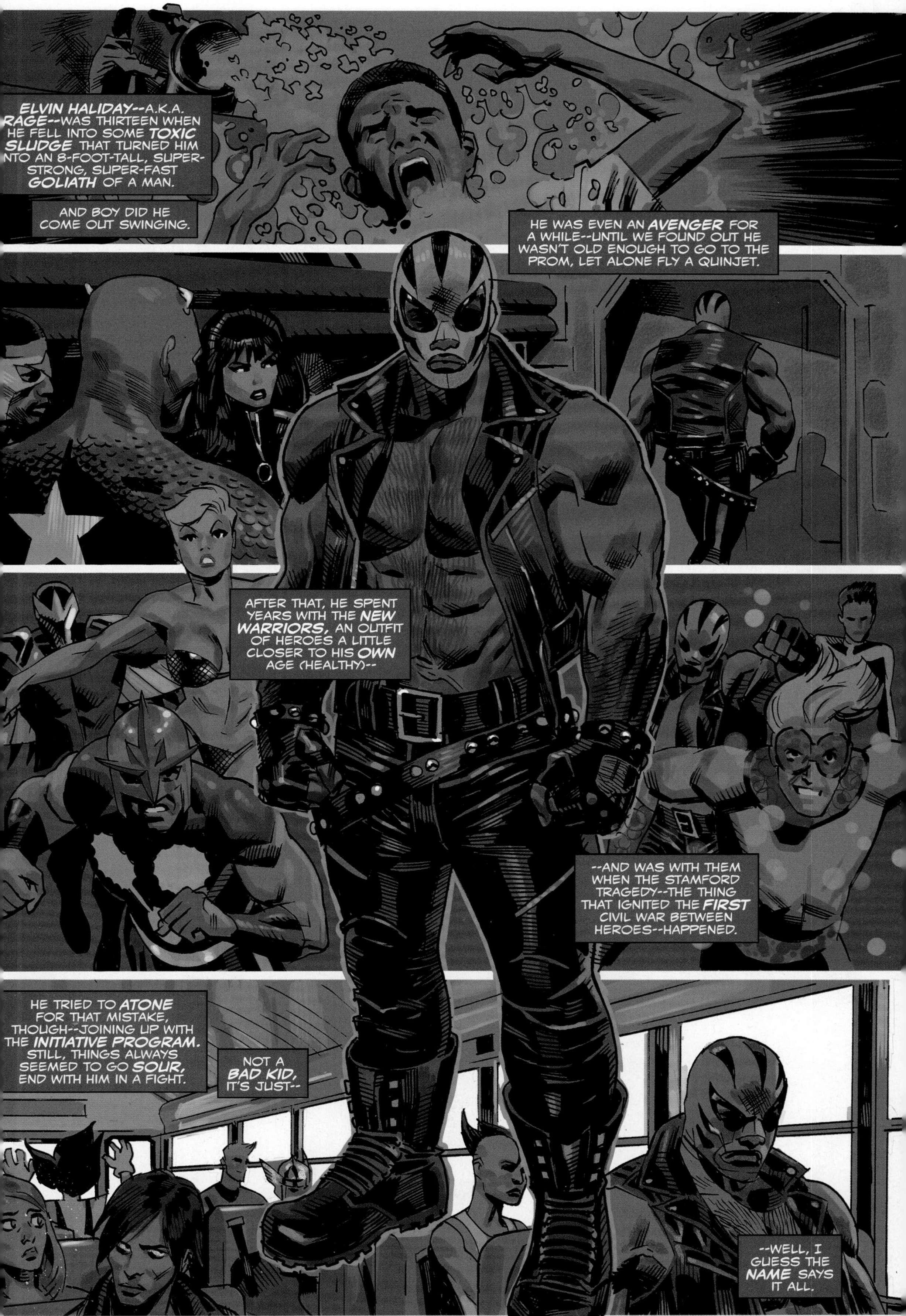
ELVIN HALIDAY--A.K.A. RAGE--WAS THIRTEEN WHEN HE FELL INTO SOME TOXIC SLUDGE THAT TURNED HIM INTO AN 8-FOOT-TALL, SUPER-STRONG, SUPER-FAST GOLIATH OF A MAN.
AND BOY DID HE COME OUT SWINGING.
HE WAS EVEN AN AVENGER FOR A WHILE--UNTIL WE FOUND OUT HE WASN'T OLD ENOUGH TO GO TO THE PROM, LET ALONE FLY A QUINJET.
AFTER THAT, HE SPENT YEARS WITH THE NEW WARRIORS, AN OUTFIT OF HEROES A LITTLE CLOSER TO HIS OWN AGE (HEALTHY)--
--AND WAS WITH THEM WHEN THE STAMFORD TRAGEDY--THE THING THAT IGNITED THE FIRST CIVIL WAR BETWEEN HEROES--HAPPENED.
HE TRIED TO ATONE FOR THAT MISTAKE, THOUGH--JOINING UP WITH THE INITIATIVE PROGRAM. STILL, THINGS ALWAYS SEEMED TO GO SOUR, END WITH HIM IN A FIGHT.
NOT A BAD KID, IT'S JUST--
--WELL, I GUESS THE NAME SAYS IT ALL.

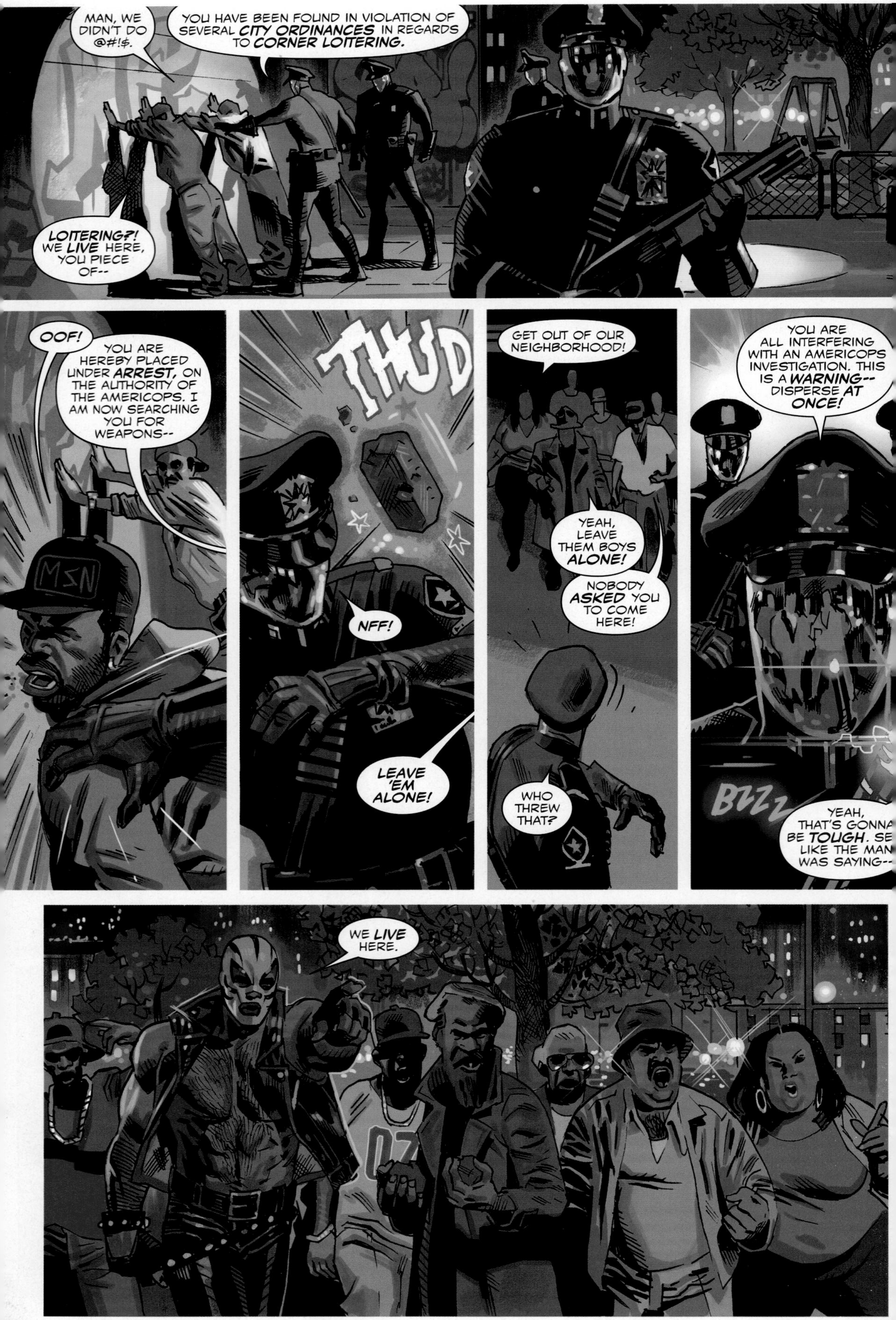
MAN, WE DIDN'T DO @#!$.
YOU HAVE BEEN FOUND IN VIOLATION OF SEVERAL CITY ORDINANCES IN REGARDS TO CORNER LOITERING.
LOITERING?! WE LIVE HERE, YOU PIECE OF--
OOF!
YOU ARE HEREBY PLACED UNDER ARREST, ON THE AUTHORITY OF THE AMERICOPS. I AM NOW SEARCHING YOU FOR WEAPONS--
THUD
NFF!
LEAVE 'EM ALONE!
GET OUT OF OUR NEIGHBORHOOD!
YEAH, LEAVE THEM BOYS ALONE!
NOBODY ASKED YOU TO COME HERE!
WHO THREW THAT?
YOU ARE ALL INTERFERING WITH AN AMERICOPS INVESTIGATION. THIS IS A WARNING-- DISPERSE AT ONCE!
BZZZ
YEAH, THAT'S GONNA BE TOUGH. SE LIKE THE MAN WAS SAYING--
WE LIVE HERE.

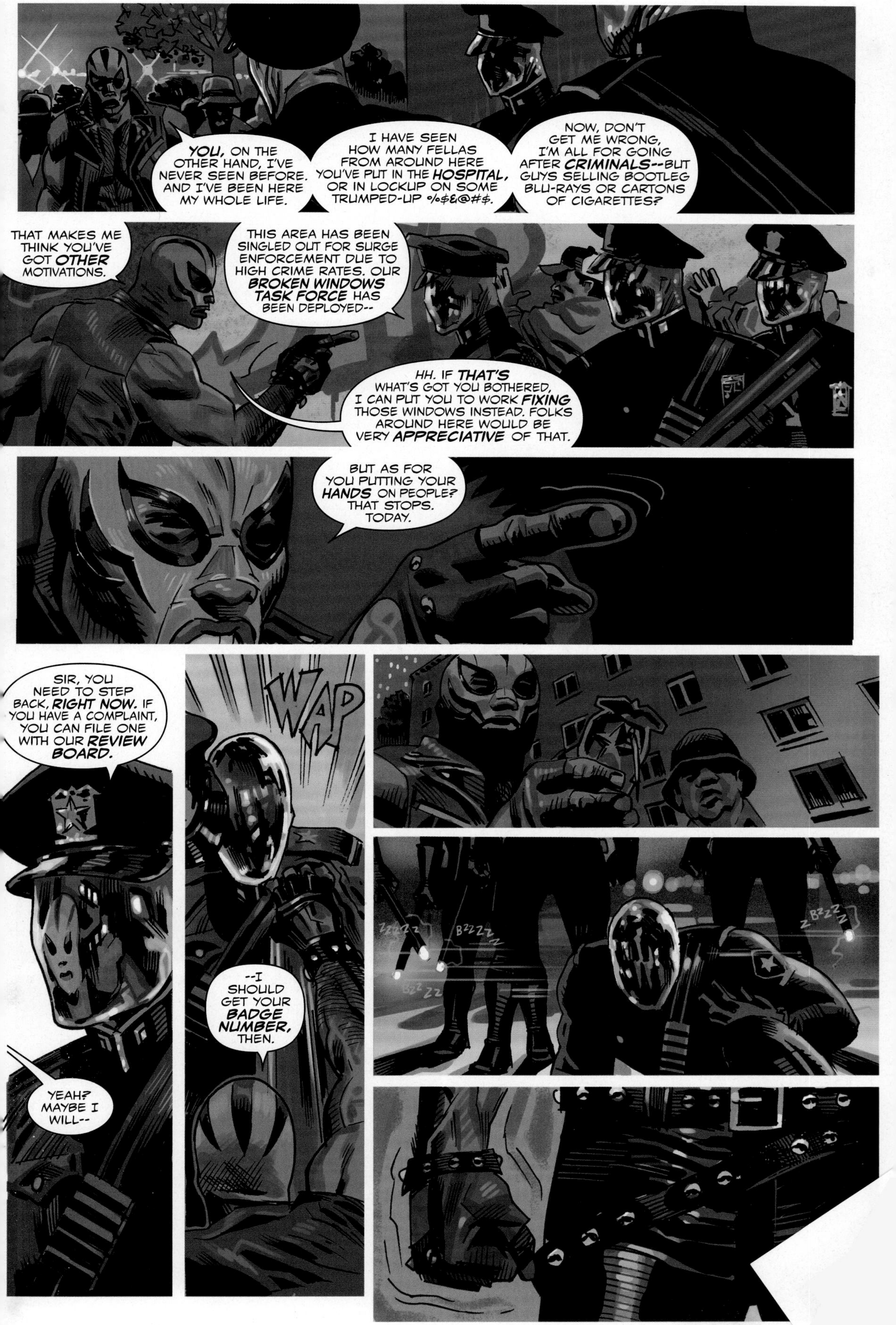
YOU, ON THE OTHER HAND, I'VE NEVER SEEN BEFORE. AND I'VE BEEN HERE MY WHOLE LIFE.
I HAVE SEEN HOW MANY FELLAS FROM AROUND HERE YOU'VE PUT IN THE HOSPITAL, OR IN LOCKUP ON SOME TRUMPED-UP %$£@#$.
NOW, DON'T GET ME WRONG, I'M ALL FOR GOING AFTER CRIMINALS--BUT GUYS SELLING BOOTLEG BLU-RAYS OR CARTONS OF CIGARETTES?
THAT MAKES ME THINK YOU'VE GOT OTHER MOTIVATIONS.
THIS AREA HAS BEEN SINGLED OUT FOR SURGE ENFORCEMENT DUE TO HIGH CRIME RATES. OUR BROKEN WINDOWS TASK FORCE HAS BEEN DEPLOYED--
HH. IF THAT'S WHAT'S GOT YOU BOTHERED, I CAN PUT YOU TO WORK FIXING THOSE WINDOWS INSTEAD. FOLKS AROUND HERE WOULD BE VERY APPRECIATIVE OF THAT.
BUT AS FOR YOU PUTTING YOUR HANDS ON PEOPLE? THAT STOPS. TODAY.
SIR, YOU NEED TO STEP BACK, RIGHT NOW. IF YOU HAVE A COMPLAINT, YOU CAN FILE ONE WITH OUR REVIEW BOARD.
YEAH? MAYBE I WILL--
WAP
--I SHOULD GET YOUR BADGE NUMBER, THEN.
BZZZZ
ZBZZZ

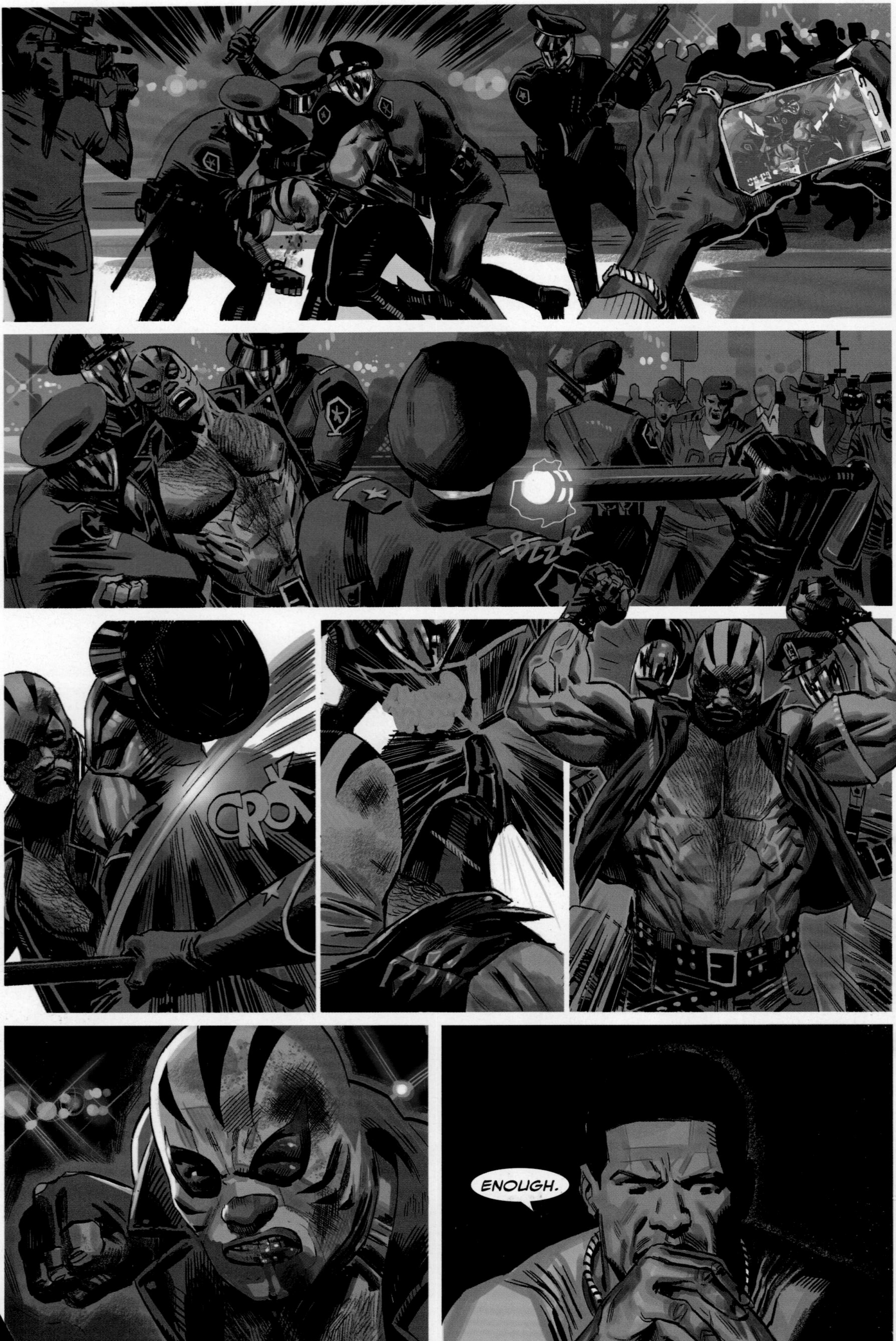
BZZZZ
CROK
ENOUGH.

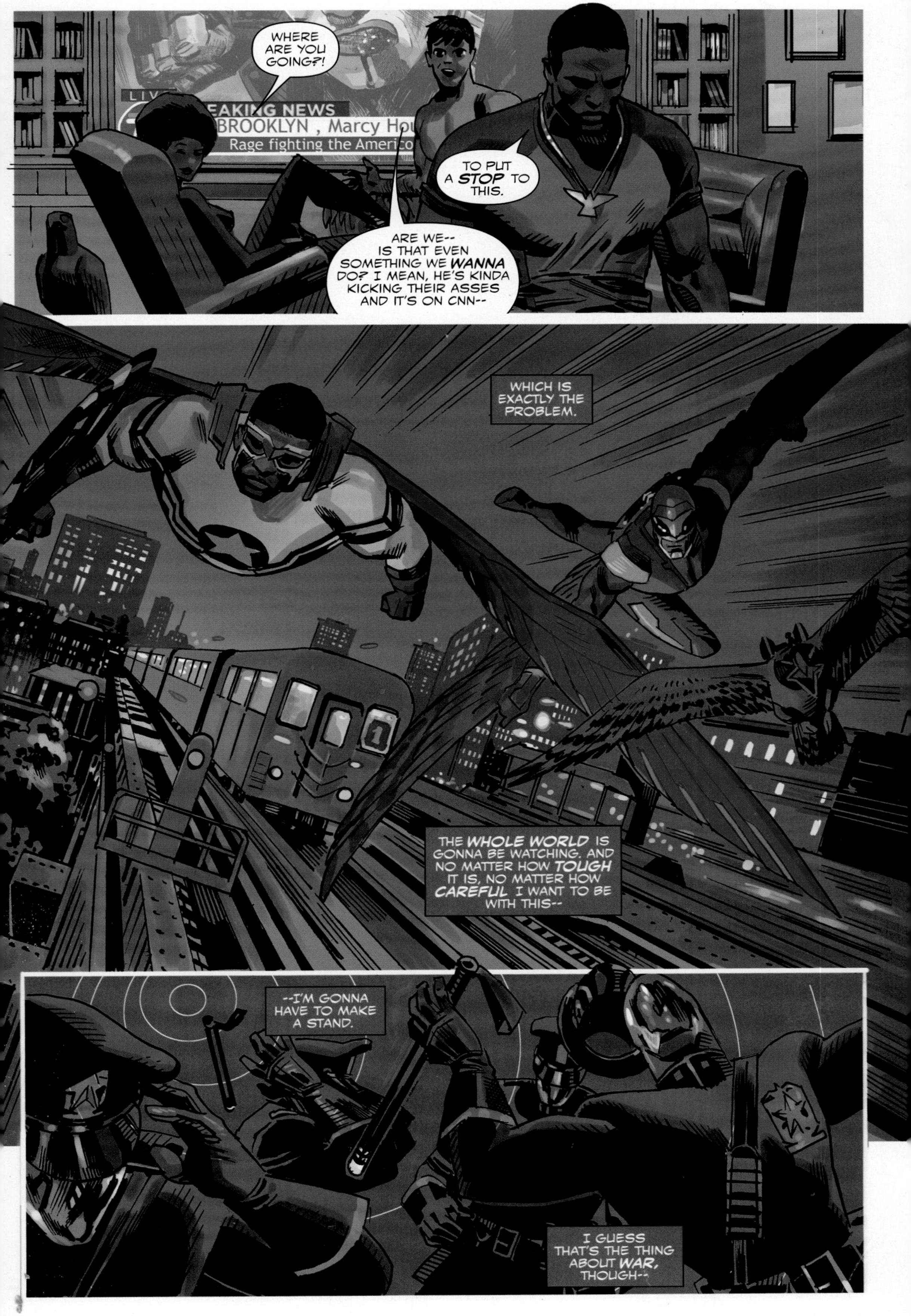
LIVE
BREAKING NEWS
BROOKLYN , Marcy Hou
Rage fighting the Americo
WHERE ARE YOU GOING?!
TO PUT A STOP TO THIS.
ARE WE-- IS THAT EVEN SOMETHING WE WANNA DO? I MEAN, HE'S KINDA KICKING THEIR ASSES AND IT'S ON CNN--
WHICH IS EXACTLY THE PROBLEM.
THE WHOLE WORLD IS GONNA BE WATCHING, AND NO MATTER HOW TOUGH IT IS, NO MATTER HOW CAREFUL I WANT TO BE WITH THIS--
--I'M GONNA HAVE TO MAKE A STAND.
I GUESS THAT'S THE THING ABOUT WAR, THOUGH--

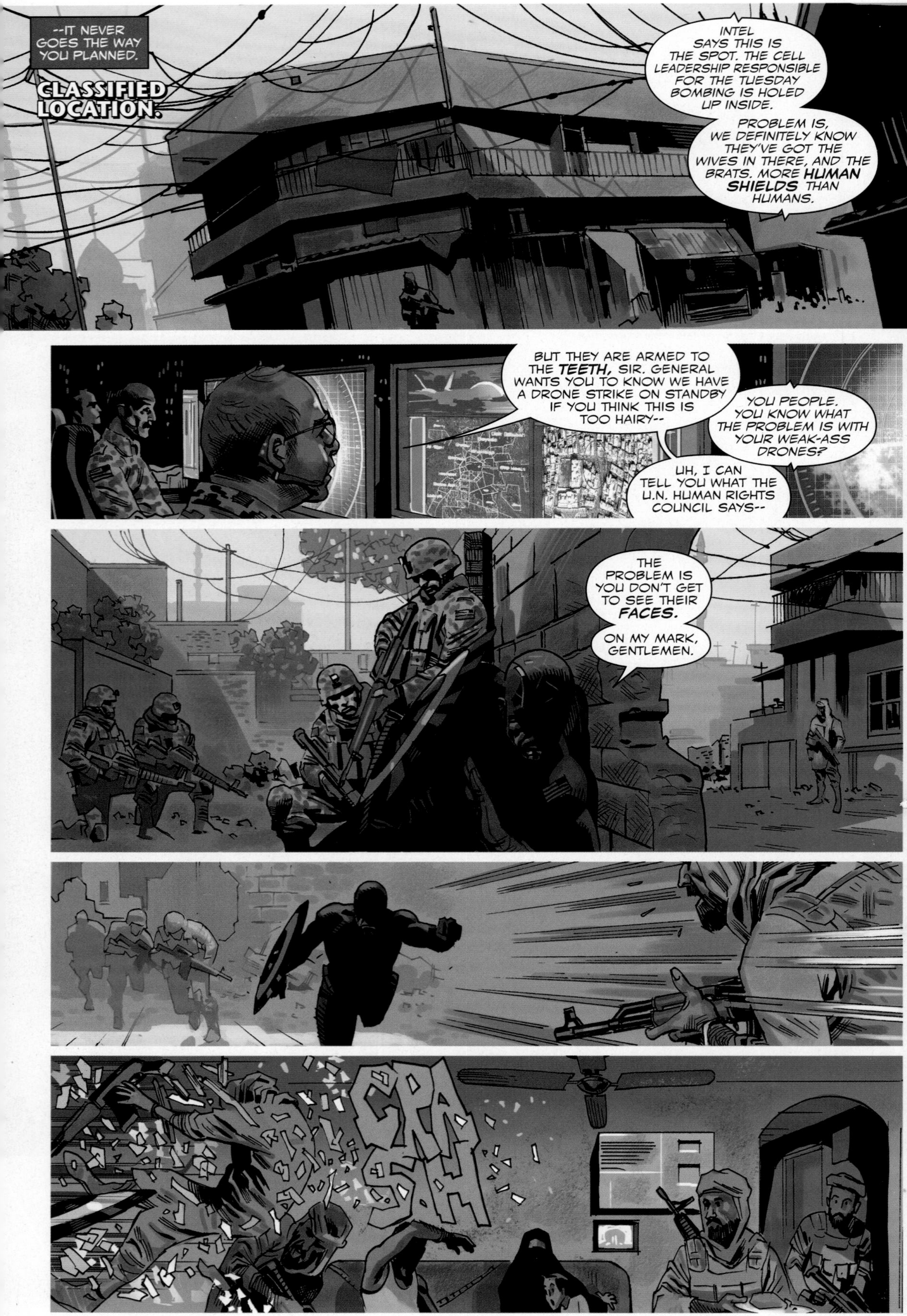

--IT NEVER GOES THE WAY YOU PLANNED.
CLASSIFIED LOCATION.
INTEL SAYS THIS IS THE SPOT. THE CELL LEADERSHIP RESPONSIBLE FOR THE TUESDAY BOMBING IS HOLED UP INSIDE.
PROBLEM IS, WE DEFINITELY KNOW THEY'VE GOT THE WIVES IN THERE, AND THE BRATS. MORE HUMAN SHIELDS THAN HUMANS.
BUT THEY ARE ARMED TO THE TEETH, SIR. GENERAL WANTS YOU TO KNOW WE HAVE A DRONE STRIKE ON STANDBY IF YOU THINK THIS IS TOO HAIRY--
YOU PEOPLE. YOU KNOW WHAT THE PROBLEM IS WITH YOUR WEAK-ASS DRONES?
UH, I CAN TELL YOU WHAT THE U.N. HUMAN RIGHTS COUNCIL SAYS--
THE PROBLEM IS YOU DON'T GET TO SEE THEIR FACES.
ON MY MARK, GENTLEMEN.
CRASH

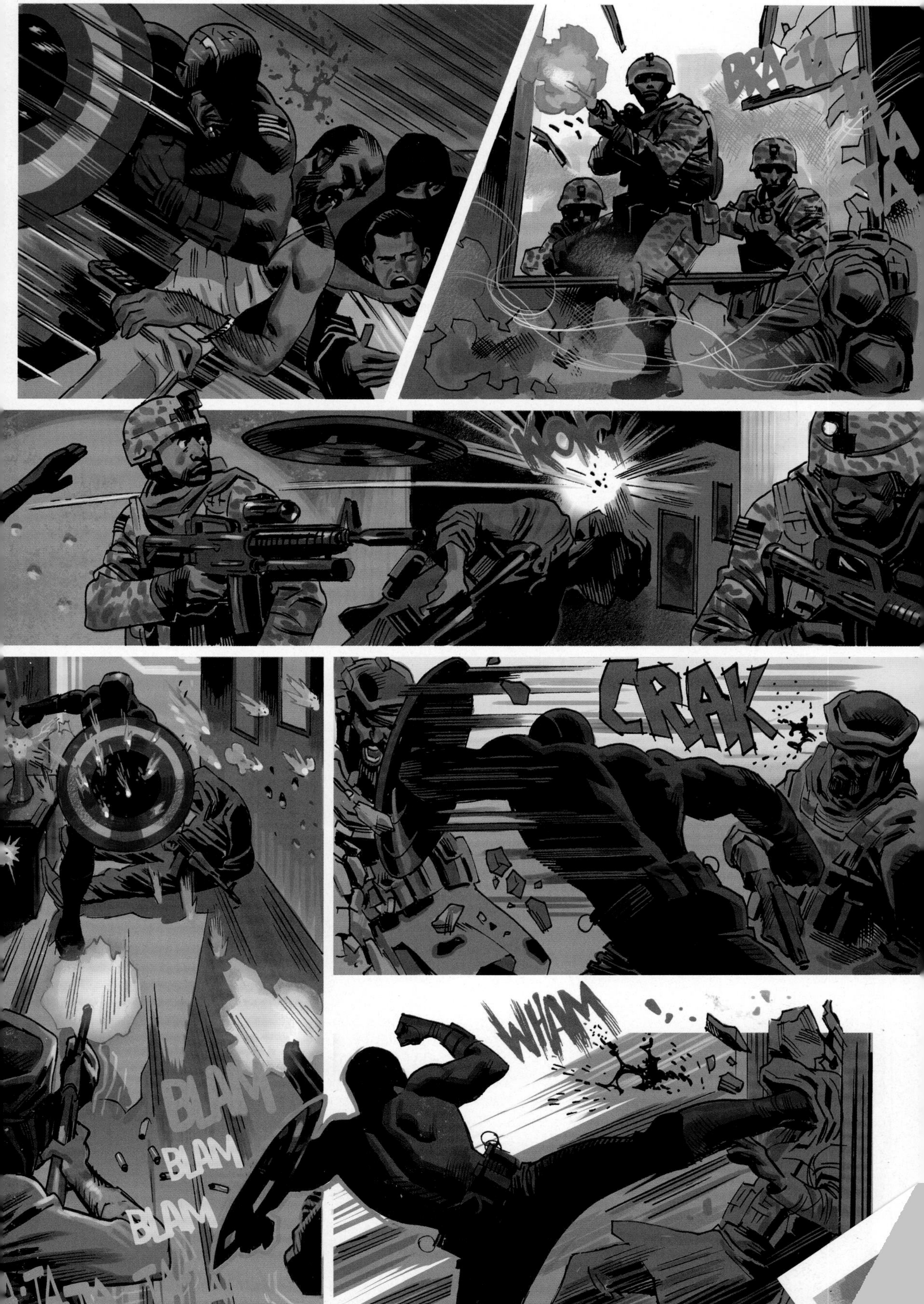

BRA-TA
TA
TA
TA
KONG
CRAK
BLAM
BLAM
BLAM
WHAM

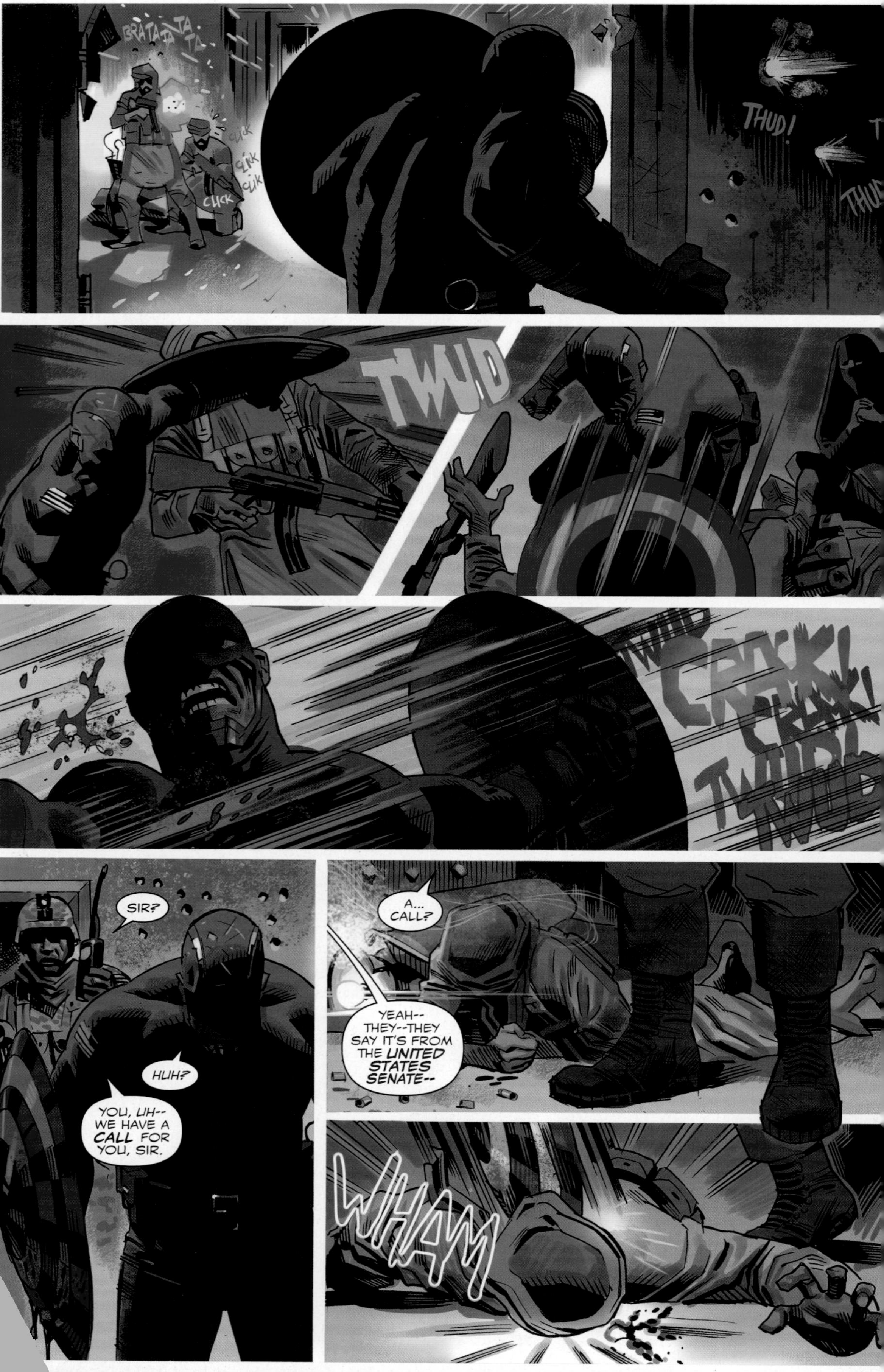
THUD!
TWUD
SIR?
HUH?
YOU, UH-- WE HAVE A CALL FOR YOU, SIR.
A... CALL?
YEAH-- THEY--THEY SAY IT'S FROM THE UNITED STATES SENATE--
WHAM

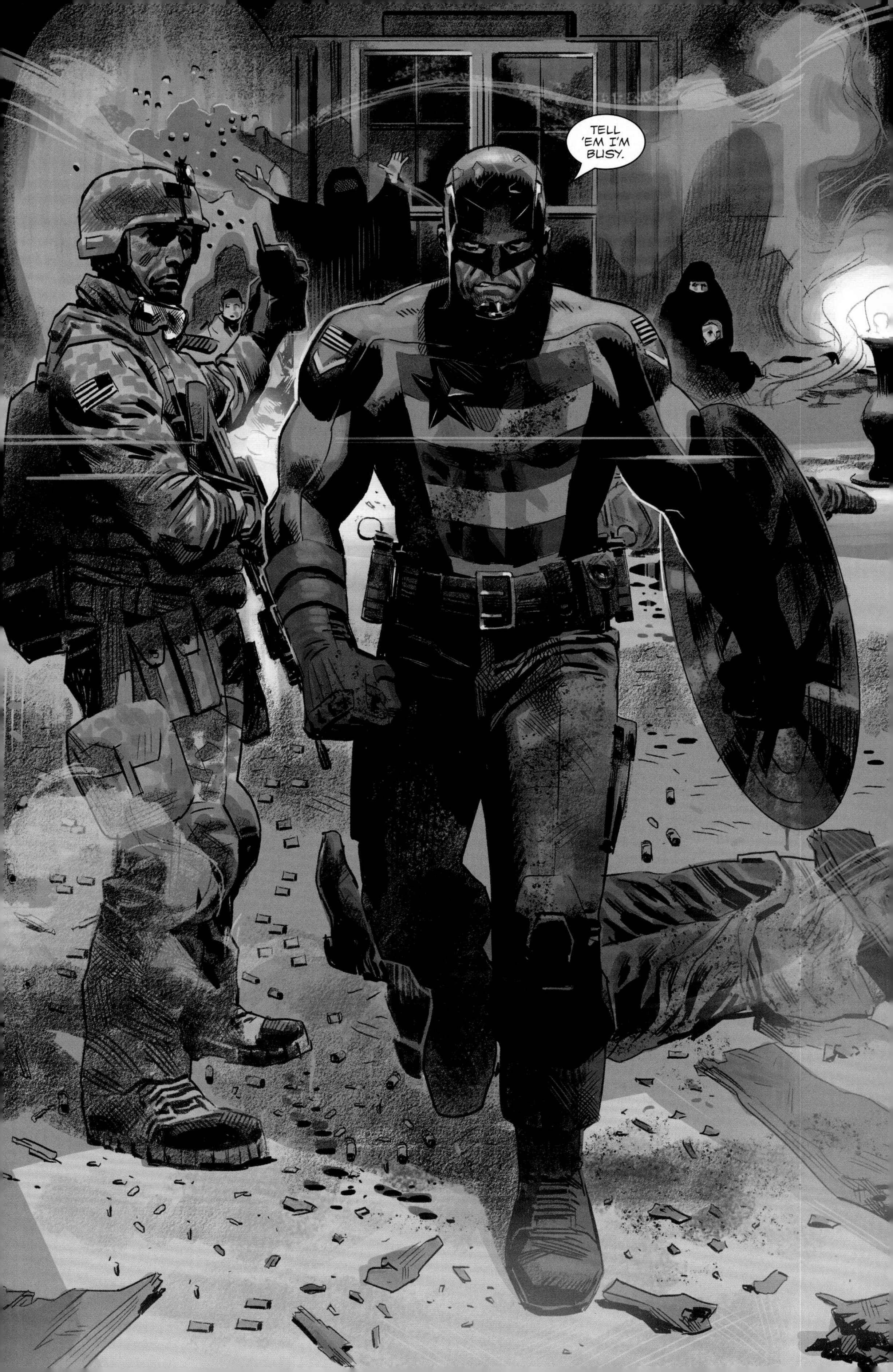
TELL 'EM I'M BUSY.

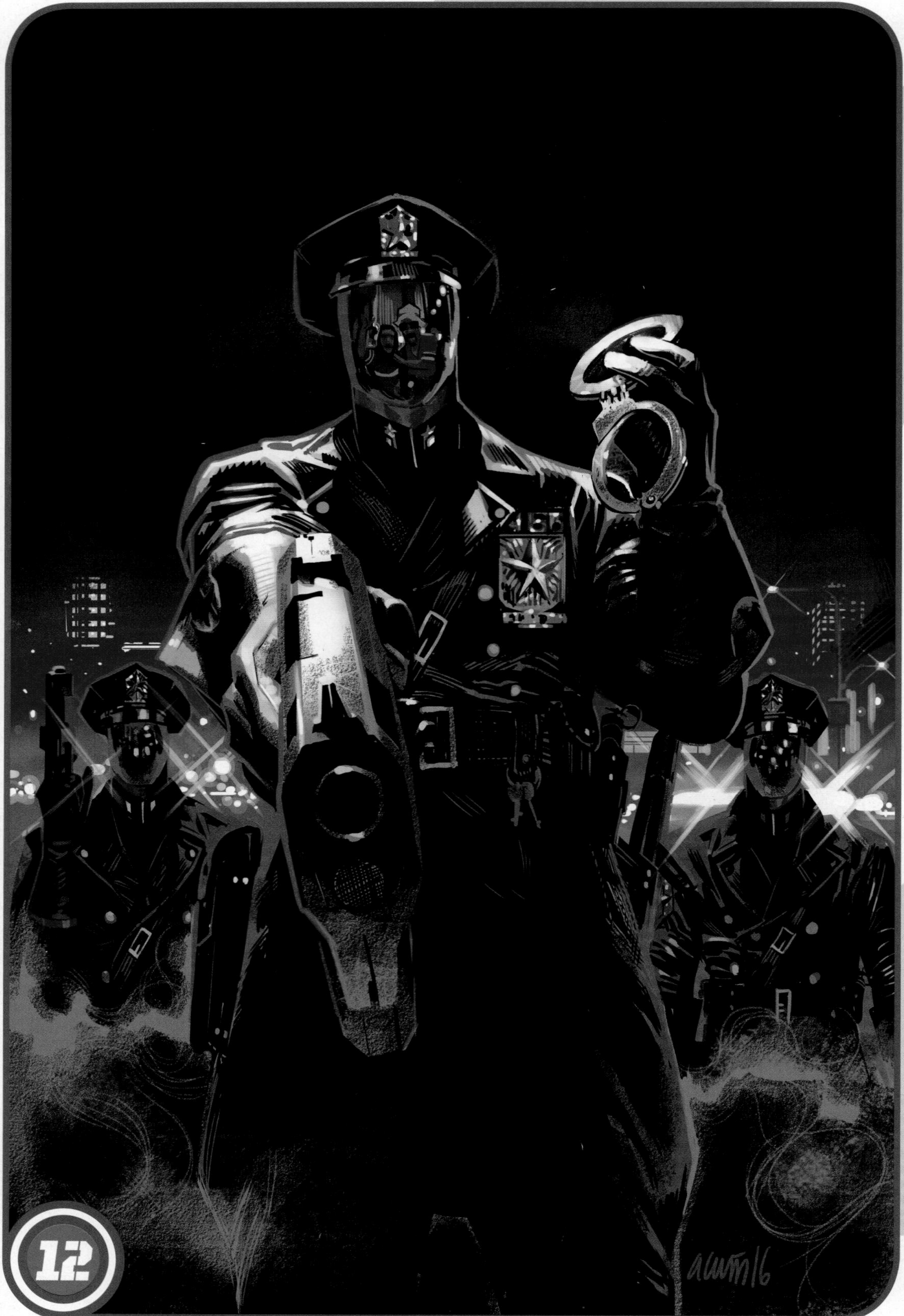
12

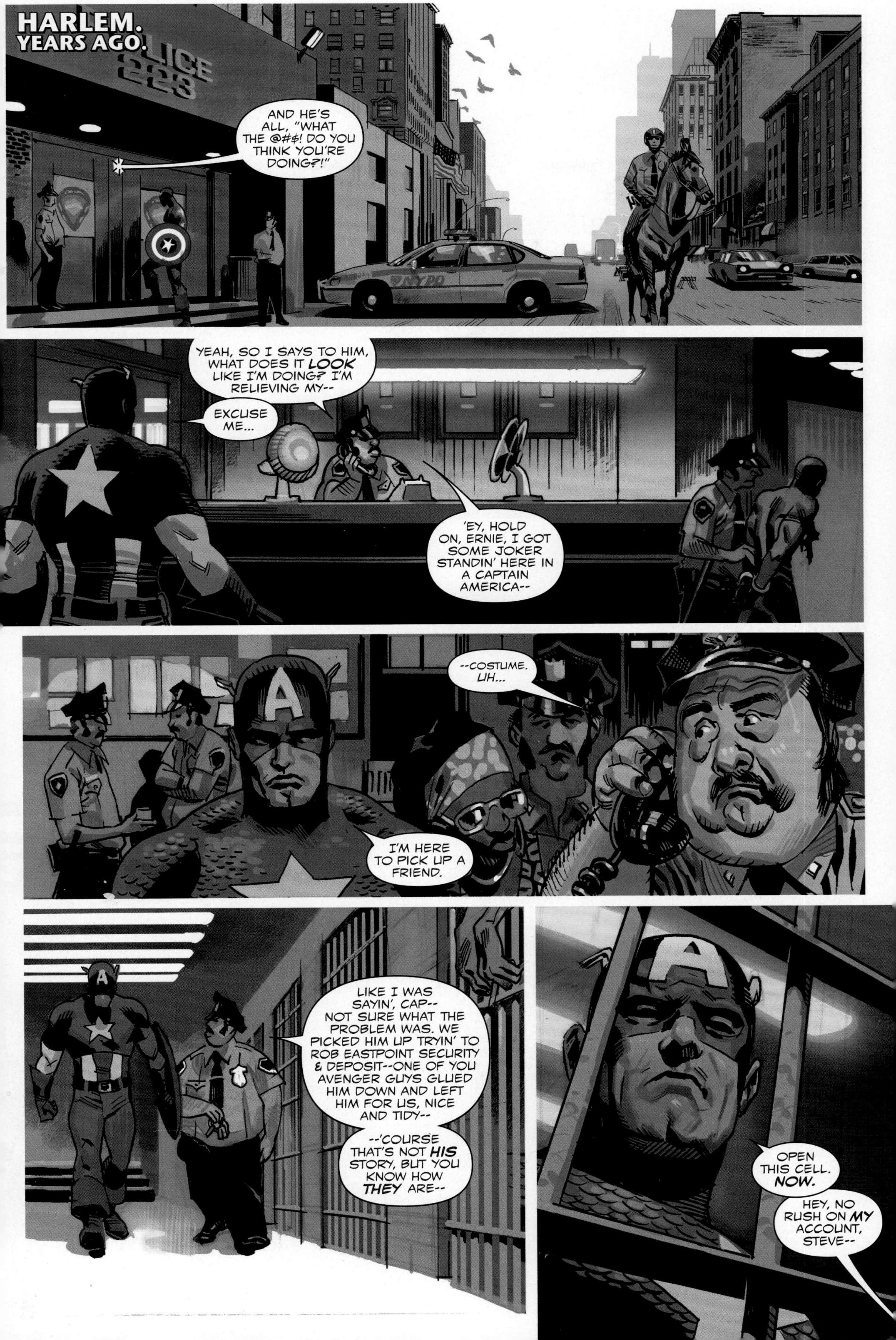
HARLEM.
YEARS AGO.
POLICE 223
AND HE'S ALL, "WHAT THE @#$! DO YOU THINK YOU'RE DOING?!"
NYPD
YEAH, SO I SAYS TO HIM, WHAT DOES IT LOOK LIKE I'M DOING? I'M RELIEVING MY--
EXCUSE ME...
'EY, HOLD ON, ERNIE, I GOT SOME JOKER STANDIN' HERE IN A CAPTAIN AMERICA--
--COSTUME. UH...
I'M HERE TO PICK UP A FRIEND.
LIKE I WAS SAYIN', CAP-- NOT SURE WHAT THE PROBLEM WAS. WE PICKED HIM UP TRYIN' TO ROB EASTPOINT SECURITY & DEPOSIT--ONE OF YOU AVENGER GUYS GLUED HIM DOWN AND LEFT HIM FOR US, NICE AND TIDY--
--'COURSE THAT'S NOT HIS STORY, BUT YOU KNOW HOW THEY ARE--
OPEN THIS CELL. NOW.
HEY, NO RUSH ON MY ACCOUNT, STEVE--

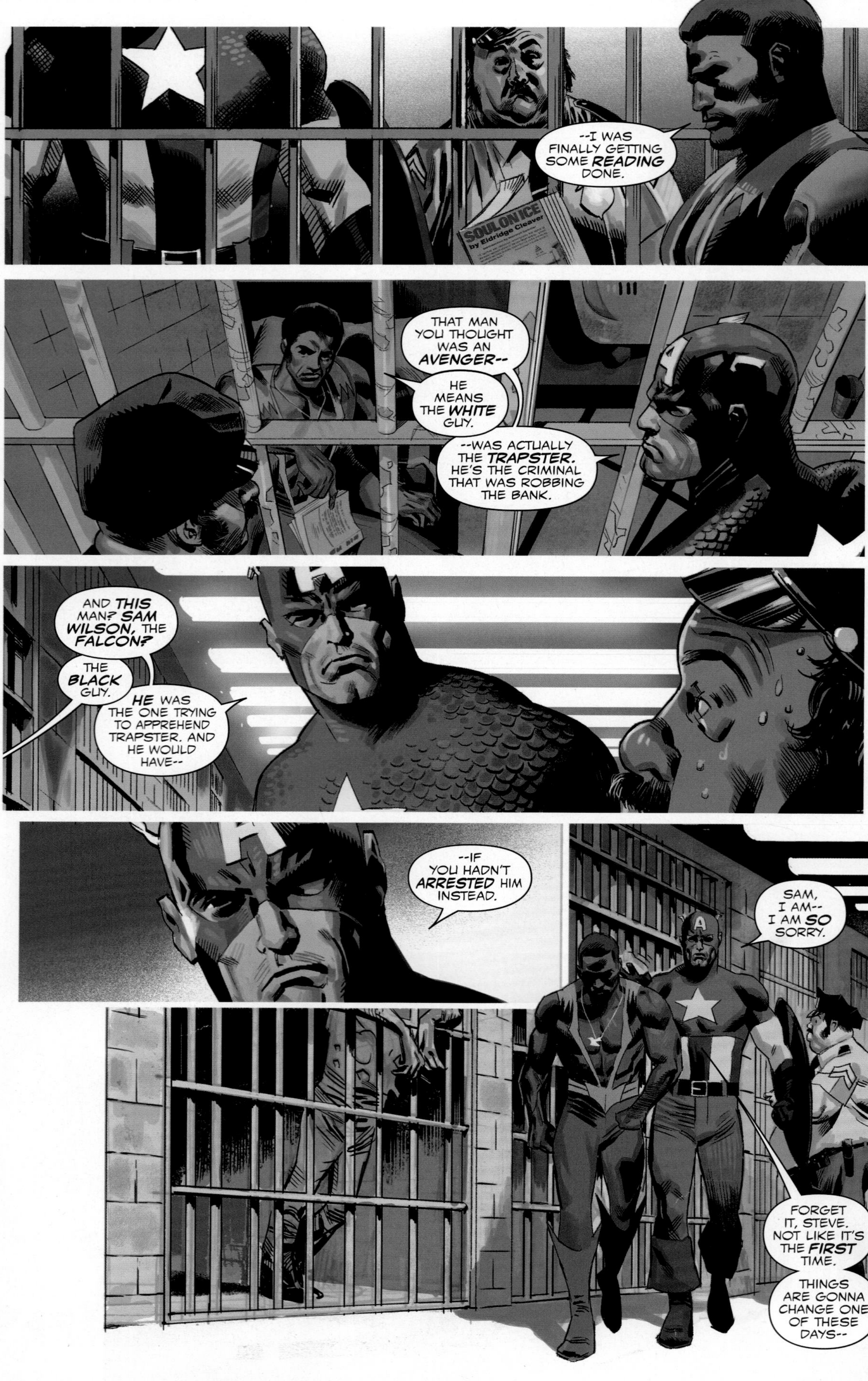
--I WAS FINALLY GETTING SOME READING DONE.
SOUL ON ICE by Eldridge Cleaver
THAT MAN YOU THOUGHT WAS AN AVENGER--
HE MEANS THE WHITE GUY.
--WAS ACTUALLY THE TRAPSTER. HE'S THE CRIMINAL THAT WAS ROBBING THE BANK.
AND THIS MAN? SAM WILSON, THE FALCON?
THE BLACK GUY.
HE WAS THE ONE TRYING TO APPREHEND TRAPSTER. AND HE WOULD HAVE--
--IF YOU HADN'T ARRESTED HIM INSTEAD.
SAM, I AM-- I AM SO SORRY.
FORGET IT, STEVE. NOT LIKE IT'S THE FIRST TIME.
THINGS ARE GONNA CHANGE ONE OF THESE DAYS--

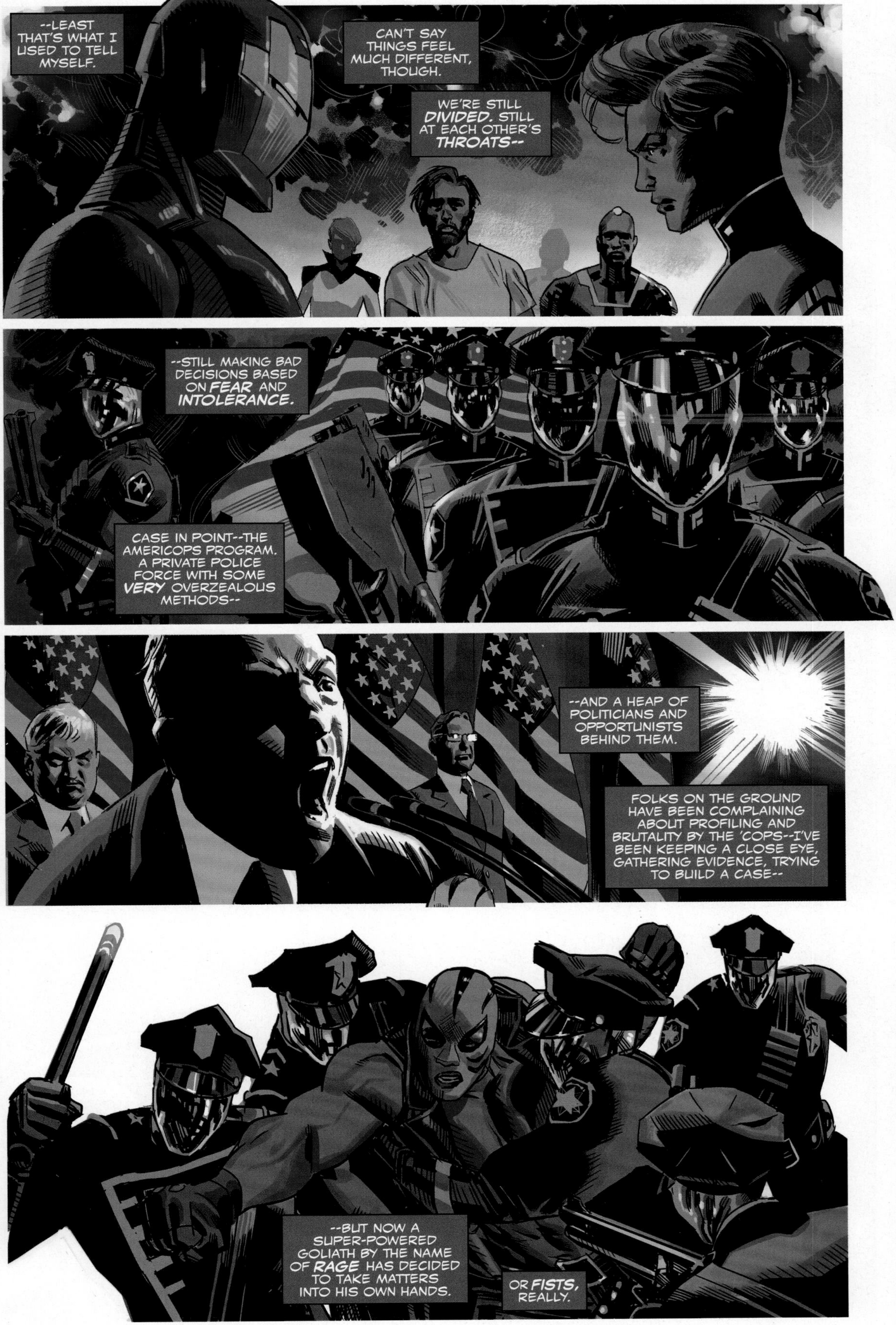
--LEAST THAT'S WHAT I USED TO TELL MYSELF.
CAN'T SAY THINGS FEEL MUCH DIFFERENT, THOUGH.
WE'RE STILL DIVIDED. STILL AT EACH OTHER'S THROATS--
--STILL MAKING BAD DECISIONS BASED ON FEAR AND INTOLERANCE.
CASE IN POINT--THE AMERICOPS PROGRAM. A PRIVATE POLICE FORCE WITH SOME VERY OVERZEALOUS METHODS--
--AND A HEAP OF POLITICIANS AND OPPORTUNISTS BEHIND THEM.
FOLKS ON THE GROUND HAVE BEEN COMPLAINING ABOUT PROFILING AND BRUTALITY BY THE 'COPS--I'VE BEEN KEEPING A CLOSE EYE, GATHERING EVIDENCE, TRYING TO BUILD A CASE--
--BUT NOW A SUPER-POWERED GOLIATH BY THE NAME OF RAGE HAS DECIDED TO TAKE MATTERS INTO HIS OWN HANDS.
OR FISTS, REALLY.

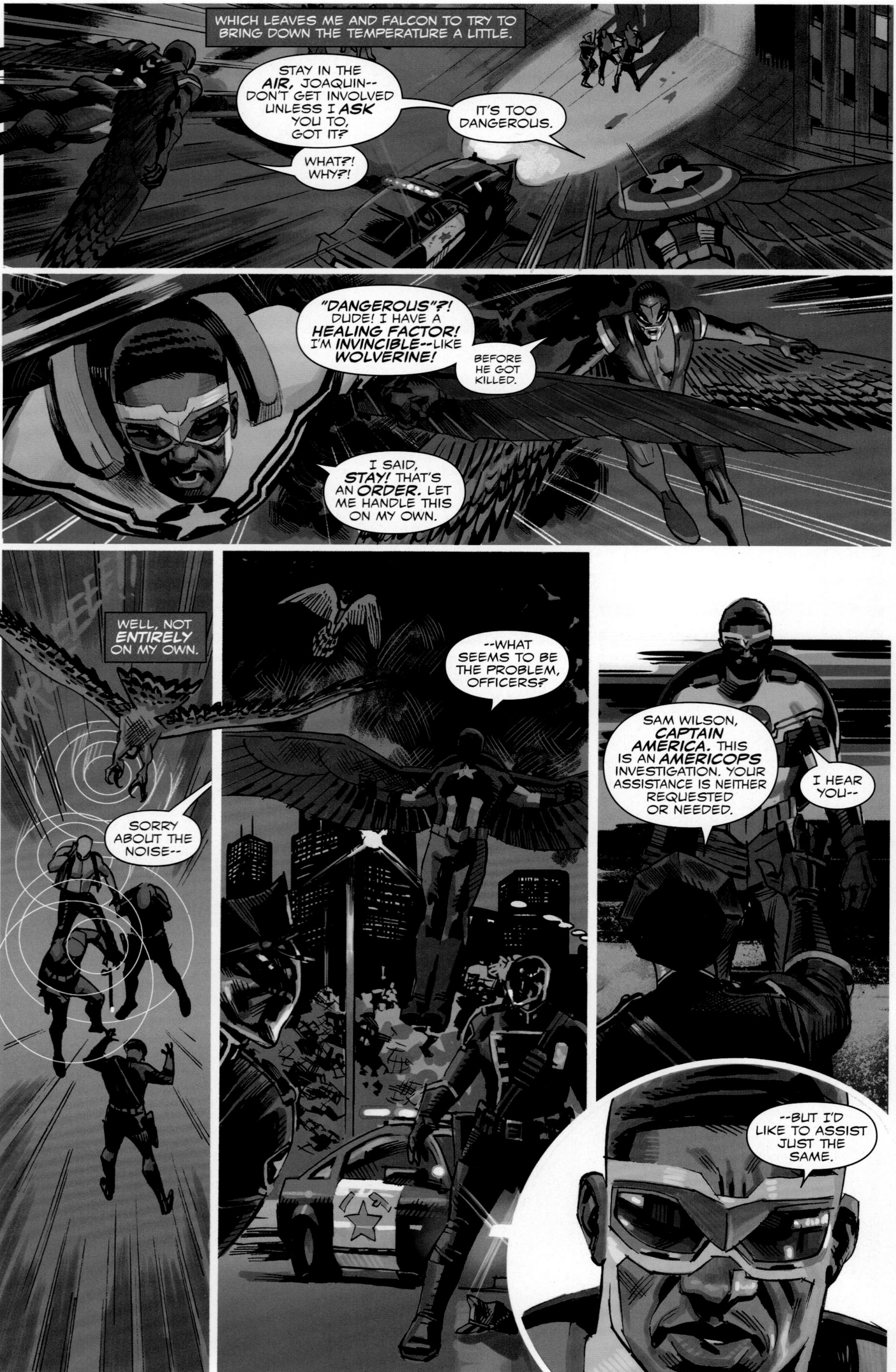
WHICH LEAVES ME AND FALCON TO TRY TO BRING DOWN THE TEMPERATURE A LITTLE.
STAY IN THE AIR, JOAQUIN--DON'T GET INVOLVED UNLESS I ASK YOU TO, GOT IT?
IT'S TOO DANGEROUS.
WHAT?! WHY?!
"DANGEROUS"?! DUDE! I HAVE A HEALING FACTOR! I'M INVINCIBLE--LIKE WOLVERINE!
BEFORE HE GOT KILLED.
I SAID, STAY! THAT'S AN ORDER. LET ME HANDLE THIS ON MY OWN.
WELL, NOT ENTIRELY ON MY OWN.
SORRY ABOUT THE NOISE--
--WHAT SEEMS TO BE THE PROBLEM, OFFICERS?
SAM WILSON, CAPTAIN AMERICA. THIS IS AN AMERICOPS INVESTIGATION. YOUR ASSISTANCE IS NEITHER REQUESTED OR NEEDED.
I HEAR YOU--
--BUT I'D LIKE TO ASSIST JUST THE SAME.

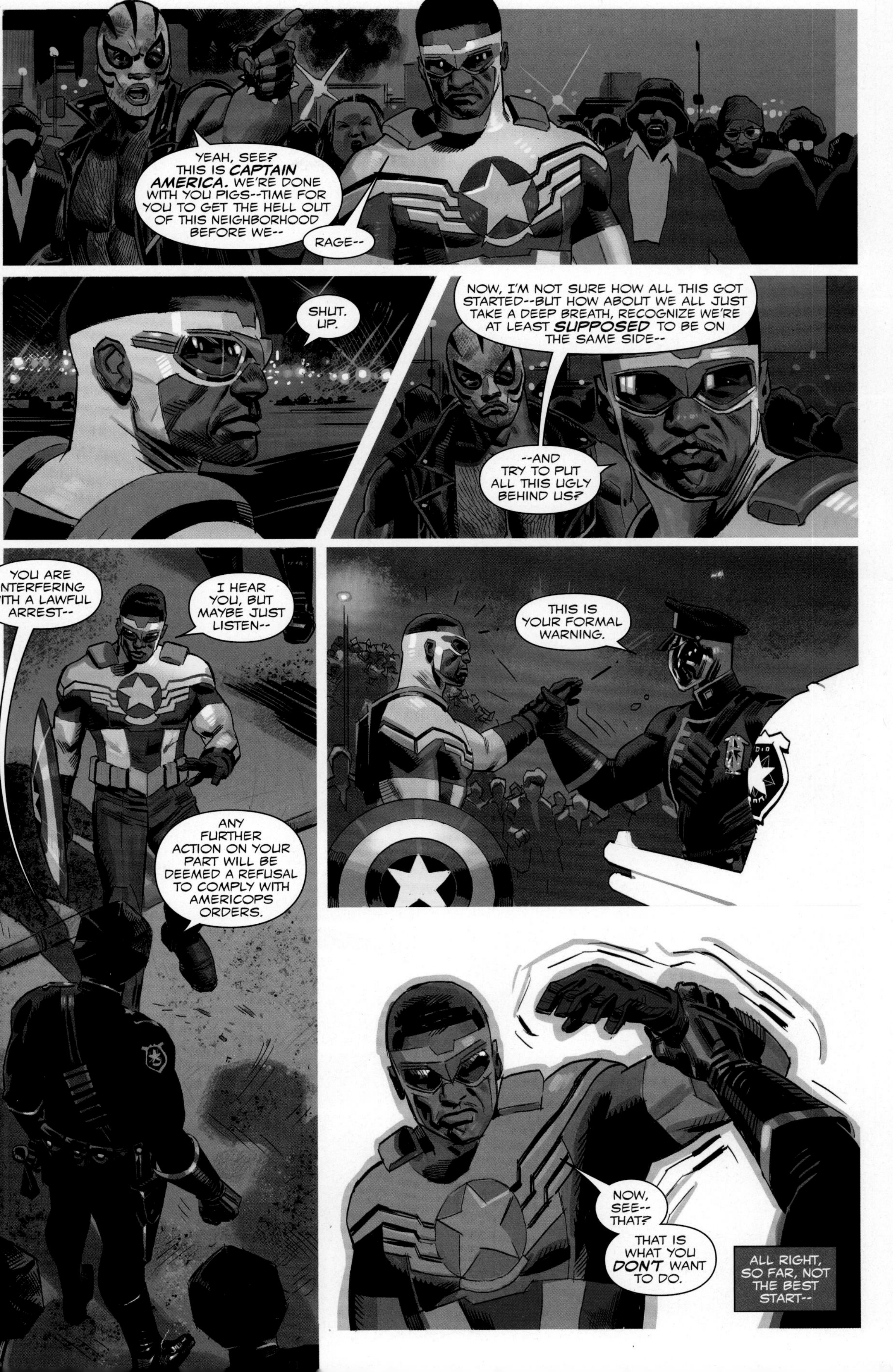
YEAH, SEE? THIS IS CAPTAIN AMERICA. WE'RE DONE WITH YOU PIGS--TIME FOR YOU TO GET THE HELL OUT OF THIS NEIGHBORHOOD BEFORE WE--
RAGE--
SHUT. UP.
NOW, I'M NOT SURE HOW ALL THIS GOT STARTED--BUT HOW ABOUT WE ALL JUST TAKE A DEEP BREATH, RECOGNIZE WE'RE AT LEAST SUPPOSED TO BE ON THE SAME SIDE--
--AND TRY TO PUT ALL THIS UGLY BEHIND US?
YOU ARE INTERFERING WITH A LAWFUL ARREST--
I HEAR YOU, BUT MAYBE JUST LISTEN--
ANY FURTHER ACTION ON YOUR PART WILL BE DEEMED A REFUSAL TO COMPLY WITH AMERICOPS ORDERS.
THIS IS YOUR FORMAL WARNING.
NOW, SEE-- THAT?
THAT IS WHAT YOU DON'T WANT TO DO.
ALL RIGHT, SO FAR, NOT THE BEST START--

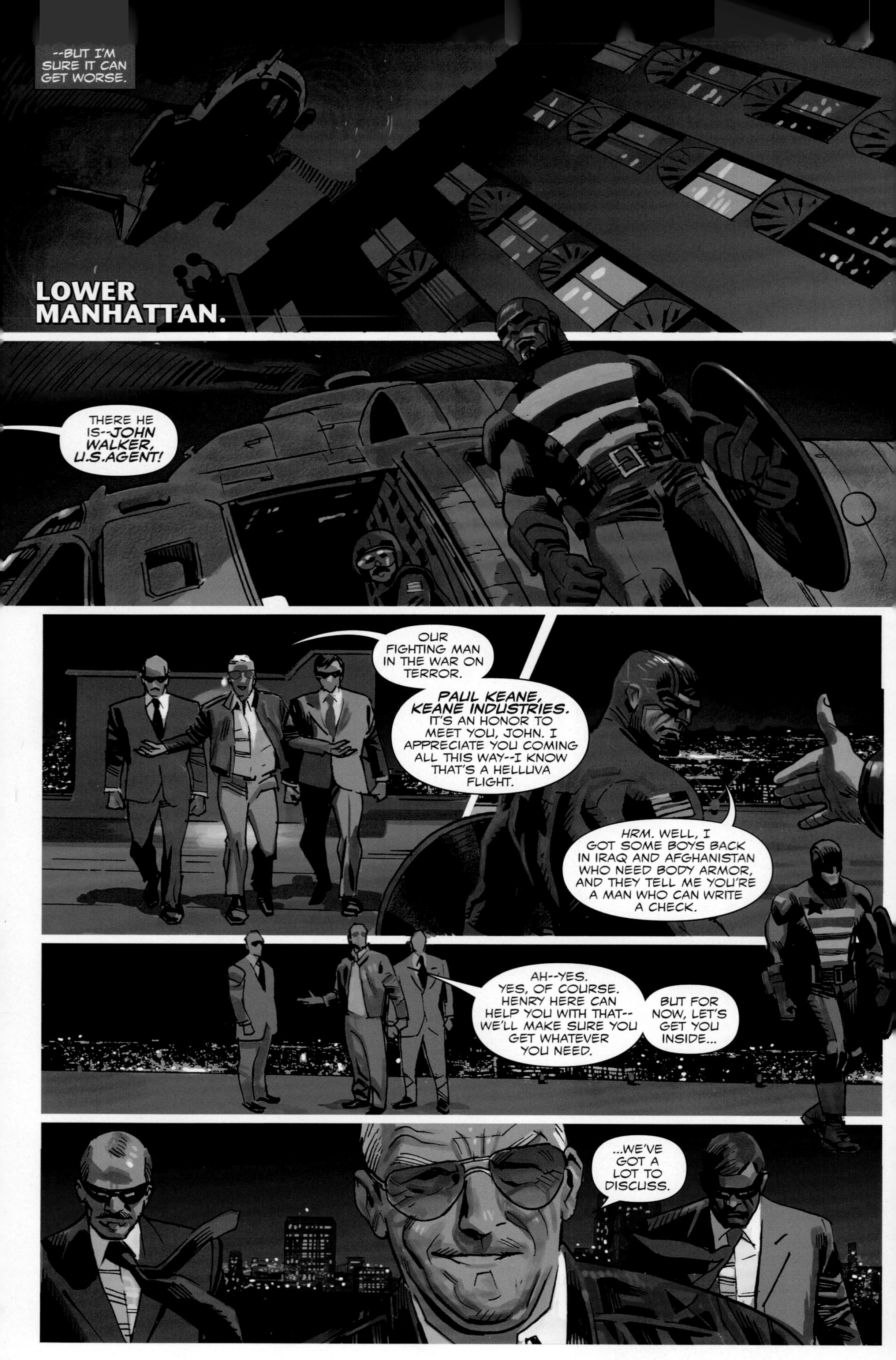
--BUT I'M SURE IT CAN GET WORSE.
LOWER MANHATTAN.
THERE HE IS--JOHN WALKER, U.S.AGENT!
OUR FIGHTING MAN IN THE WAR ON TERROR.
PAUL KEANE, KEANE INDUSTRIES. IT'S AN HONOR TO MEET YOU, JOHN. I APPRECIATE YOU COMING ALL THIS WAY--I KNOW THAT'S A HELLUVA FLIGHT.
HRM. WELL, I GOT SOME BOYS BACK IN IRAQ AND AFGHANISTAN WHO NEED BODY ARMOR, AND THEY TELL ME YOU'RE A MAN WHO CAN WRITE A CHECK.
AH--YES. YES, OF COURSE. HENRY HERE CAN HELP YOU WITH THAT--WE'LL MAKE SURE YOU GET WHATEVER YOU NEED.
BUT FOR NOW, LET'S GET YOU INSIDE...
...WE'VE GOT A LOT TO DISCUSS.

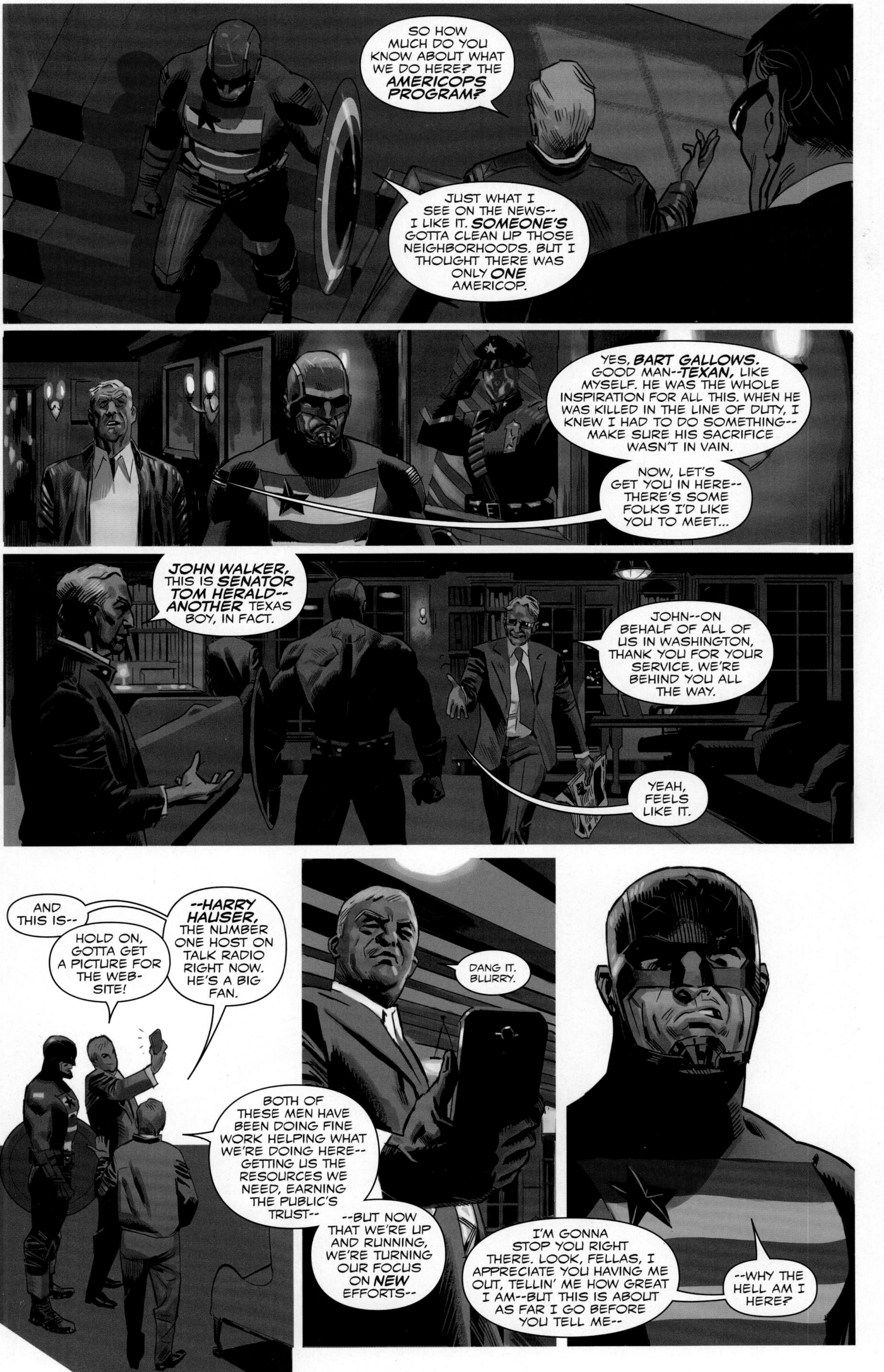
SO HOW MUCH DO YOU KNOW ABOUT WHAT WE DO HERE? THE AMERICOPS PROGRAM?
JUST WHAT I SEE ON THE NEWS-- I LIKE IT. SOMEONE'S GOTTA CLEAN UP THOSE NEIGHBORHOODS. BUT I THOUGHT THERE WAS ONLY ONE AMERICOP.
YES, BART GALLOWS. GOOD MAN--TEXAN, LIKE MYSELF. HE WAS THE WHOLE INSPIRATION FOR ALL THIS. WHEN HE WAS KILLED IN THE LINE OF DUTY, I KNEW I HAD TO DO SOMETHING-- MAKE SURE HIS SACRIFICE WASN'T IN VAIN.
NOW, LET'S GET YOU IN HERE-- THERE'S SOME FOLKS I'D LIKE YOU TO MEET...
JOHN WALKER, THIS IS SENATOR TOM HERALD-- ANOTHER TEXAS BOY, IN FACT.
JOHN--ON BEHALF OF ALL OF US IN WASHINGTON, THANK YOU FOR YOUR SERVICE. WE'RE BEHIND YOU ALL THE WAY.
YEAH, FEELS LIKE IT.
AND THIS IS--
HOLD ON, GOTTA GET A PICTURE FOR THE WEB-SITE!
--HARRY HAUSER, THE NUMBER ONE HOST ON TALK RADIO RIGHT NOW. HE'S A BIG FAN.
DANG IT. BLURRY.
BOTH OF THESE MEN HAVE BEEN DOING FINE WORK HELPING WHAT WE'RE DOING HERE-- GETTING US THE RESOURCES WE NEED, EARNING THE PUBLIC'S TRUST--
--BUT NOW THAT WE'RE UP AND RUNNING, WE'RE TURNING OUR FOCUS ON NEW EFFORTS--
I'M GONNA STOP YOU RIGHT THERE. LOOK, FELLAS, I APPRECIATE YOU HAVING ME OUT, TELLIN' ME HOW GREAT I AM--BUT THIS IS ABOUT AS FAR I GO BEFORE YOU TELL ME--
--WHY THE HELL AM I HERE?

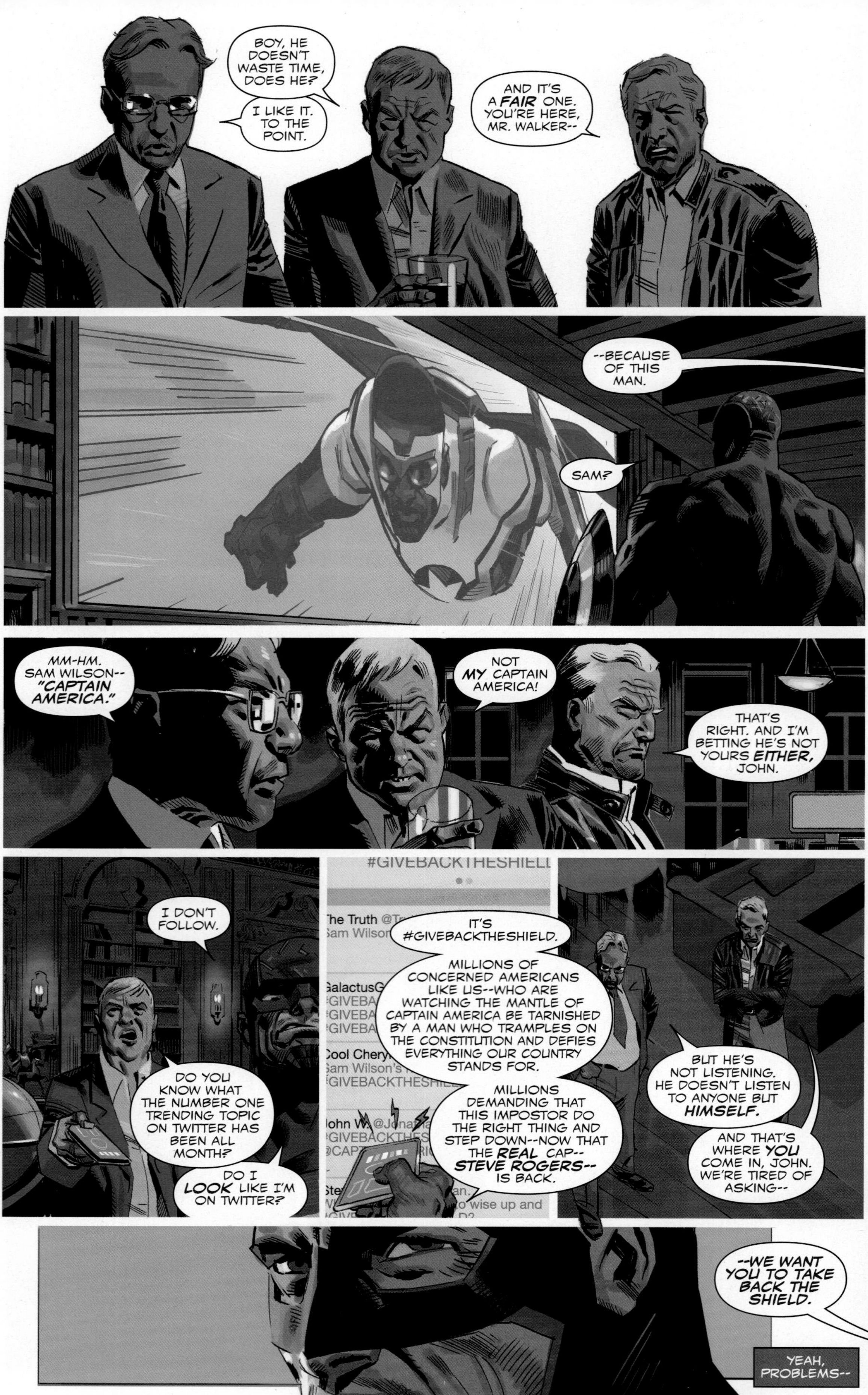

BOY, HE DOESN'T WASTE TIME, DOES HE?
I LIKE IT. TO THE POINT.
AND IT'S A FAIR ONE. YOU'RE HERE, MR. WALKER--
--BECAUSE OF THIS MAN.
SAM?
MM-HM. SAM WILSON-- "CAPTAIN AMERICA."
NOT MY CAPTAIN AMERICA!
THAT'S RIGHT. AND I'M BETTING HE'S NOT YOURS EITHER, JOHN.
I DON'T FOLLOW.
DO YOU KNOW WHAT THE NUMBER ONE TRENDING TOPIC ON TWITTER HAS BEEN ALL MONTH?
DO I LOOK LIKE I'M ON TWITTER?
IT'S #GIVEBACKTHESHIELD.
MILLIONS OF CONCERNED AMERICANS LIKE US--WHO ARE WATCHING THE MANTLE OF CAPTAIN AMERICA BE TARNISHED BY A MAN WHO TRAMPLES ON THE CONSTITUTION AND DEFIES EVERYTHING OUR COUNTRY STANDS FOR.
MILLIONS DEMANDING THAT THIS IMPOSTOR DO THE RIGHT THING AND STEP DOWN--NOW THAT THE REAL CAP-- STEVE ROGERS-- IS BACK.
BUT HE'S NOT LISTENING. HE DOESN'T LISTEN TO ANYONE BUT HIMSELF.
AND THAT'S WHERE YOU COME IN, JOHN. WE'RE TIRED OF ASKING--
--WE WANT YOU TO TAKE BACK THE SHIELD.
YEAH, PROBLEMS--

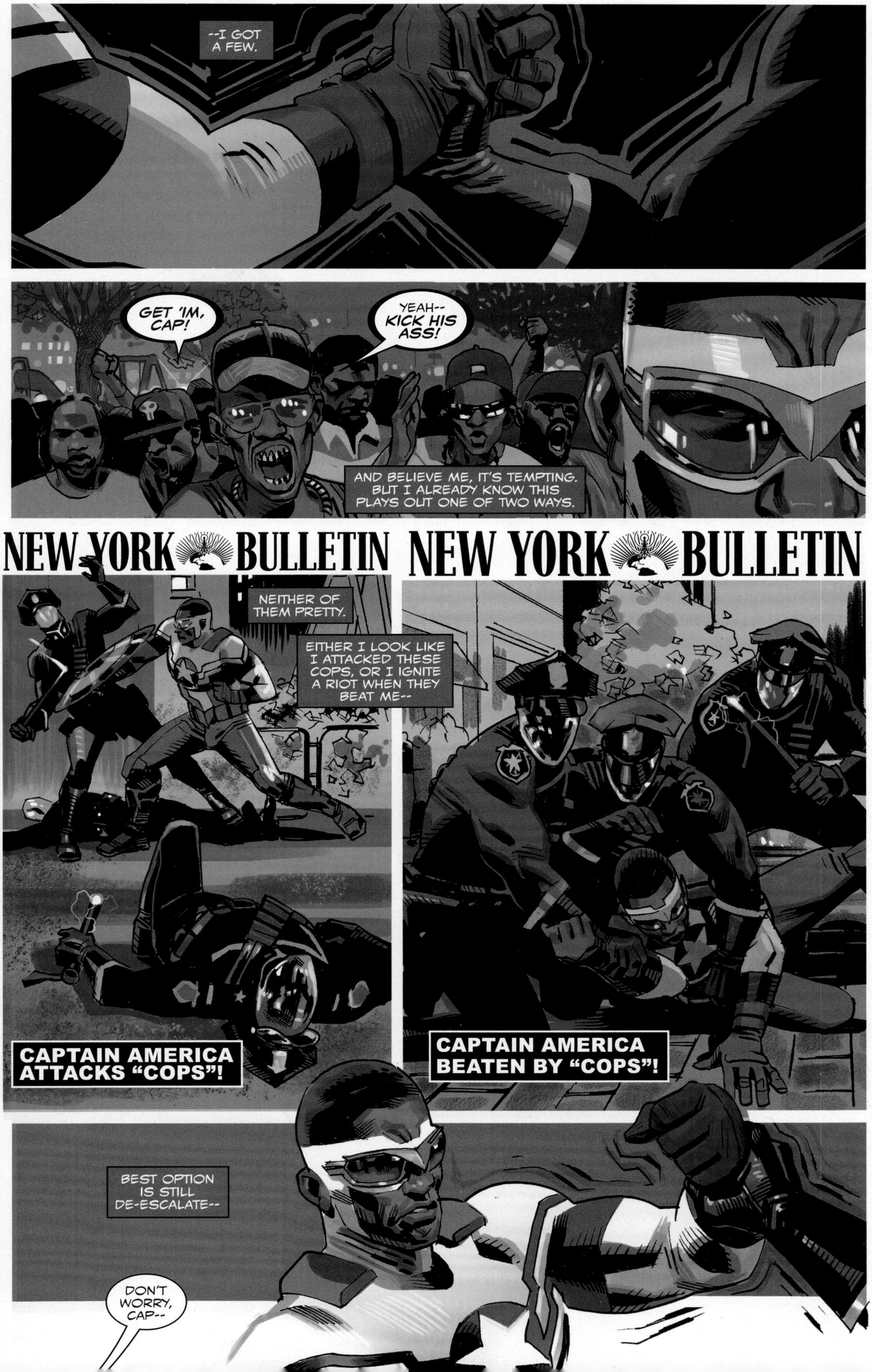
--I GOT A FEW.
GET 'IM, CAP!
YEAH-- KICK HIS ASS!
AND BELIEVE ME, IT'S TEMPTING. BUT I ALREADY KNOW THIS PLAYS OUT ONE OF TWO WAYS.
NEW YORK BULLETIN
NEITHER OF THEM PRETTY.
EITHER I LOOK LIKE I ATTACKED THESE COPS, OR I IGNITE A RIOT WHEN THEY BEAT ME--
CAPTAIN AMERICA ATTACKS "COPS"!
NEW YORK BULLETIN
CAPTAIN AMERICA BEATEN BY "COPS"!
BEST OPTION IS STILL DE-ESCALATE--
DON'T WORRY, CAP--

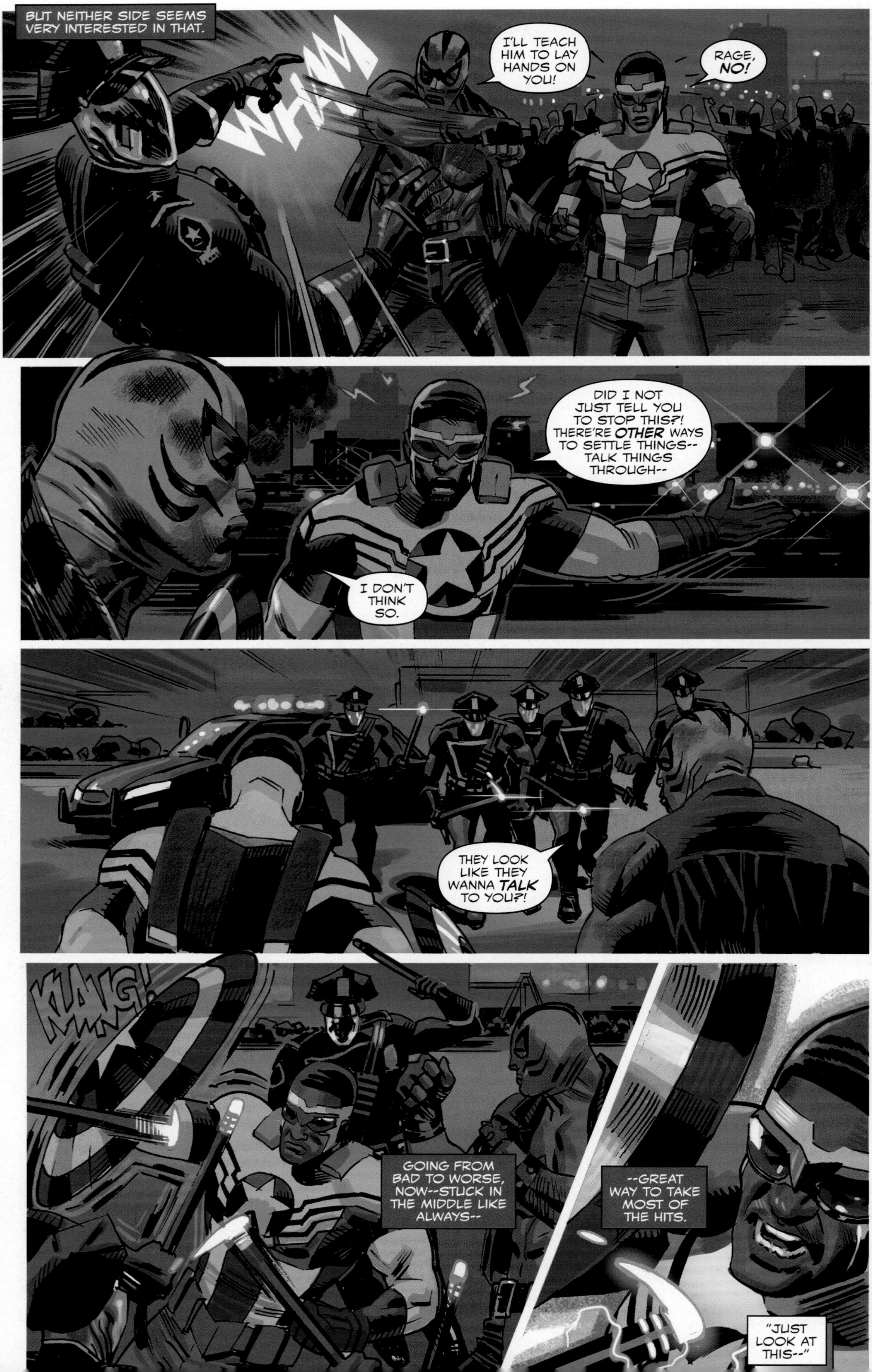

BUT NEITHER SIDE SEEMS VERY INTERESTED IN THAT.
WHAM
I'LL TEACH HIM TO LAY HANDS ON YOU!
RAGE, NO!
DID I NOT JUST TELL YOU TO STOP THIS?! THERE'RE OTHER WAYS TO SETTLE THINGS-- TALK THINGS THROUGH--
I DON'T THINK SO.
THEY LOOK LIKE THEY WANNA TALK TO YOU?!
KLANG!
GOING FROM BAD TO WORSE, NOW--STUCK IN THE MIDDLE LIKE ALWAYS--
--GREAT WAY TO TAKE MOST OF THE HITS.
"JUST LOOK AT THIS--"

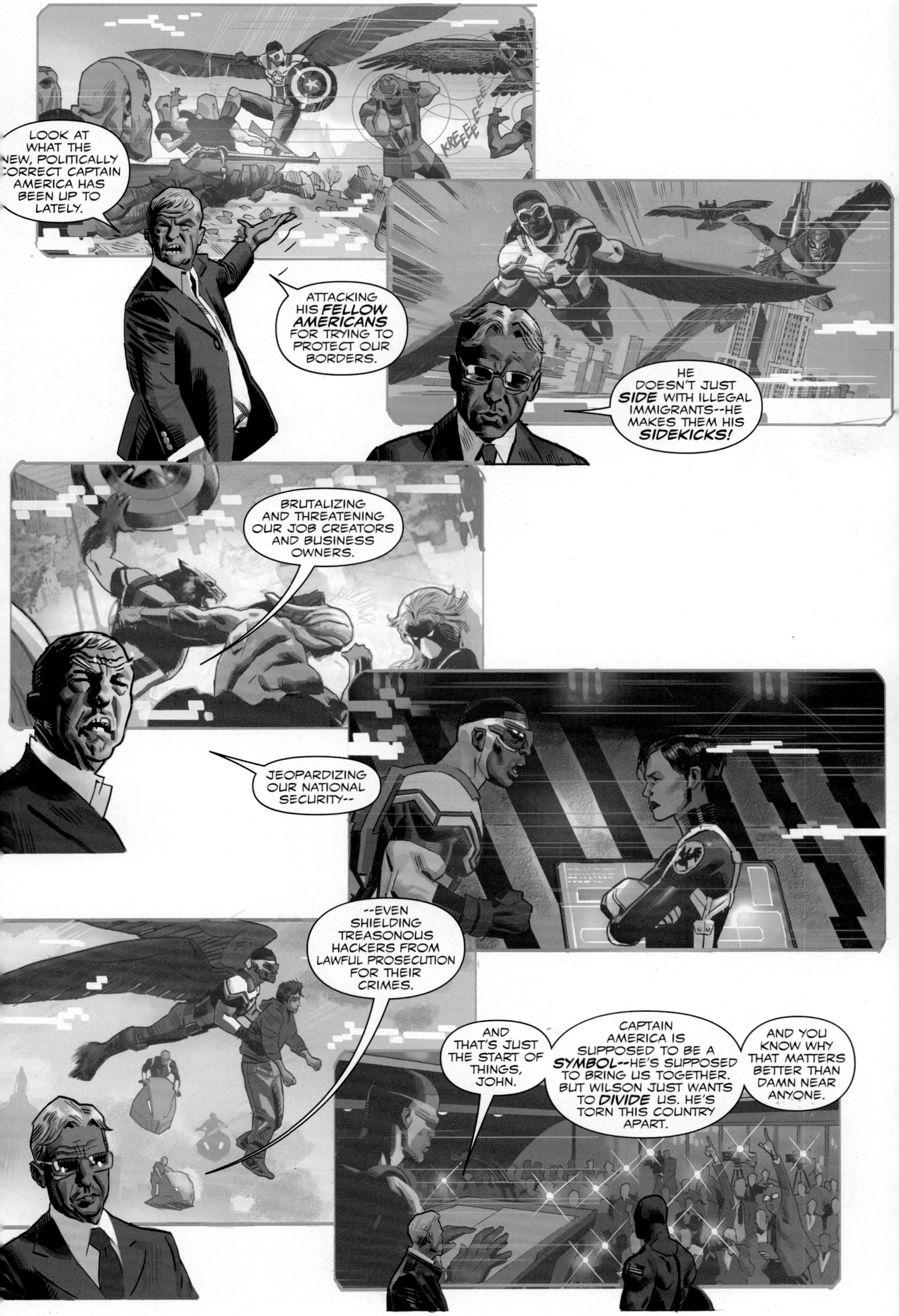

KREEEEEEE
LOOK AT WHAT THE NEW, POLITICALLY CORRECT CAPTAIN AMERICA HAS BEEN UP TO LATELY.
ATTACKING HIS FELLOW AMERICANS FOR TRYING TO PROTECT OUR BORDERS.
HE DOESN'T JUST SIDE WITH ILLEGAL IMMIGRANTS--HE MAKES THEM HIS SIDEKICKS!
BRUTALIZING AND THREATENING OUR JOB CREATORS AND BUSINESS OWNERS.
JEOPARDIZING OUR NATIONAL SECURITY--
--EVEN SHIELDING TREASONOUS HACKERS FROM LAWFUL PROSECUTION FOR THEIR CRIMES.
AND THAT'S JUST THE START OF THINGS, JOHN.
CAPTAIN AMERICA IS SUPPOSED TO BE A SYMBOL--HE'S SUPPOSED TO BRING US TOGETHER. BUT WILSON JUST WANTS TO DIVIDE US. HE'S TORN THIS COUNTRY APART.
AND YOU KNOW WHY THAT MATTERS BETTER THAN DAMN NEAR ANYONE.

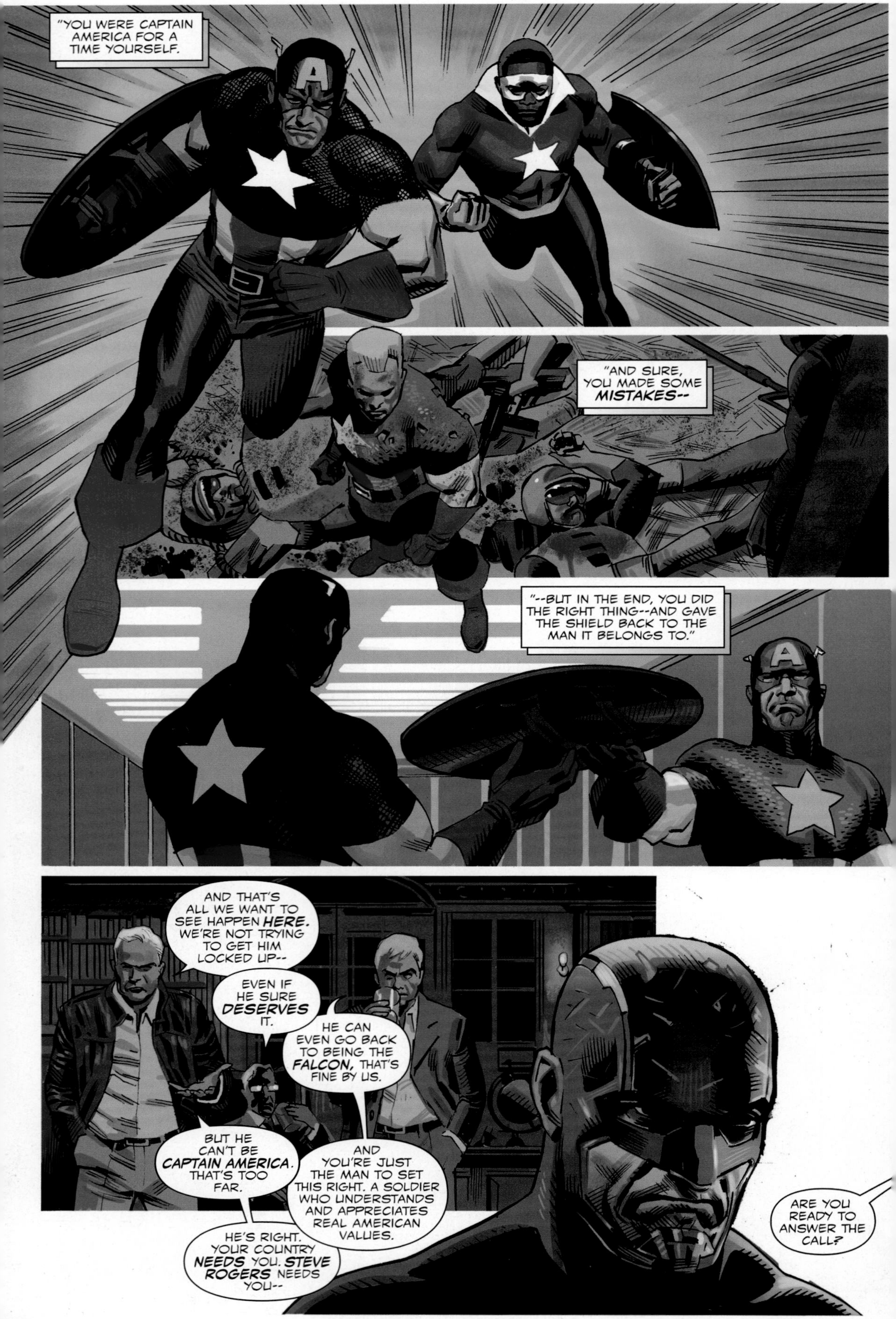
"YOU WERE CAPTAIN AMERICA FOR A TIME YOURSELF.
"AND SURE, YOU MADE SOME MISTAKES--
"--BUT IN THE END, YOU DID THE RIGHT THING--AND GAVE THE SHIELD BACK TO THE MAN IT BELONGS TO."
AND THAT'S ALL WE WANT TO SEE HAPPEN HERE. WE'RE NOT TRYING TO GET HIM LOCKED UP--
EVEN IF HE SURE DESERVES IT.
HE CAN EVEN GO BACK TO BEING THE FALCON, THAT'S FINE BY US.
BUT HE CAN'T BE CAPTAIN AMERICA. THAT'S TOO FAR.
AND YOU'RE JUST THE MAN TO SET THIS RIGHT. A SOLDIER WHO UNDERSTANDS AND APPRECIATES REAL AMERICAN VALUES.
HE'S RIGHT. YOUR COUNTRY NEEDS YOU. STEVE ROGERS NEEDS YOU--
ARE YOU READY TO ANSWER THE CALL?

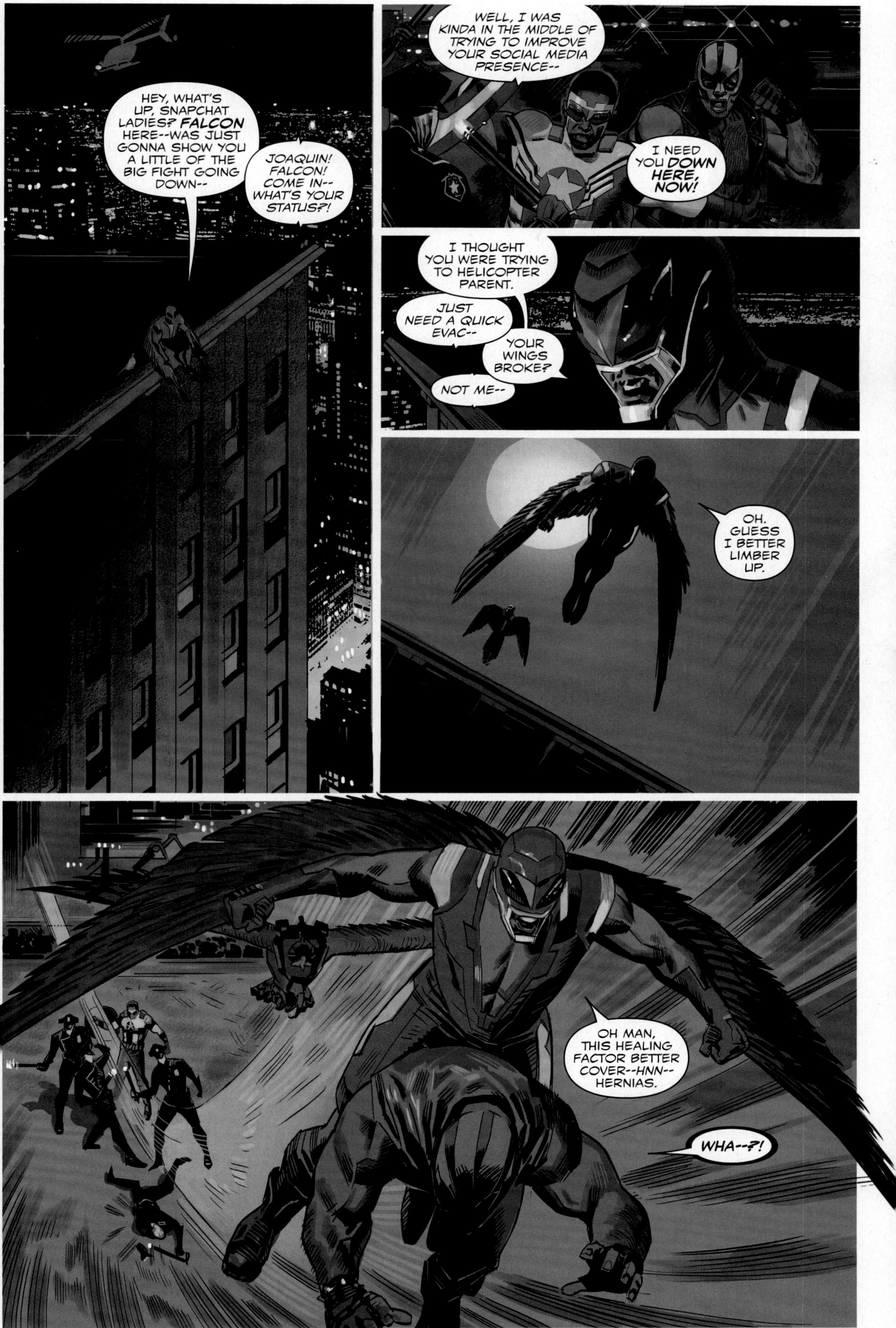
HEY, WHAT'S UP, SNAPCHAT LADIES? FALCON HERE--WAS JUST GONNA SHOW YOU A LITTLE OF THE BIG FIGHT GOING DOWN--
JOAQUIN! FALCON! COME IN--WHAT'S YOUR STATUS?!
WELL, I WAS KINDA IN THE MIDDLE OF TRYING TO IMPROVE YOUR SOCIAL MEDIA PRESENCE--
I NEED YOU DOWN HERE, NOW!
I THOUGHT YOU WERE TRYING TO HELICOPTER PARENT.
JUST NEED A QUICK EVAC--
YOUR WINGS BROKE?
NOT ME--
OH. GUESS I BETTER LIMBER UP.
OH MAN, THIS HEALING FACTOR BETTER COVER--HNN--HERNIAS.
WHA--?!

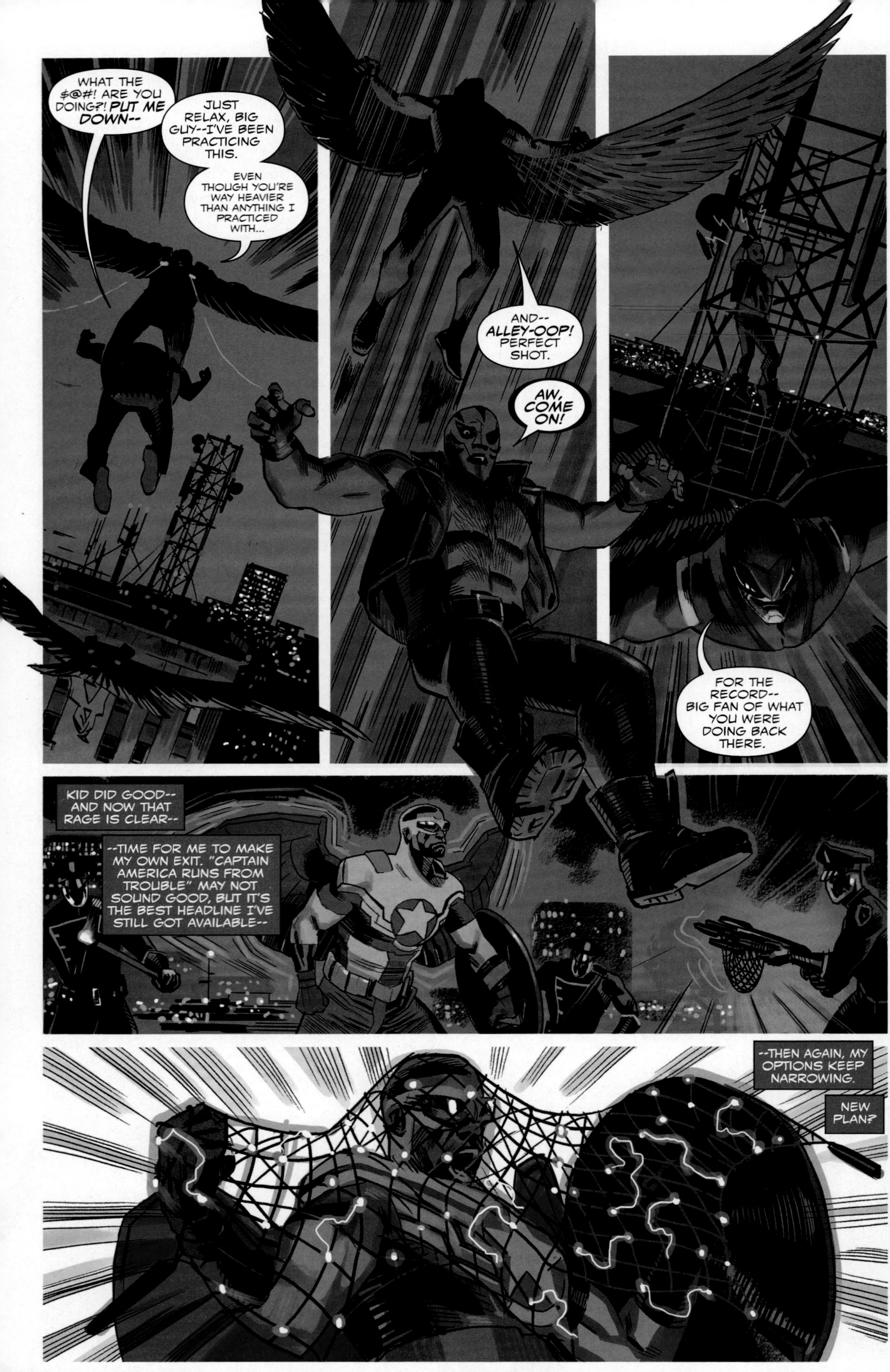
WHAT THE $@#! ARE YOU DOING?! PUT ME DOWN--
JUST RELAX, BIG GUY--I'VE BEEN PRACTICING THIS.
EVEN THOUGH YOU'RE WAY HEAVIER THAN ANYTHING I PRACTICED WITH...
AND-- ALLEY-OOP! PERFECT SHOT.
AW, COME ON!
FOR THE RECORD-- BIG FAN OF WHAT YOU WERE DOING BACK THERE.
KID DID GOOD-- AND NOW THAT RAGE IS CLEAR--
--TIME FOR ME TO MAKE MY OWN EXIT. "CAPTAIN AMERICA RUNS FROM TROUBLE" MAY NOT SOUND GOOD, BUT IT'S THE BEST HEADLINE I'VE STILL GOT AVAILABLE--
--THEN AGAIN, MY OPTIONS KEEP NARROWING.
NEW PLAN?

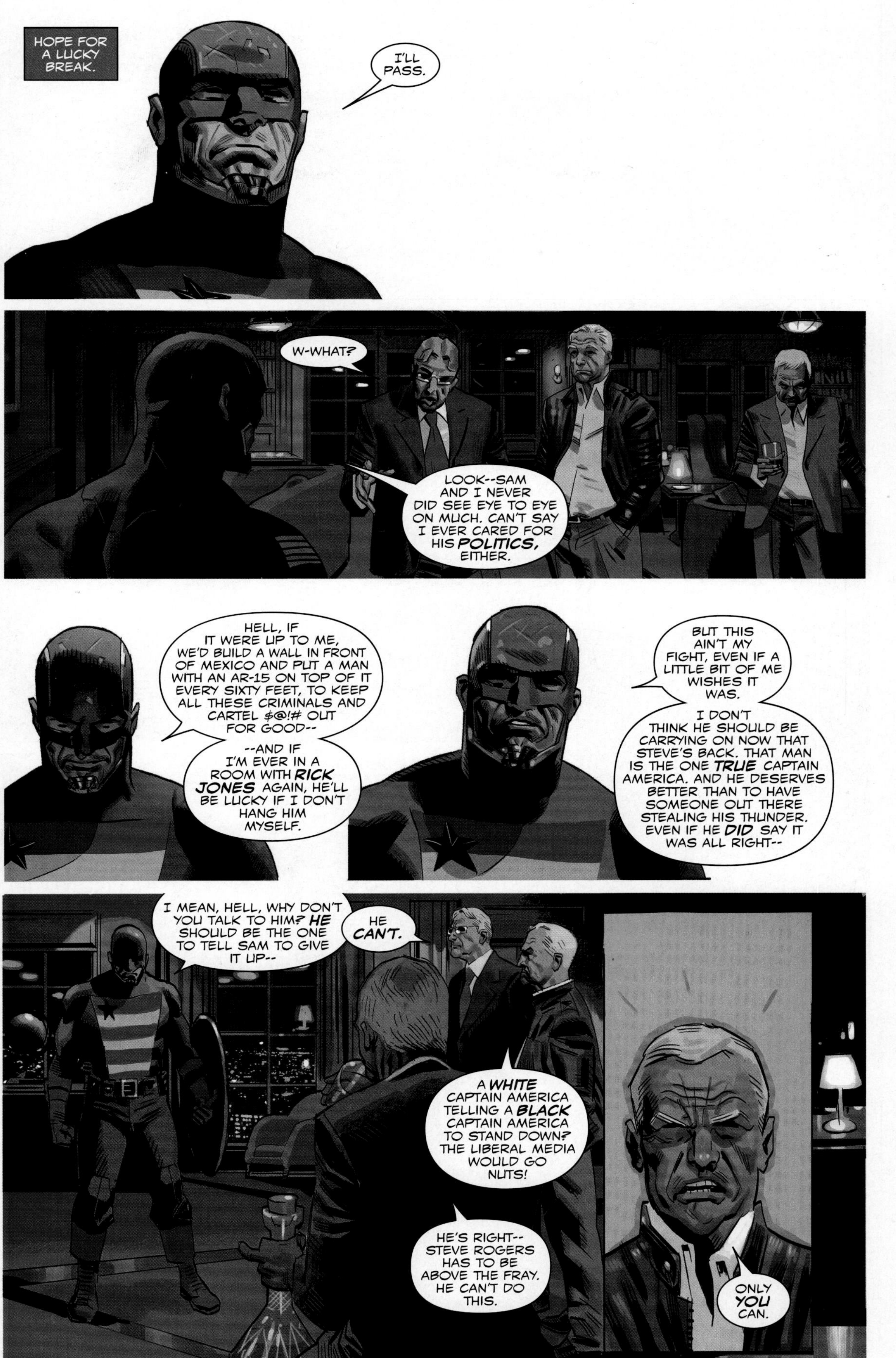
HOPE FOR A LUCKY BREAK.
I'LL PASS.
W-WHAT?
LOOK--SAM AND I NEVER DID SEE EYE TO EYE ON MUCH. CAN'T SAY I EVER CARED FOR HIS POLITICS, EITHER.
HELL, IF IT WERE UP TO ME, WE'D BUILD A WALL IN FRONT OF MEXICO AND PUT A MAN WITH AN AR-15 ON TOP OF IT EVERY SIXTY FEET, TO KEEP ALL THESE CRIMINALS AND CARTEL $@!# OUT FOR GOOD--
--AND IF I'M EVER IN A ROOM WITH RICK JONES AGAIN, HE'LL BE LUCKY IF I DON'T HANG HIM MYSELF.
BUT THIS AIN'T MY FIGHT, EVEN IF A LITTLE BIT OF ME WISHES IT WAS.
I DON'T THINK HE SHOULD BE CARRYING ON NOW THAT STEVE'S BACK. THAT MAN IS THE ONE TRUE CAPTAIN AMERICA. AND HE DESERVES BETTER THAN TO HAVE SOMEONE OUT THERE STEALING HIS THUNDER. EVEN IF HE DID SAY IT WAS ALL RIGHT--
I MEAN, HELL, WHY DON'T YOU TALK TO HIM? HE SHOULD BE THE ONE TO TELL SAM TO GIVE IT UP--
HE CAN'T.
A WHITE CAPTAIN AMERICA TELLING A BLACK CAPTAIN AMERICA TO STAND DOWN? THE LIBERAL MEDIA WOULD GO NUTS!
HE'S RIGHT-- STEVE ROGERS HAS TO BE ABOVE THE FRAY. HE CAN'T DO THIS.
ONLY YOU CAN.

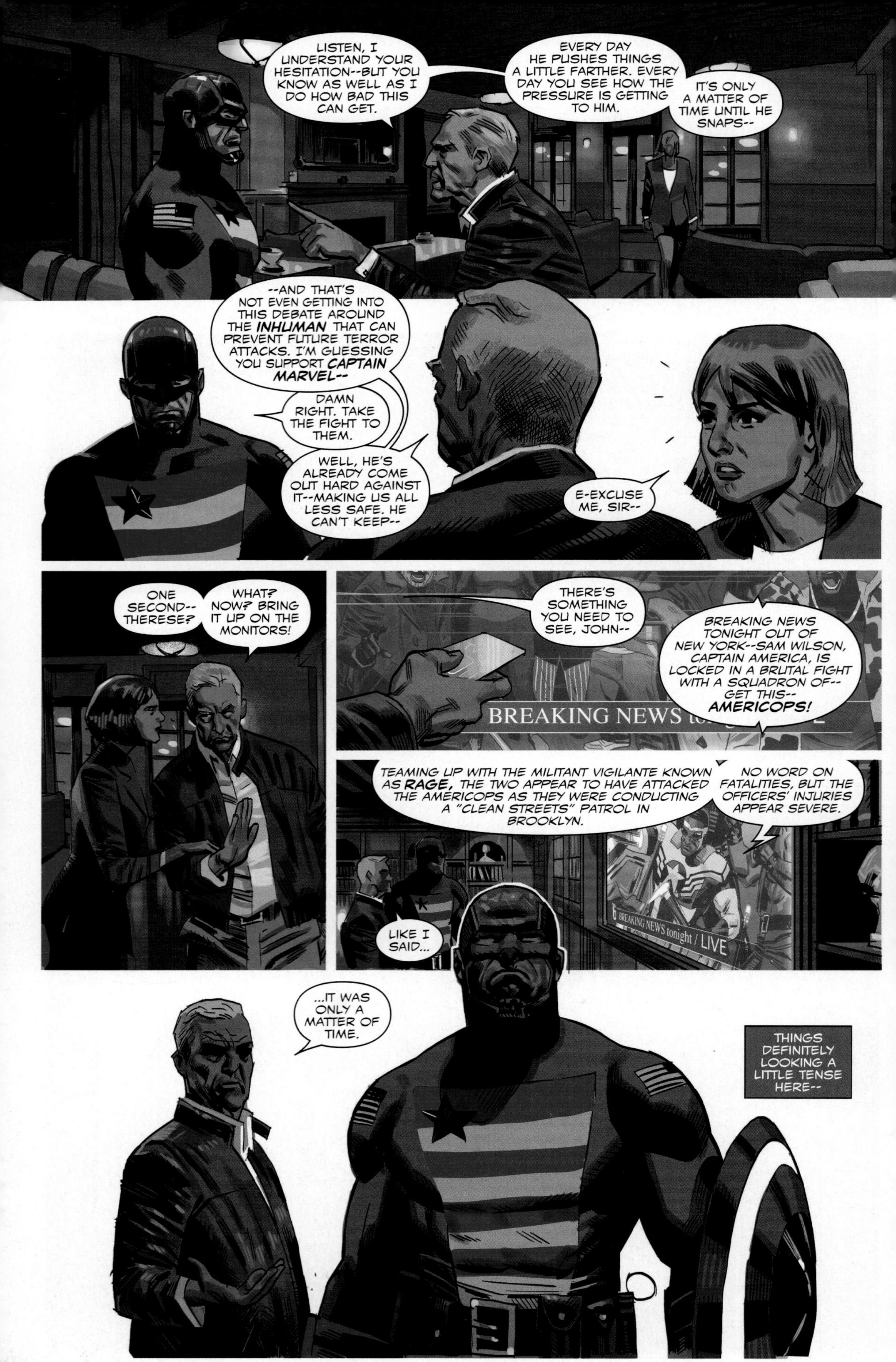
LISTEN, I UNDERSTAND YOUR HESITATION--BUT YOU KNOW AS WELL AS I DO HOW BAD THIS CAN GET.
EVERY DAY HE PUSHES THINGS A LITTLE FARTHER. EVERY DAY YOU SEE HOW THE PRESSURE IS GETTING TO HIM.
IT'S ONLY A MATTER OF TIME UNTIL HE SNAPS--
--AND THAT'S NOT EVEN GETTING INTO THIS DEBATE AROUND THE INHUMAN THAT CAN PREVENT FUTURE TERROR ATTACKS. I'M GUESSING YOU SUPPORT CAPTAIN MARVEL--
DAMN RIGHT. TAKE THE FIGHT TO THEM.
WELL, HE'S ALREADY COME OUT HARD AGAINST IT--MAKING US ALL LESS SAFE. HE CAN'T KEEP--
E-EXCUSE ME, SIR--
ONE SECOND-- THERESE?
WHAT? NOW? BRING IT UP ON THE MONITORS!
THERE'S SOMETHING YOU NEED TO SEE, JOHN--
BREAKING NEWS TONIGHT OUT OF NEW YORK--SAM WILSON, CAPTAIN AMERICA, IS LOCKED IN A BRUTAL FIGHT WITH A SQUADRON OF-- GET THIS-- AMERICOPS!
BREAKING NEWS
TEAMING UP WITH THE MILITANT VIGILANTE KNOWN AS RAGE, THE TWO APPEAR TO HAVE ATTACKED THE AMERICOPS AS THEY WERE CONDUCTING A "CLEAN STREETS" PATROL IN BROOKLYN.
NO WORD ON FATALITIES, BUT THE OFFICERS' INJURIES APPEAR SEVERE.
BREAKING NEWS tonight / LIVE
LIKE I SAID...
...IT WAS ONLY A MATTER OF TIME.
THINGS DEFINITELY LOOKING A LITTLE TENSE HERE--

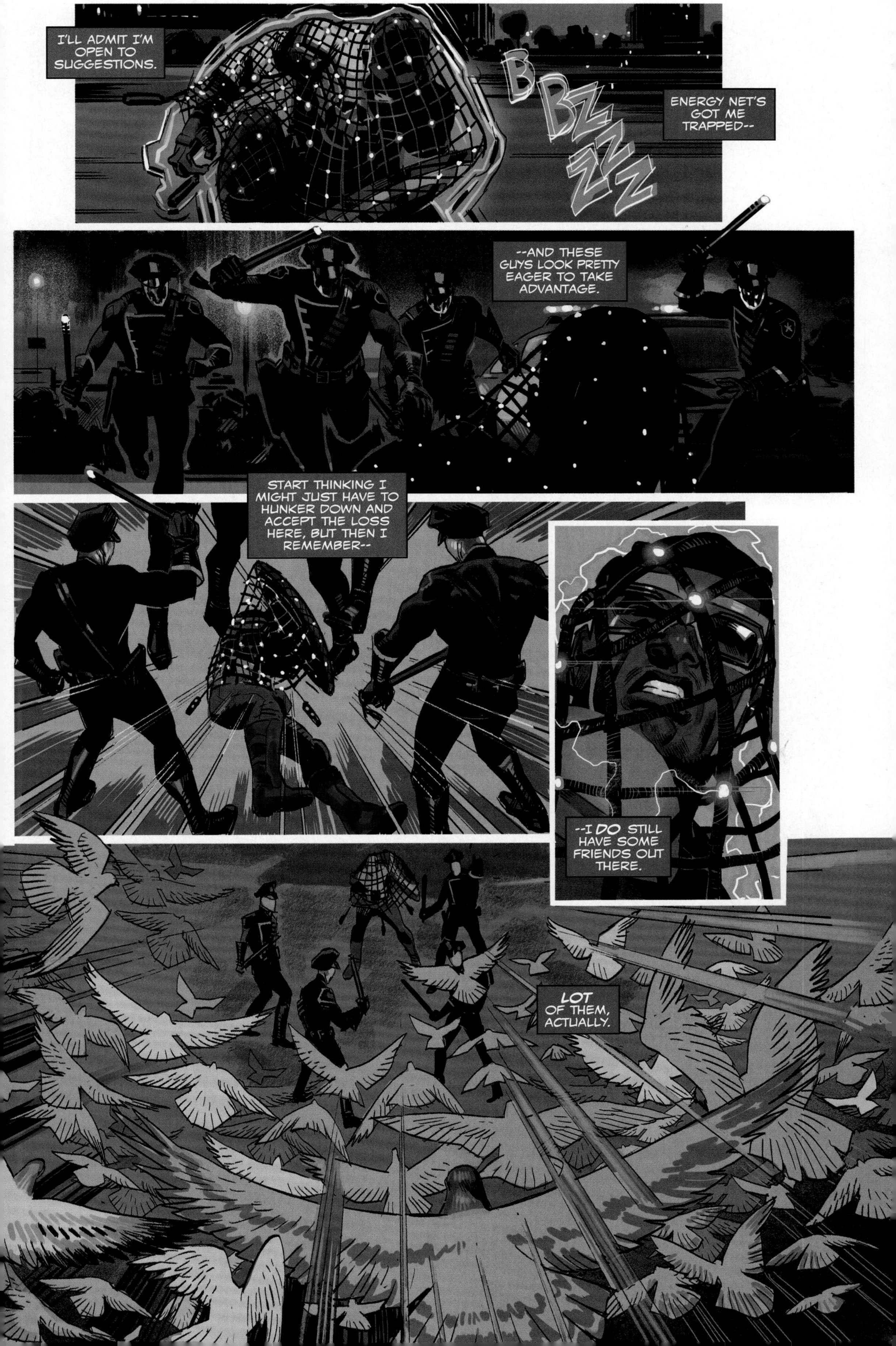
I'LL ADMIT I'M OPEN TO SUGGESTIONS.
BBZZZZ
ENERGY NET'S GOT ME TRAPPED--
--AND THESE GUYS LOOK PRETTY EAGER TO TAKE ADVANTAGE.
START THINKING I MIGHT JUST HAVE TO HUNKER DOWN AND ACCEPT THE LOSS HERE, BUT THEN I REMEMBER--
--I DO STILL HAVE SOME FRIENDS OUT THERE.
LOT OF THEM, ACTUALLY.

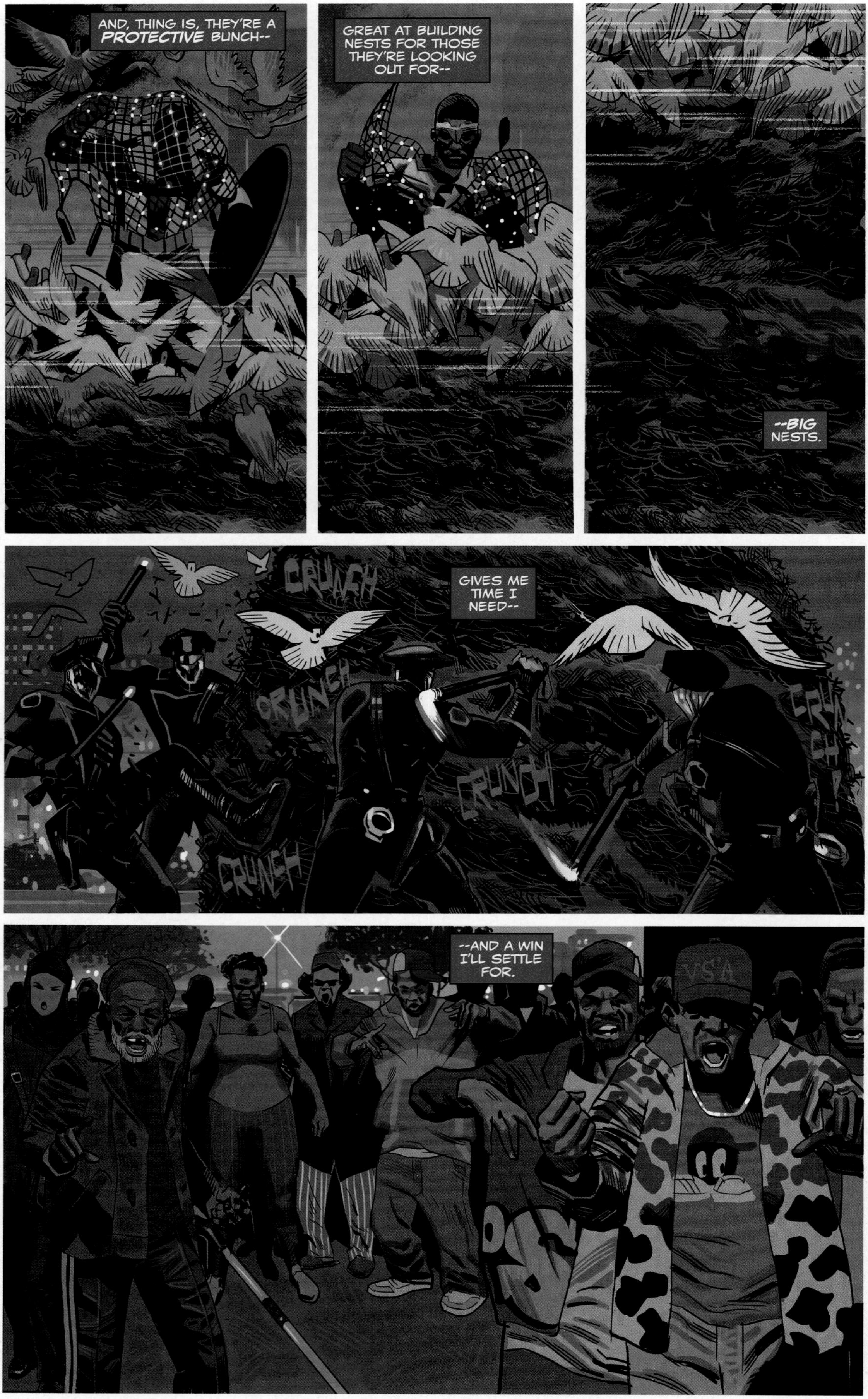
AND, THING IS, THEY'RE A PROTECTIVE BUNCH--
GREAT AT BUILDING NESTS FOR THOSE THEY'RE LOOKING OUT FOR--
--BIG NESTS.
CRUNCH
GIVES ME TIME I NEED--
CRUNCH
CRUNCH
CRUNCH
CRUNCH
--AND A WIN I'LL SETTLE FOR.

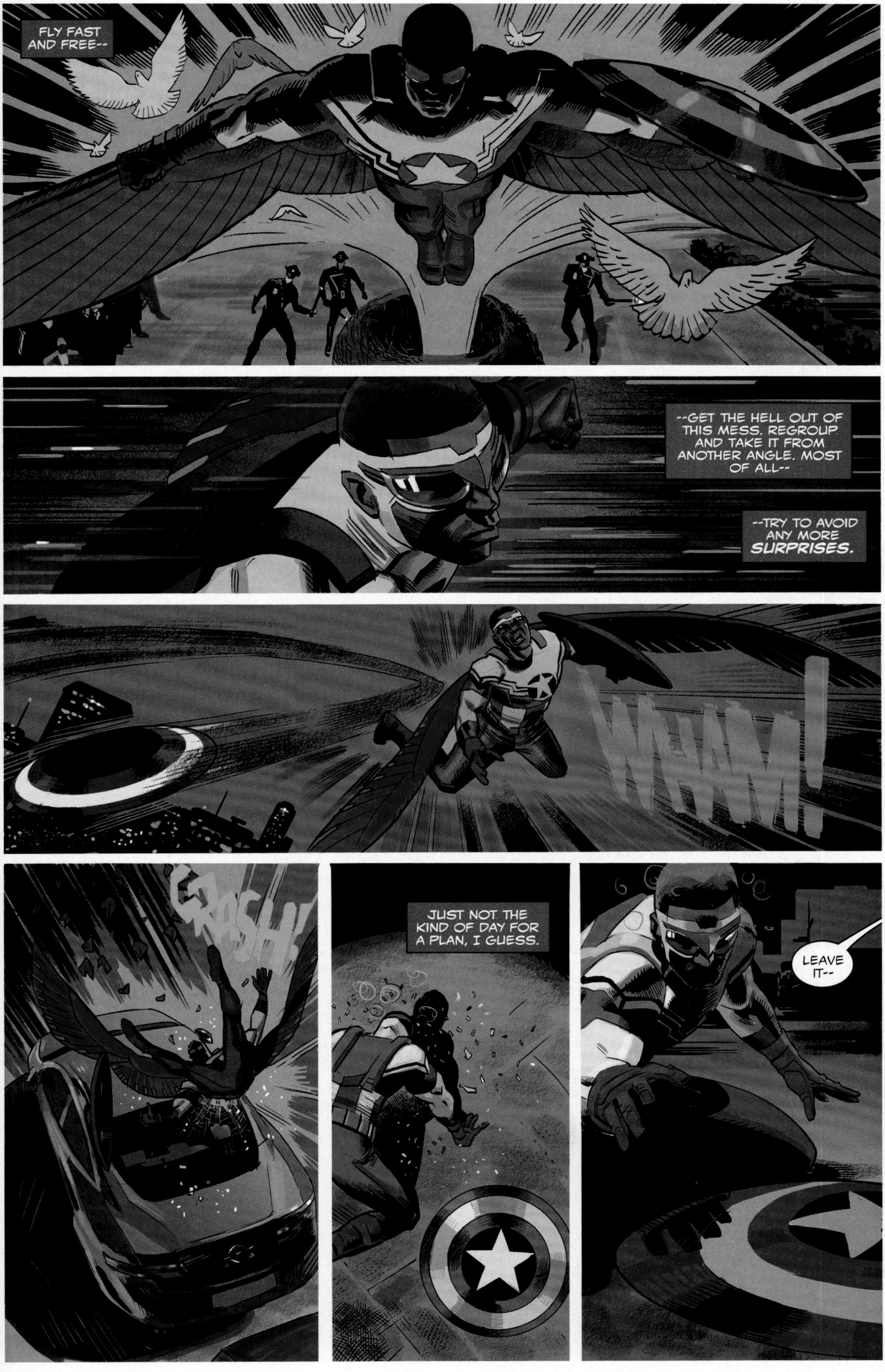
FLY FAST AND FREE--
--GET THE HELL OUT OF THIS MESS. REGROUP AND TAKE IT FROM ANOTHER ANGLE. MOST OF ALL--
--TRY TO AVOID ANY MORE SURPRISES.
WHAM!
CRASH!
JUST NOT THE KIND OF DAY FOR A PLAN, I GUESS.
LEAVE IT--

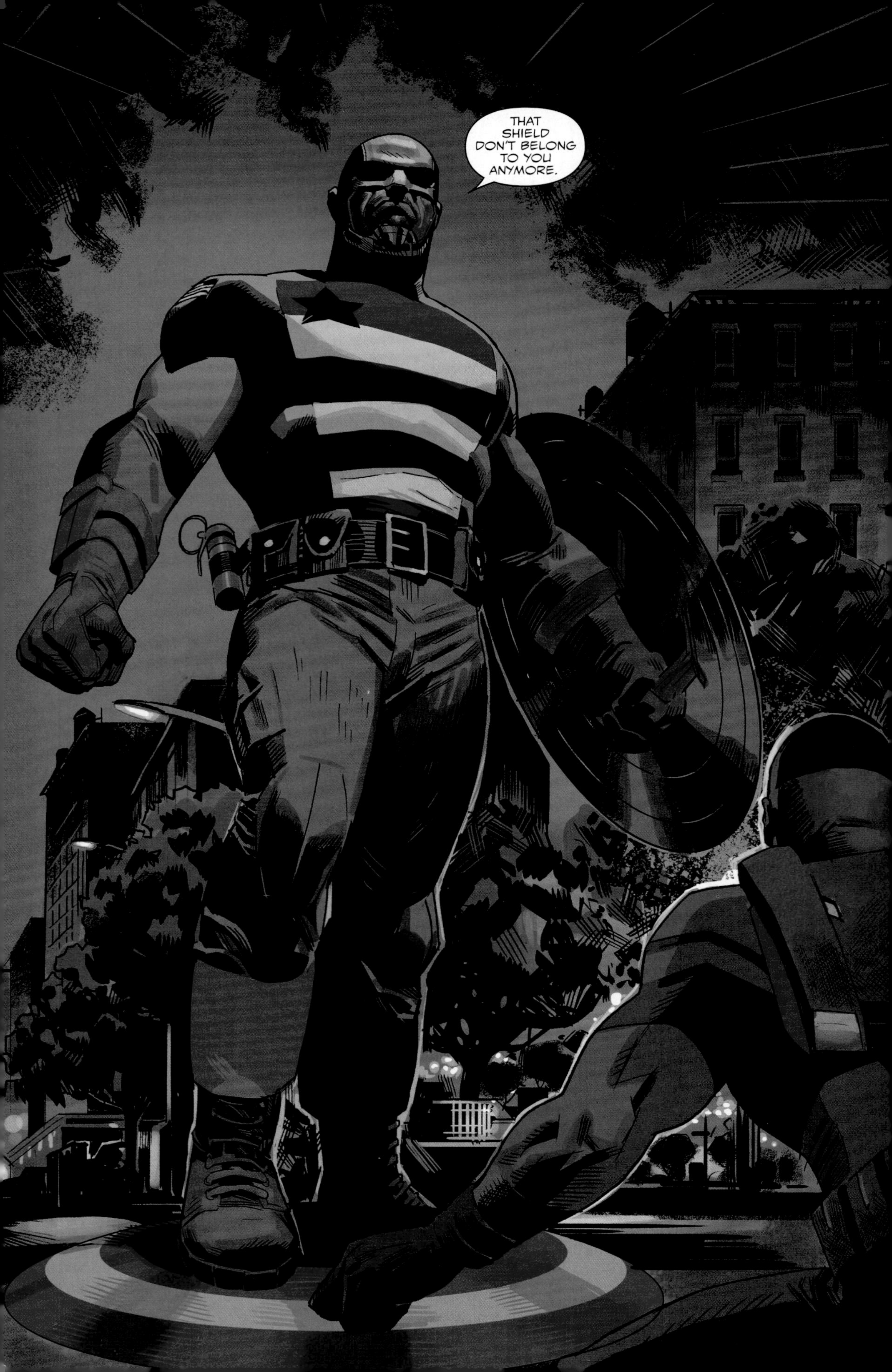
THAT SHIELD DON'T BELONG TO YOU ANYMORE.

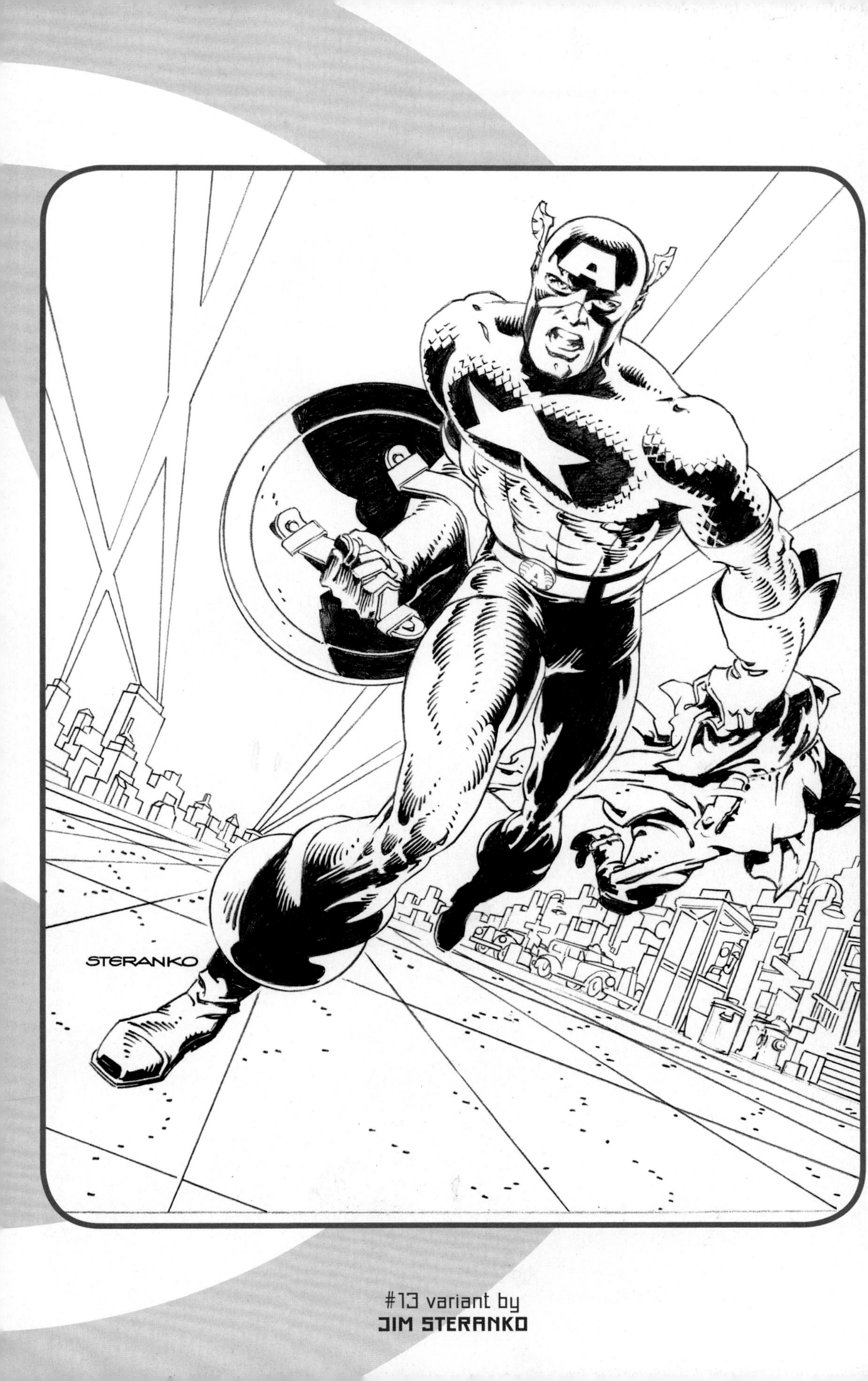
STERANKO

#13 variant by
JIM STERANKO

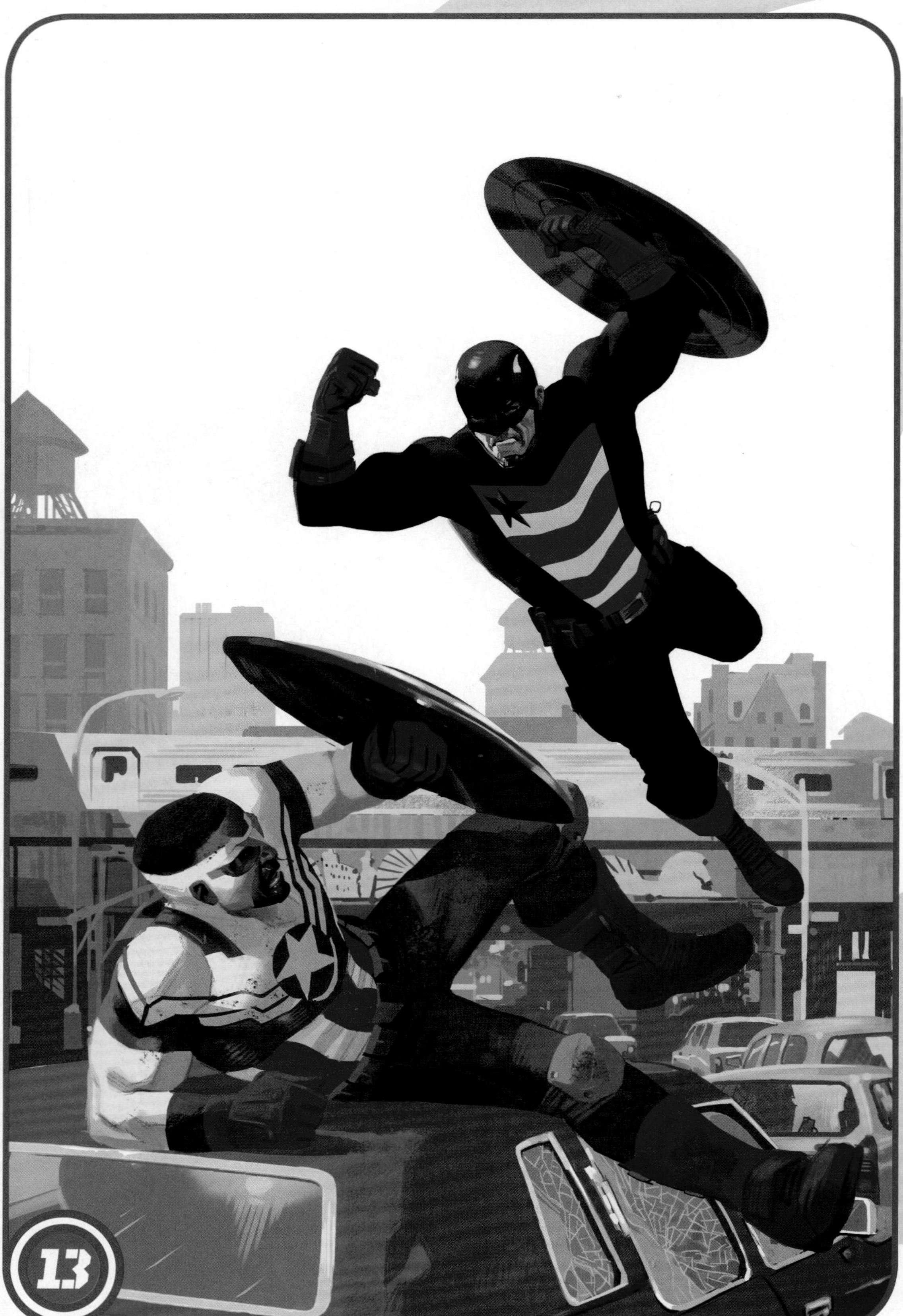
13

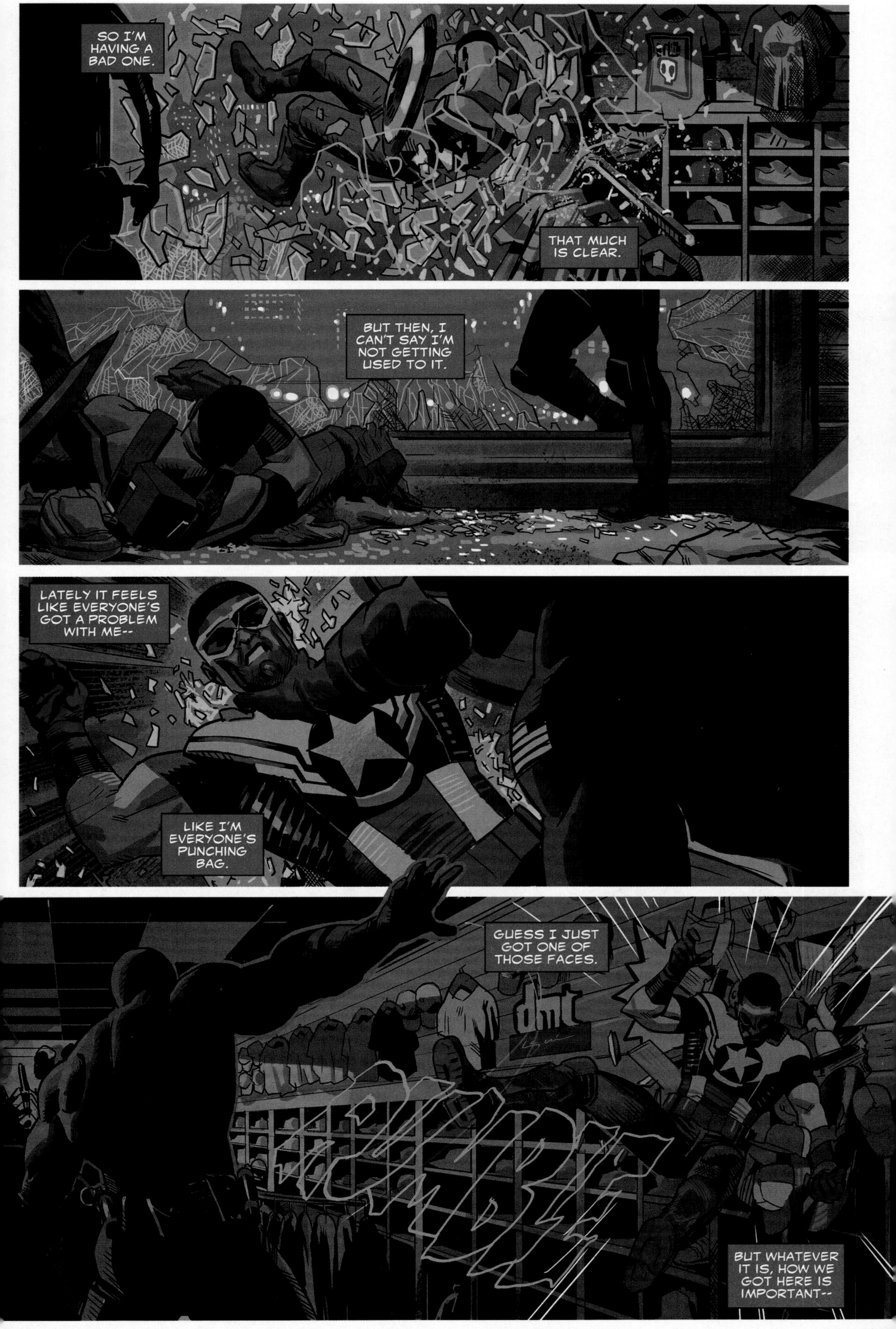

SO I'M HAVING A BAD ONE.
THAT MUCH IS CLEAR.
BUT THEN, I CAN'T SAY I'M NOT GETTING USED TO IT.
LATELY IT FEELS LIKE EVERYONE'S GOT A PROBLEM WITH ME--
LIKE I'M EVERYONE'S PUNCHING BAG.
GUESS I JUST GOT ONE OF THOSE FACES.
BUT WHATEVER IT IS, HOW WE GOT HERE IS IMPORTANT--

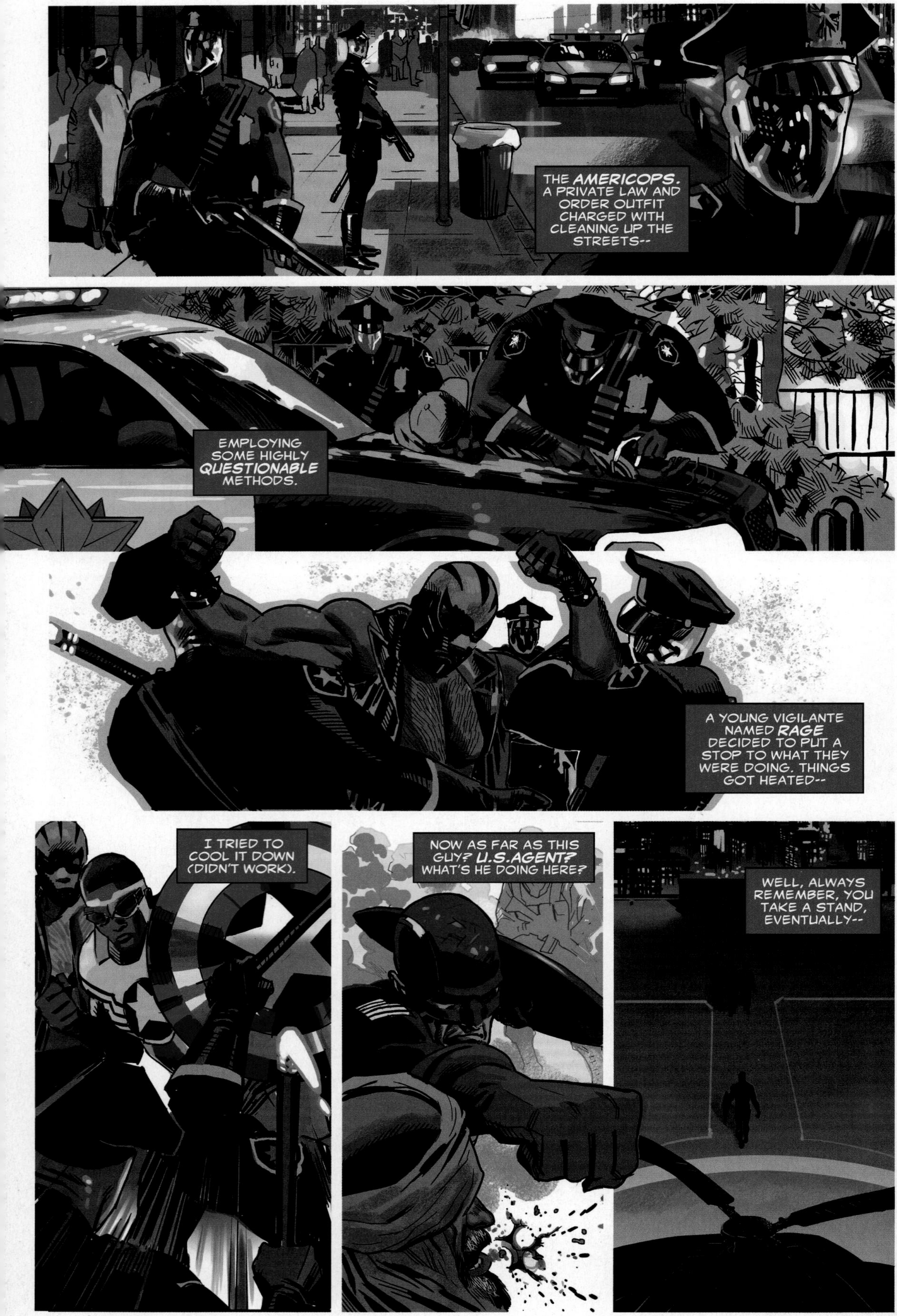
THE AMERICOPS. A PRIVATE LAW AND ORDER OUTFIT CHARGED WITH CLEANING UP THE STREETS--
EMPLOYING SOME HIGHLY QUESTIONABLE METHODS.
A YOUNG VIGILANTE NAMED RAGE DECIDED TO PUT A STOP TO WHAT THEY WERE DOING. THINGS GOT HEATED--
I TRIED TO COOL IT DOWN (DIDN'T WORK).
NOW AS FAR AS THIS GUY? U.S.AGENT? WHAT'S HE DOING HERE?
WELL, ALWAYS REMEMBER, YOU TAKE A STAND, EVENTUALLY--

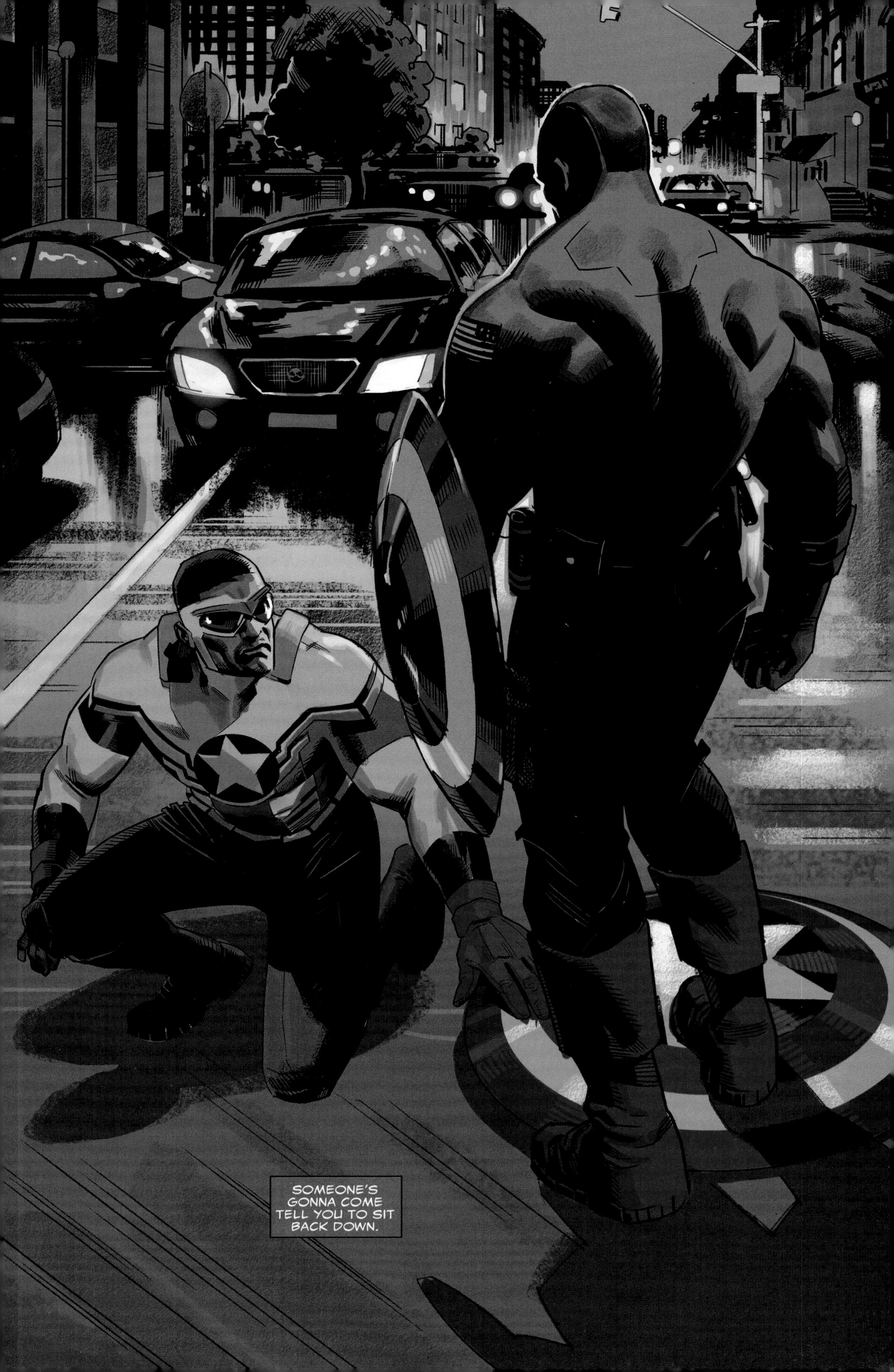
SOMEONE'S GONNA COME TELL YOU TO SIT BACK DOWN.

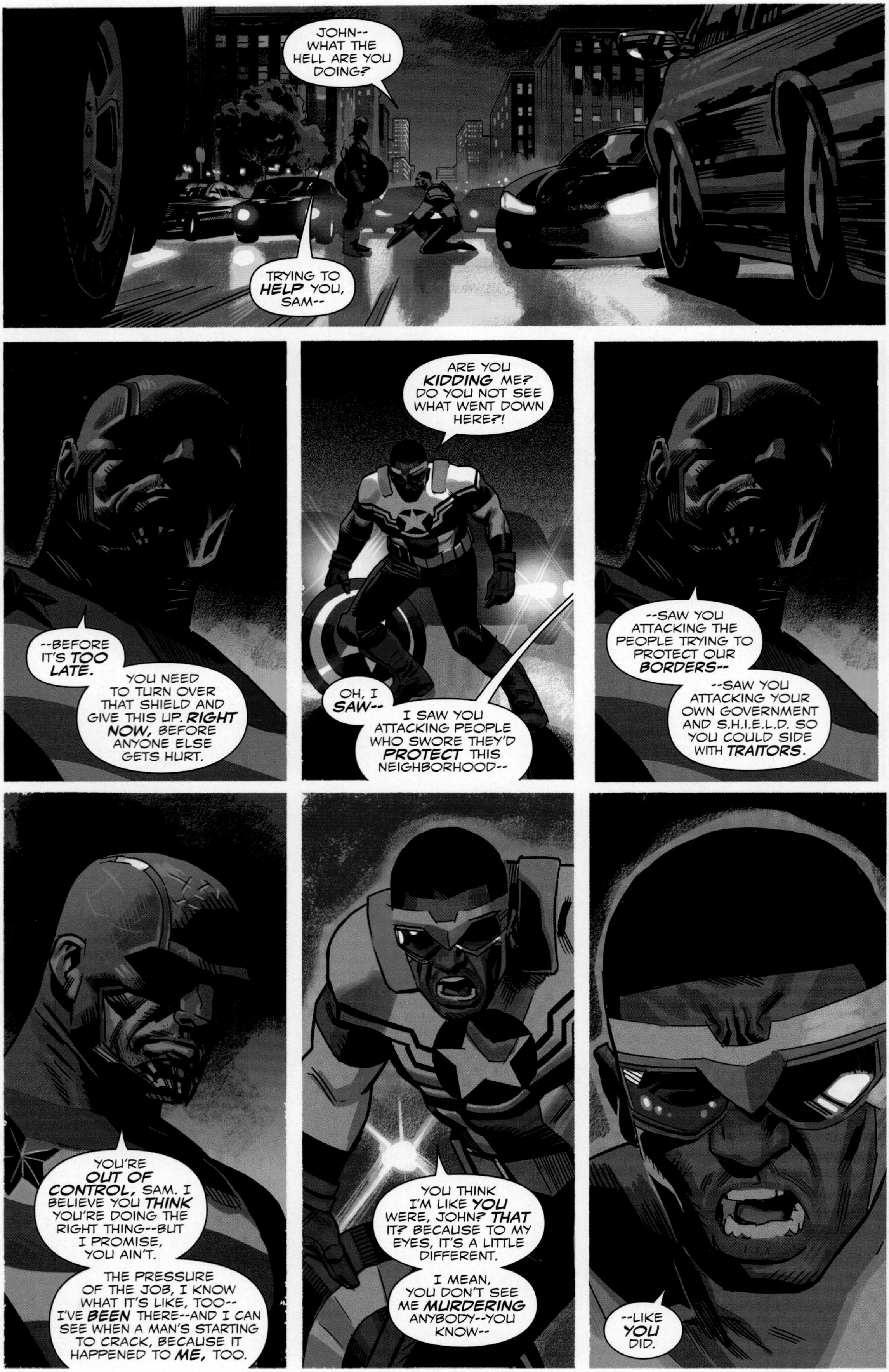
JOHN-- WHAT THE HELL ARE YOU DOING?
TRYING TO HELP YOU, SAM--
--BEFORE IT'S TOO LATE.
YOU NEED TO TURN OVER THAT SHIELD AND GIVE THIS UP. RIGHT NOW, BEFORE ANYONE ELSE GETS HURT.
ARE YOU KIDDING ME? DO YOU NOT SEE WHAT WENT DOWN HERE?!
OH, I SAW--
I SAW YOU ATTACKING PEOPLE WHO SWORE THEY'D PROTECT THIS NEIGHBORHOOD--
--SAW YOU ATTACKING THE PEOPLE TRYING TO PROTECT OUR BORDERS--
--SAW YOU ATTACKING YOUR OWN GOVERNMENT AND S.H.I.E.L.D. SO YOU COULD SIDE WITH TRAITORS.
YOU'RE OUT OF CONTROL, SAM. I BELIEVE YOU THINK YOU'RE DOING THE RIGHT THING--BUT I PROMISE, YOU AIN'T.
THE PRESSURE OF THE JOB, I KNOW WHAT IT'S LIKE, TOO-- I'VE BEEN THERE--AND I CAN SEE WHEN A MAN'S STARTING TO CRACK, BECAUSE IT HAPPENED TO ME, TOO.
YOU THINK I'M LIKE YOU WERE, JOHN? THAT IT? BECAUSE TO MY EYES, IT'S A LITTLE DIFFERENT.
I MEAN, YOU DON'T SEE ME MURDERING ANYBODY--YOU KNOW--
--LIKE YOU DID.

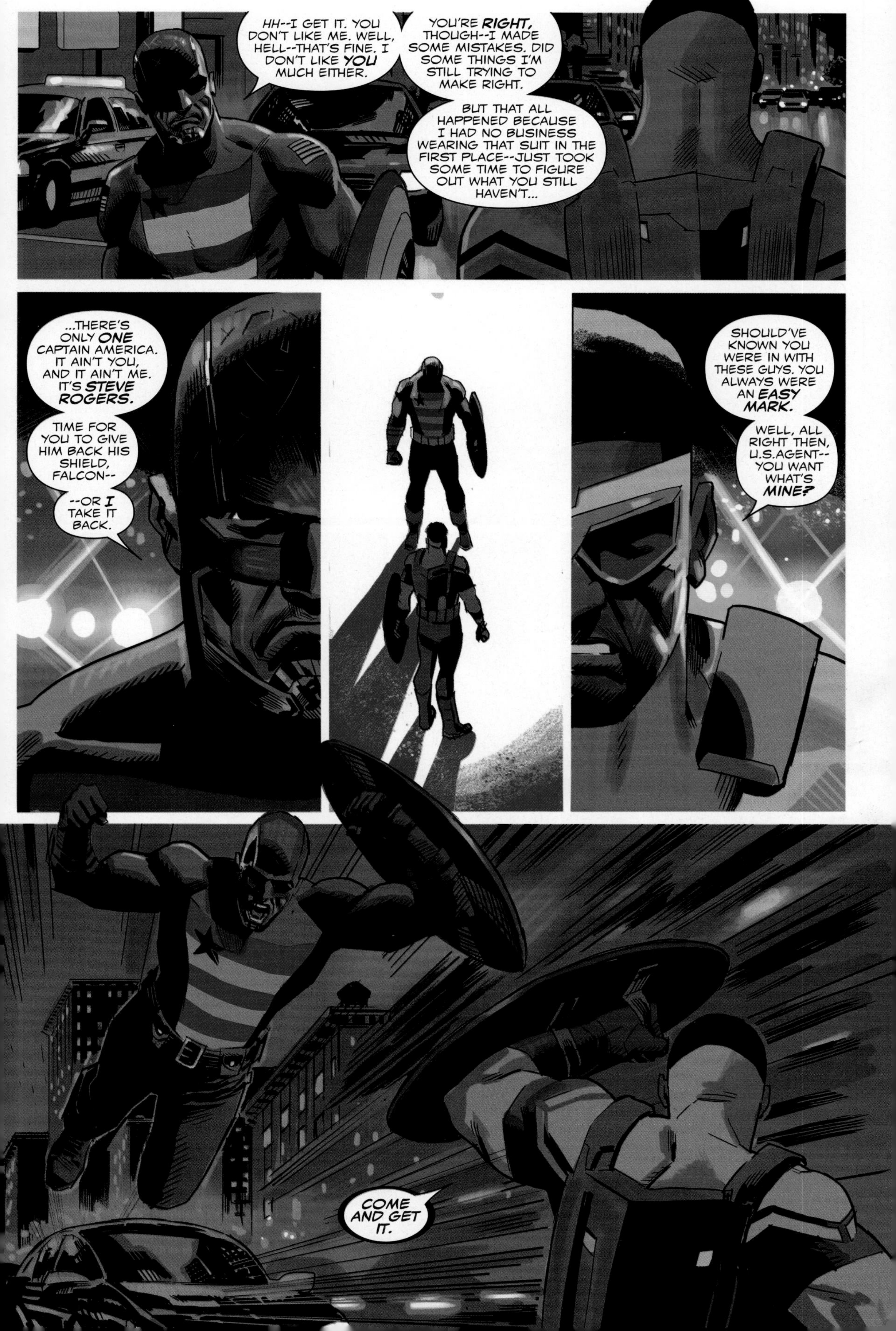
HH--I GET IT. YOU DON'T LIKE ME. WELL, HELL--THAT'S FINE. I DON'T LIKE YOU MUCH EITHER.
YOU'RE RIGHT, THOUGH--I MADE SOME MISTAKES. DID SOME THINGS I'M STILL TRYING TO MAKE RIGHT.
BUT THAT ALL HAPPENED BECAUSE I HAD NO BUSINESS WEARING THAT SUIT IN THE FIRST PLACE--JUST TOOK SOME TIME TO FIGURE OUT WHAT YOU STILL HAVEN'T...
...THERE'S ONLY ONE CAPTAIN AMERICA. IT AIN'T YOU, AND IT AIN'T ME. IT'S STEVE ROGERS.
TIME FOR YOU TO GIVE HIM BACK HIS SHIELD, FALCON--
--OR I TAKE IT BACK.
SHOULD'VE KNOWN YOU WERE IN WITH THESE GUYS. YOU ALWAYS WERE AN EASY MARK.
WELL, ALL RIGHT THEN, U.S.AGENT-- YOU WANT WHAT'S MINE?
COME AND GET IT.

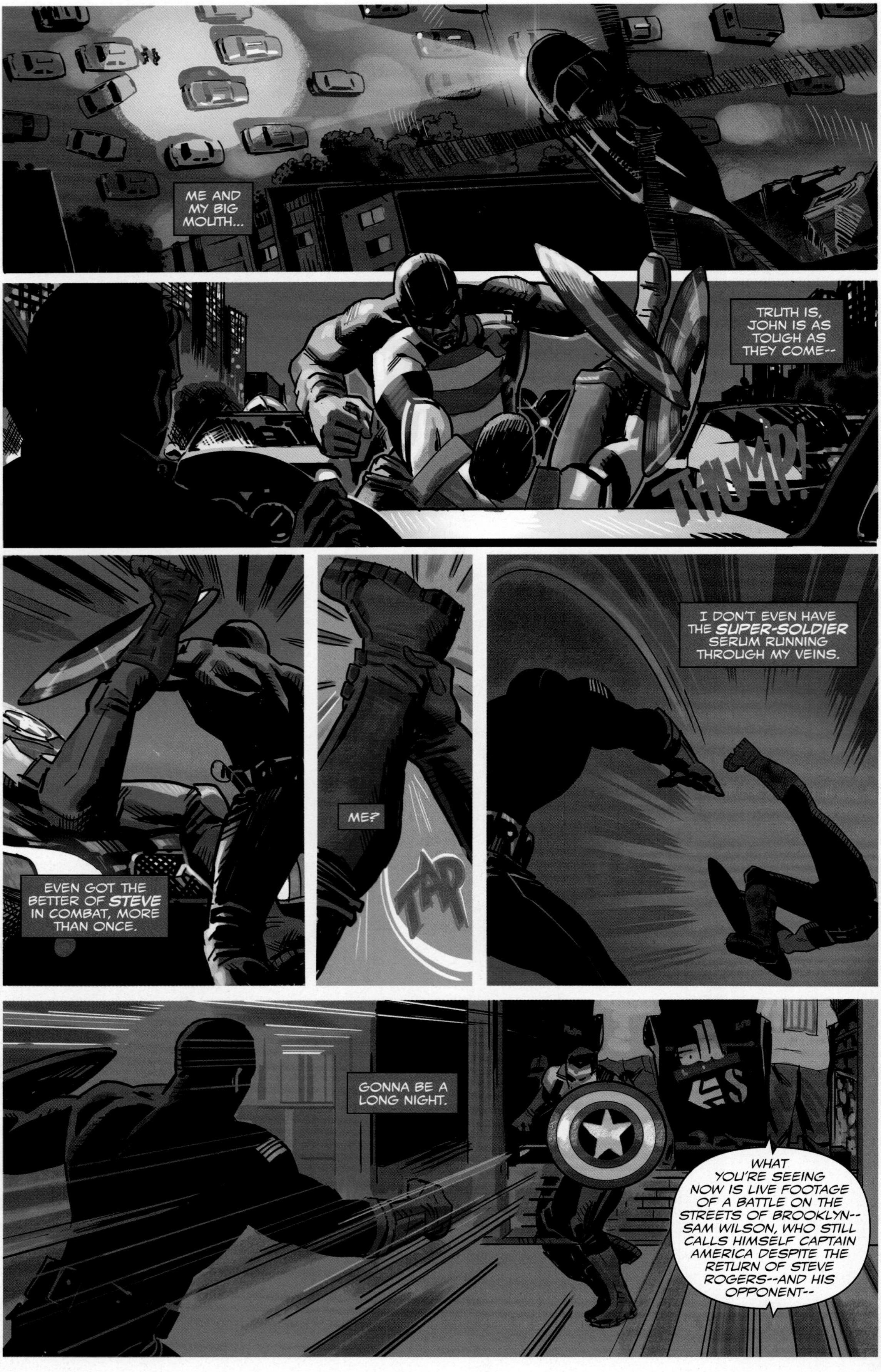
ME AND MY BIG MOUTH...
TRUTH IS, JOHN IS AS TOUGH AS THEY COME--
THUMP!
EVEN GOT THE BETTER OF STEVE IN COMBAT, MORE THAN ONCE.
ME?
TAP
I DON'T EVEN HAVE THE SUPER-SOLDIER SERUM RUNNING THROUGH MY VEINS.
GONNA BE A LONG NIGHT.
WHAT YOU'RE SEEING NOW IS LIVE FOOTAGE OF A BATTLE ON THE STREETS OF BROOKLYN--SAM WILSON, WHO STILL CALLS HIMSELF CAPTAIN AMERICA DESPITE THE RETURN OF STEVE ROGERS--AND HIS OPPONENT--

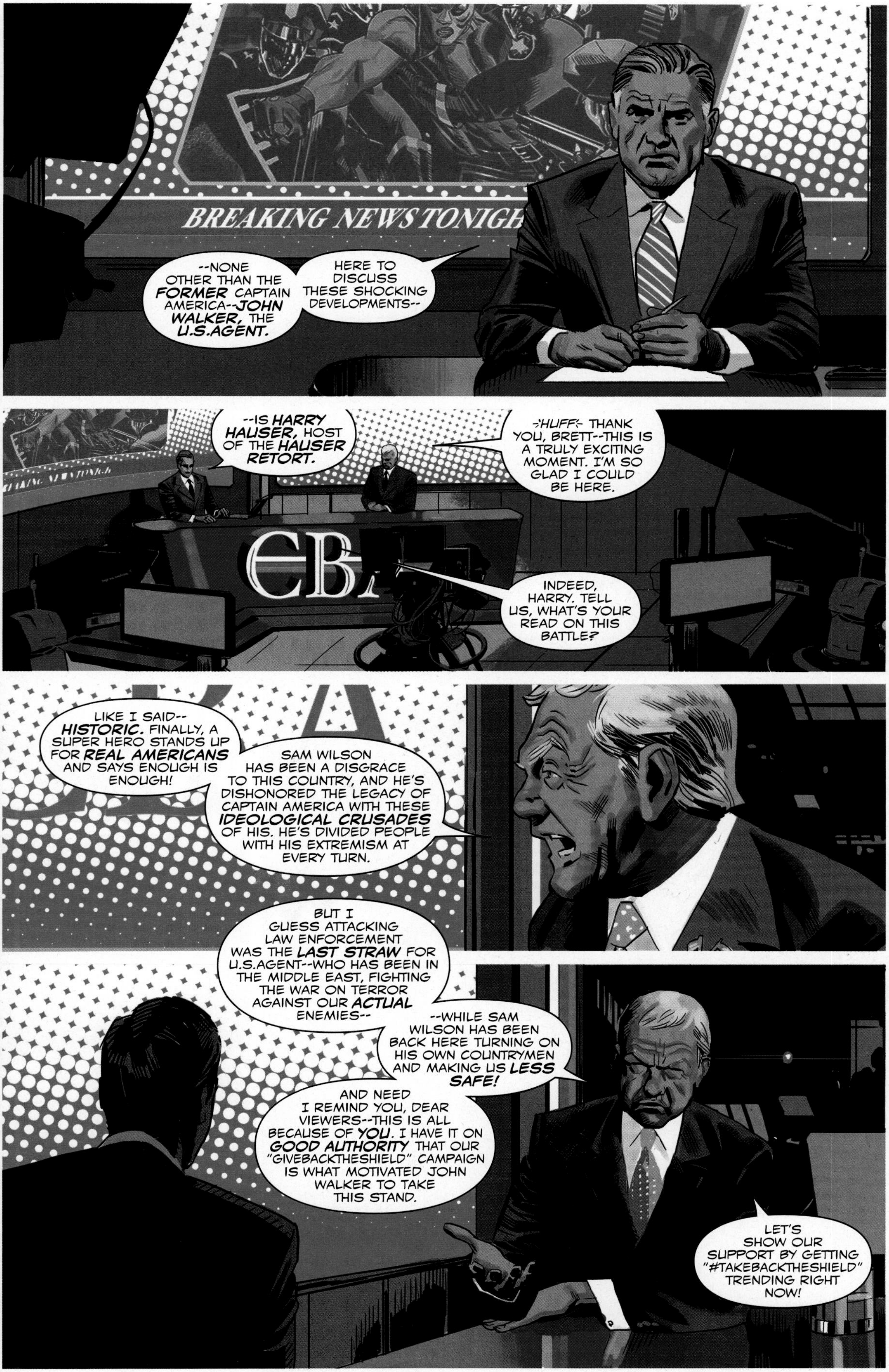
BREAKING NEWS TONIGH
HERE TO DISCUSS THESE SHOCKING DEVELOPMENTS--
--NONE OTHER THAN THE FORMER CAPTAIN AMERICA--JOHN WALKER, THE U.S.AGENT.
--IS HARRY HAUSER, HOST OF THE HAUSER RETORT.
-HUFF- THANK YOU, BRETT--THIS IS A TRULY EXCITING MOMENT. I'M SO GLAD I COULD BE HERE.
INDEED, HARRY. TELL US, WHAT'S YOUR READ ON THIS BATTLE?
LIKE I SAID--HISTORIC. FINALLY, A SUPER HERO STANDS UP FOR REAL AMERICANS AND SAYS ENOUGH IS ENOUGH!
SAM WILSON HAS BEEN A DISGRACE TO THIS COUNTRY, AND HE'S DISHONORED THE LEGACY OF CAPTAIN AMERICA WITH THESE IDEOLOGICAL CRUSADES OF HIS. HE'S DIVIDED PEOPLE WITH HIS EXTREMISM AT EVERY TURN.
BUT I GUESS ATTACKING LAW ENFORCEMENT WAS THE LAST STRAW FOR U.S.AGENT--WHO HAS BEEN IN THE MIDDLE EAST, FIGHTING THE WAR ON TERROR AGAINST OUR ACTUAL ENEMIES--
--WHILE SAM WILSON HAS BEEN BACK HERE TURNING ON HIS OWN COUNTRYMEN AND MAKING US LESS SAFE!
AND NEED I REMIND YOU, DEAR VIEWERS--THIS IS ALL BECAUSE OF YOU. I HAVE IT ON GOOD AUTHORITY THAT OUR "GIVEBACKTHESHIELD" CAMPAIGN IS WHAT MOTIVATED JOHN WALKER TO TAKE THIS STAND.
LET'S SHOW OUR SUPPORT BY GETTING "#TAKEBACKTHESHIELD" TRENDING RIGHT NOW!

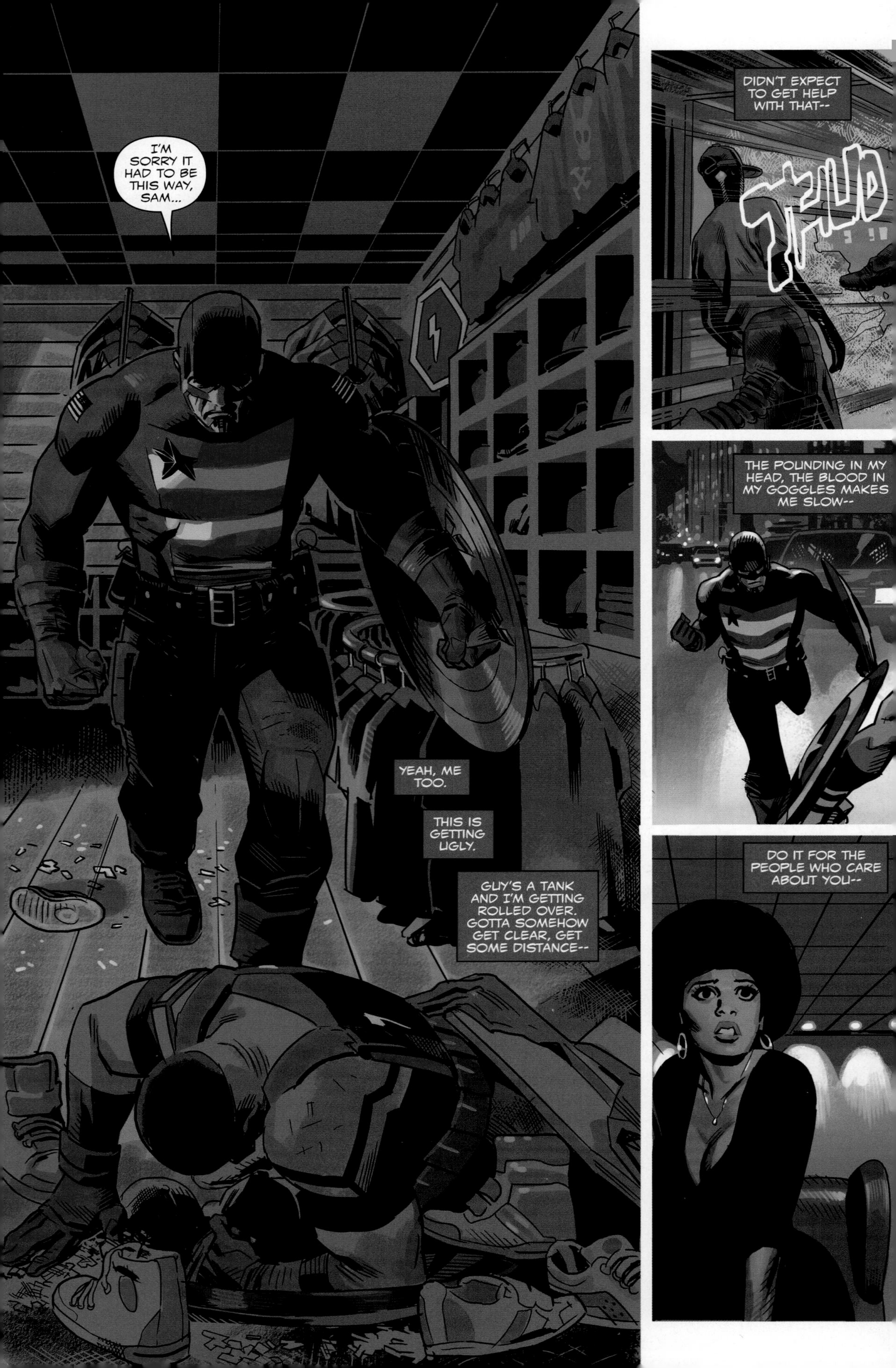
I'M SORRY IT HAD TO BE THIS WAY, SAM...
YEAH, ME TOO.
THIS IS GETTING UGLY.
GUY'S A TANK AND I'M GETTING ROLLED OVER. GOTTA SOMEHOW GET CLEAR, GET SOME DISTANCE--
DIDN'T EXPECT TO GET HELP WITH THAT--
THE POUNDING IN MY HEAD, THE BLOOD IN MY GOGGLES MAKES ME SLOW--
DO IT FOR THE PEOPLE WHO CARE ABOUT YOU--

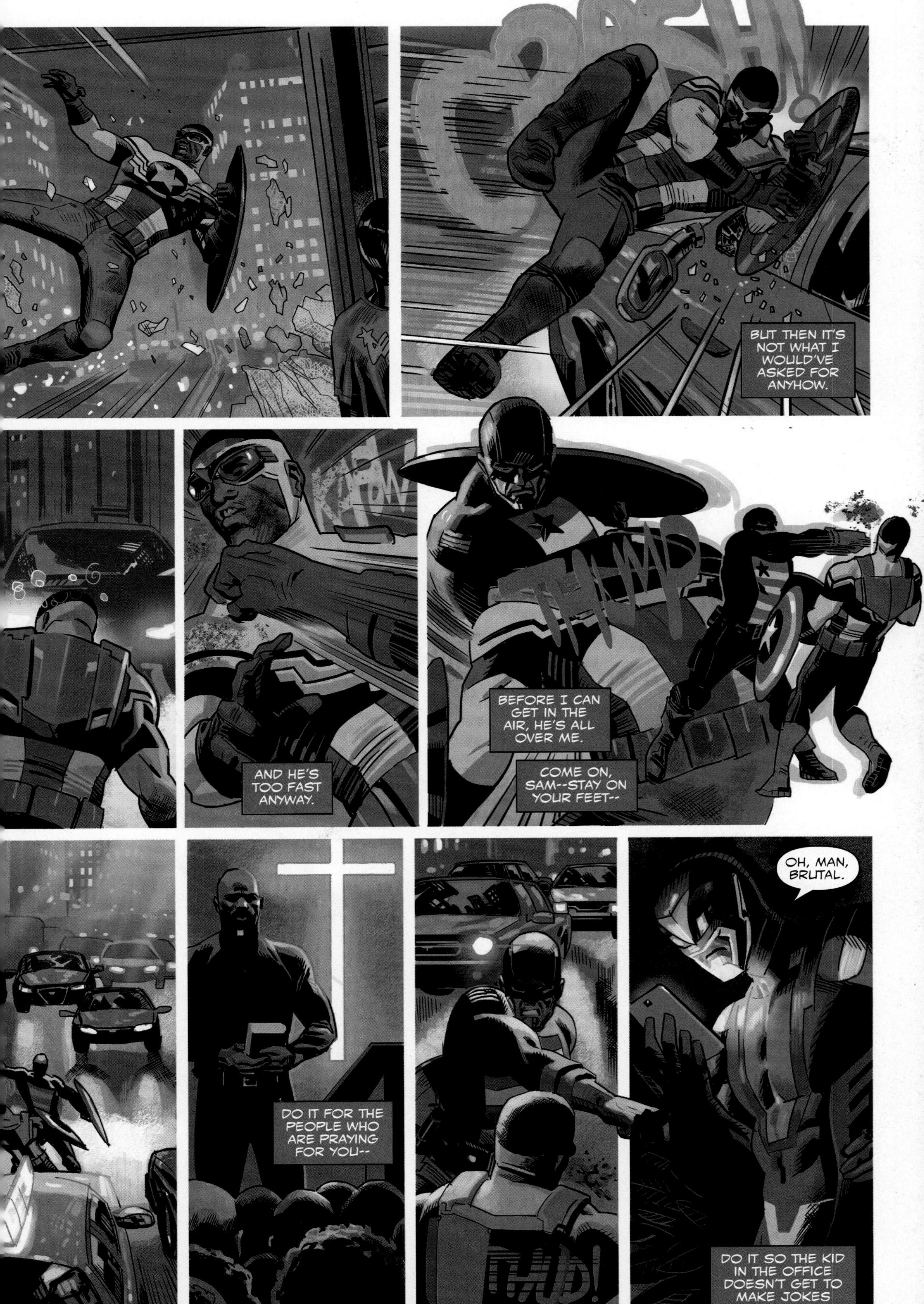
KRASH!
BUT THEN IT'S NOT WHAT I WOULD'VE ASKED FOR ANYHOW.
KAPOW
AND HE'S TOO FAST ANYWAY.
THWMP
BEFORE I CAN GET IN THE AIR, HE'S ALL OVER ME.
COME ON, SAM--STAY ON YOUR FEET--
DO IT FOR THE PEOPLE WHO ARE PRAYING FOR YOU--
THUD!
OH, MAN, BRUTAL.
DO IT SO THE KID IN THE OFFICE DOESN'T GET TO MAKE JOKES ABOUT YOU.

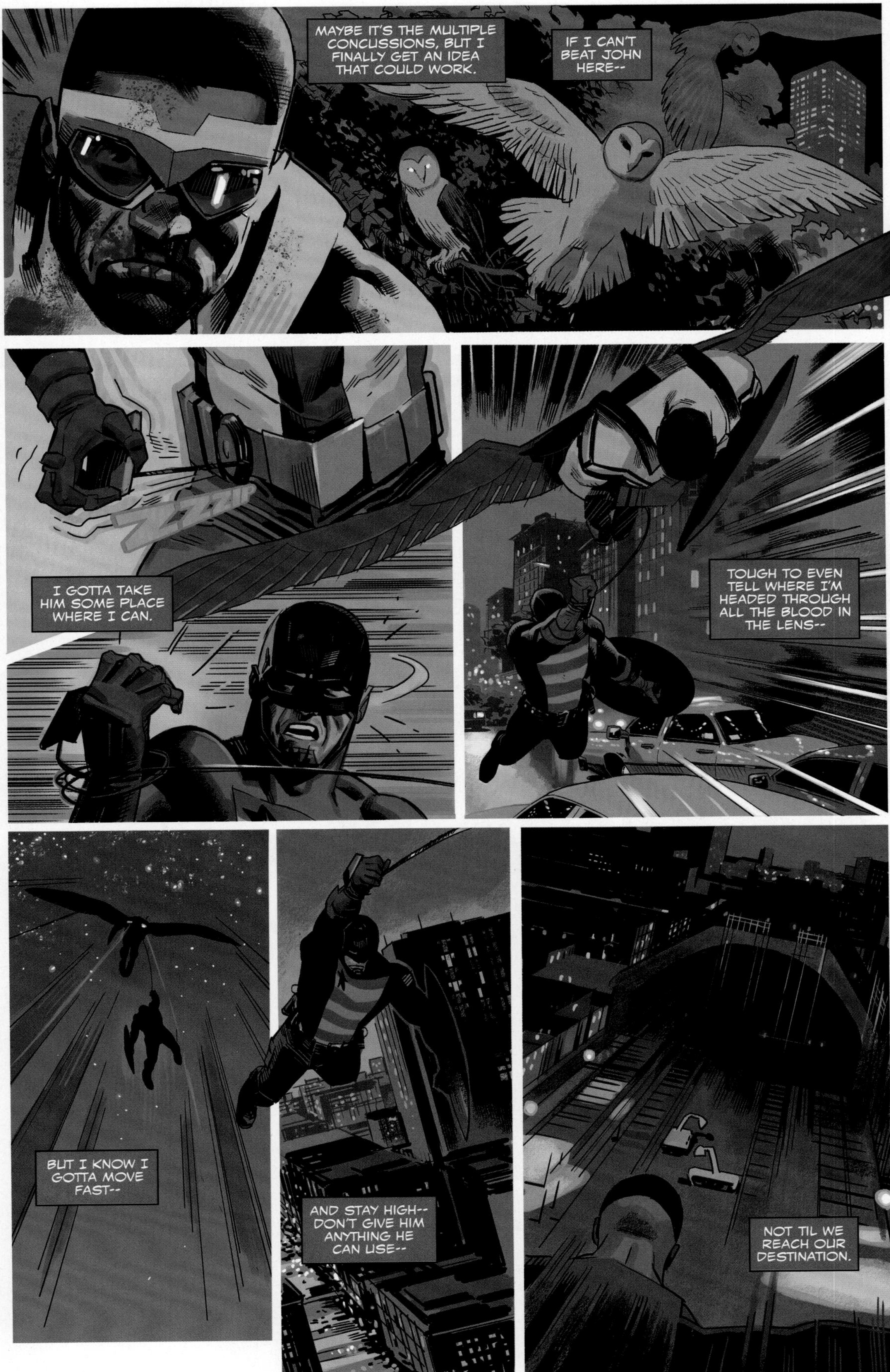
MAYBE IT'S THE MULTIPLE CONCUSSIONS, BUT I FINALLY GET AN IDEA THAT COULD WORK.
IF I CAN'T BEAT JOHN HERE--
ZZZIP
I GOTTA TAKE HIM SOME PLACE WHERE I CAN.
TOUGH TO EVEN TELL WHERE I'M HEADED THROUGH ALL THE BLOOD IN THE LENS--
BUT I KNOW I GOTTA MOVE FAST--
AND STAY HIGH--DON'T GIVE HIM ANYTHING HE CAN USE--
NOT TIL WE REACH OUR DESTINATION.

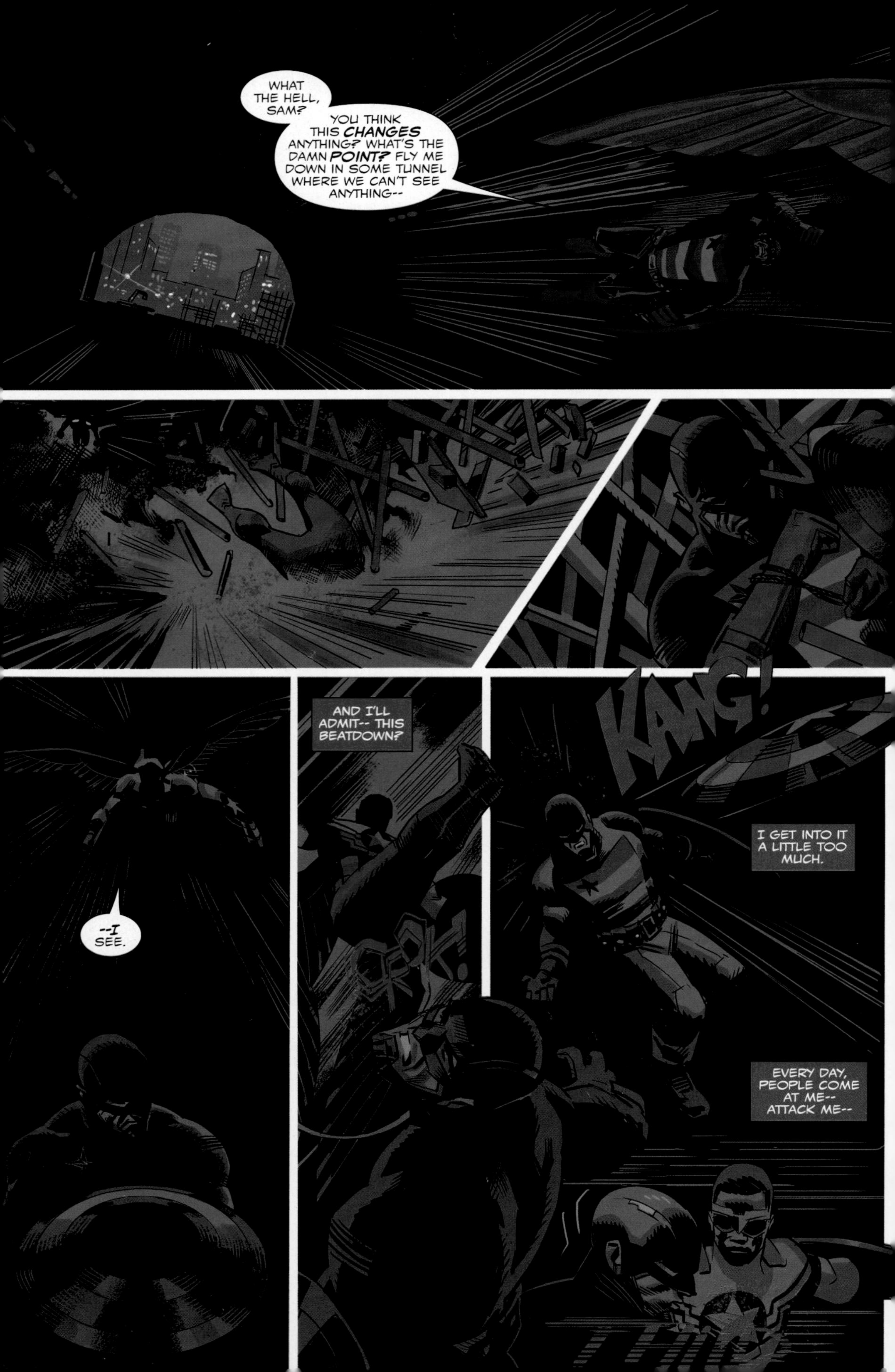

WHAT THE HELL, SAM?
YOU THINK THIS CHANGES ANYTHING? WHAT'S THE DAMN POINT? FLY ME DOWN IN SOME TUNNEL WHERE WE CAN'T SEE ANYTHING--
--I SEE.
AND I'LL ADMIT-- THIS BEATDOWN?
KANG!
I GET INTO IT A LITTLE TOO MUCH.
EVERY DAY, PEOPLE COME AT ME-- ATTACK ME--

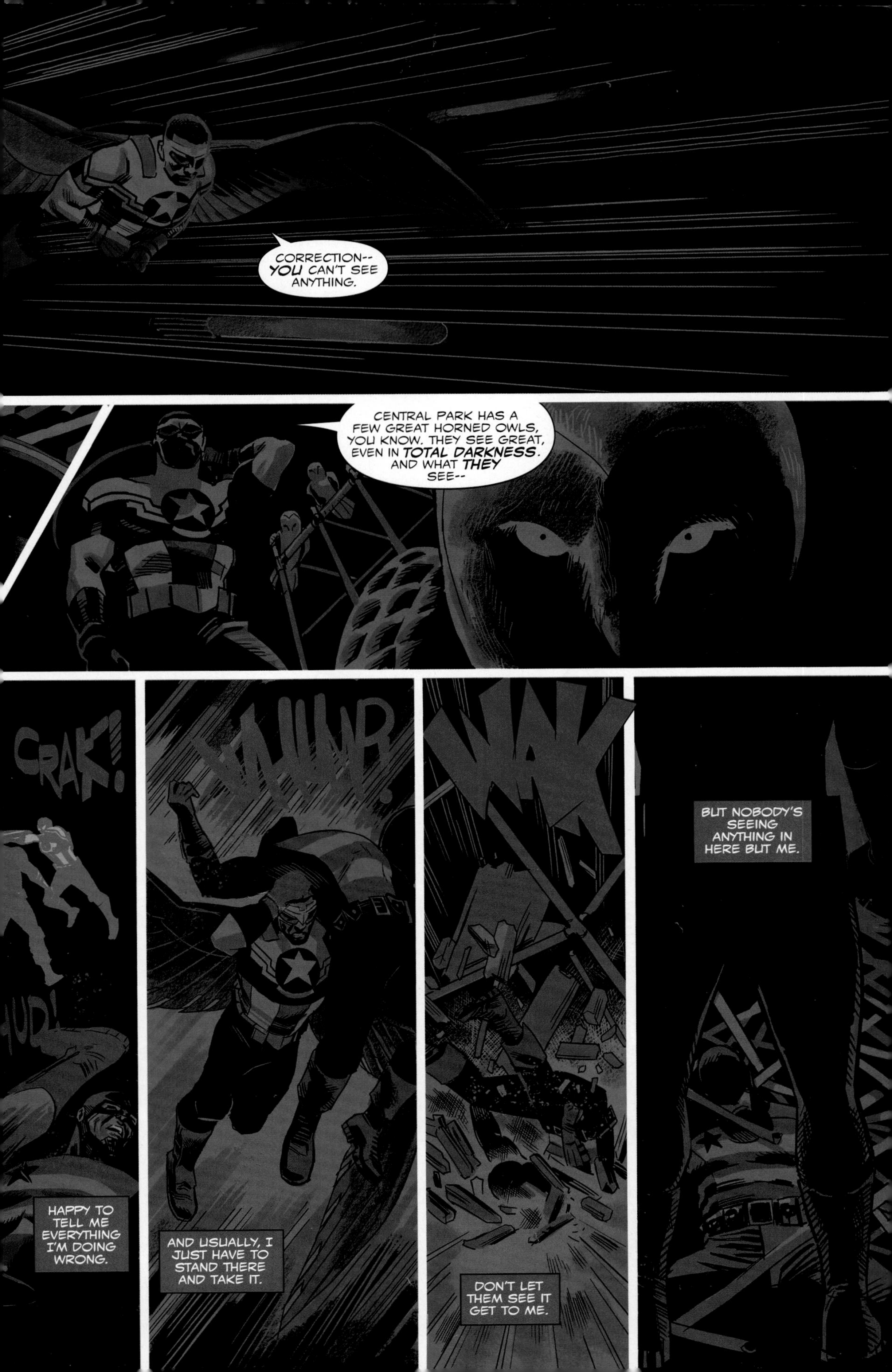
CORRECTION-- YOU CAN'T SEE ANYTHING.
CENTRAL PARK HAS A FEW GREAT HORNED OWLS, YOU KNOW. THEY SEE GREAT, EVEN IN TOTAL DARKNESS. AND WHAT THEY SEE--
CRAK!
HAPPY TO TELL ME EVERYTHING I'M DOING WRONG.
AND USUALLY, I JUST HAVE TO STAND THERE AND TAKE IT.
WAK
DON'T LET THEM SEE IT GET TO ME.
BUT NOBODY'S SEEING ANYTHING IN HERE BUT ME.

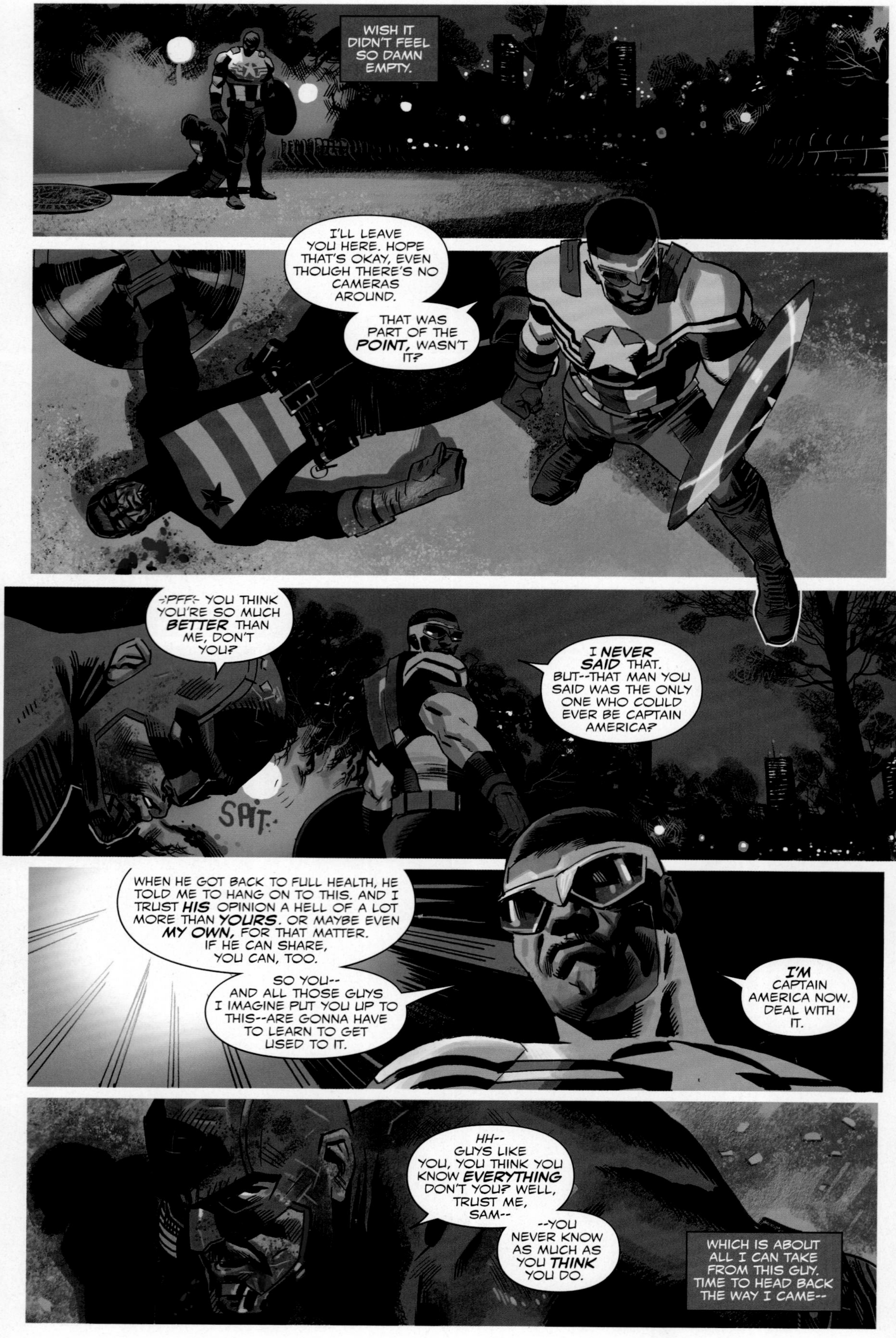
WISH IT DIDN'T FEEL SO DAMN EMPTY.
I'LL LEAVE YOU HERE. HOPE THAT'S OKAY, EVEN THOUGH THERE'S NO CAMERAS AROUND.
THAT WAS PART OF THE POINT, WASN'T IT?
-PFF- YOU THINK YOU'RE SO MUCH BETTER THAN ME, DON'T YOU?
SPIT
I NEVER SAID THAT. BUT--THAT MAN YOU SAID WAS THE ONLY ONE WHO COULD EVER BE CAPTAIN AMERICA?
WHEN HE GOT BACK TO FULL HEALTH, HE TOLD ME TO HANG ON TO THIS. AND I TRUST HIS OPINION A HELL OF A LOT MORE THAN YOURS. OR MAYBE EVEN MY OWN, FOR THAT MATTER. IF HE CAN SHARE, YOU CAN, TOO.
SO YOU-- AND ALL THOSE GUYS I IMAGINE PUT YOU UP TO THIS--ARE GONNA HAVE TO LEARN TO GET USED TO IT.
I'M CAPTAIN AMERICA NOW. DEAL WITH IT.
HH-- GUYS LIKE YOU, YOU THINK YOU KNOW EVERYTHING DON'T YOU? WELL, TRUST ME, SAM--
--YOU NEVER KNOW AS MUCH AS YOU THINK YOU DO.
WHICH IS ABOUT ALL I CAN TAKE FROM THIS GUY. TIME TO HEAD BACK THE WAY I CAME--

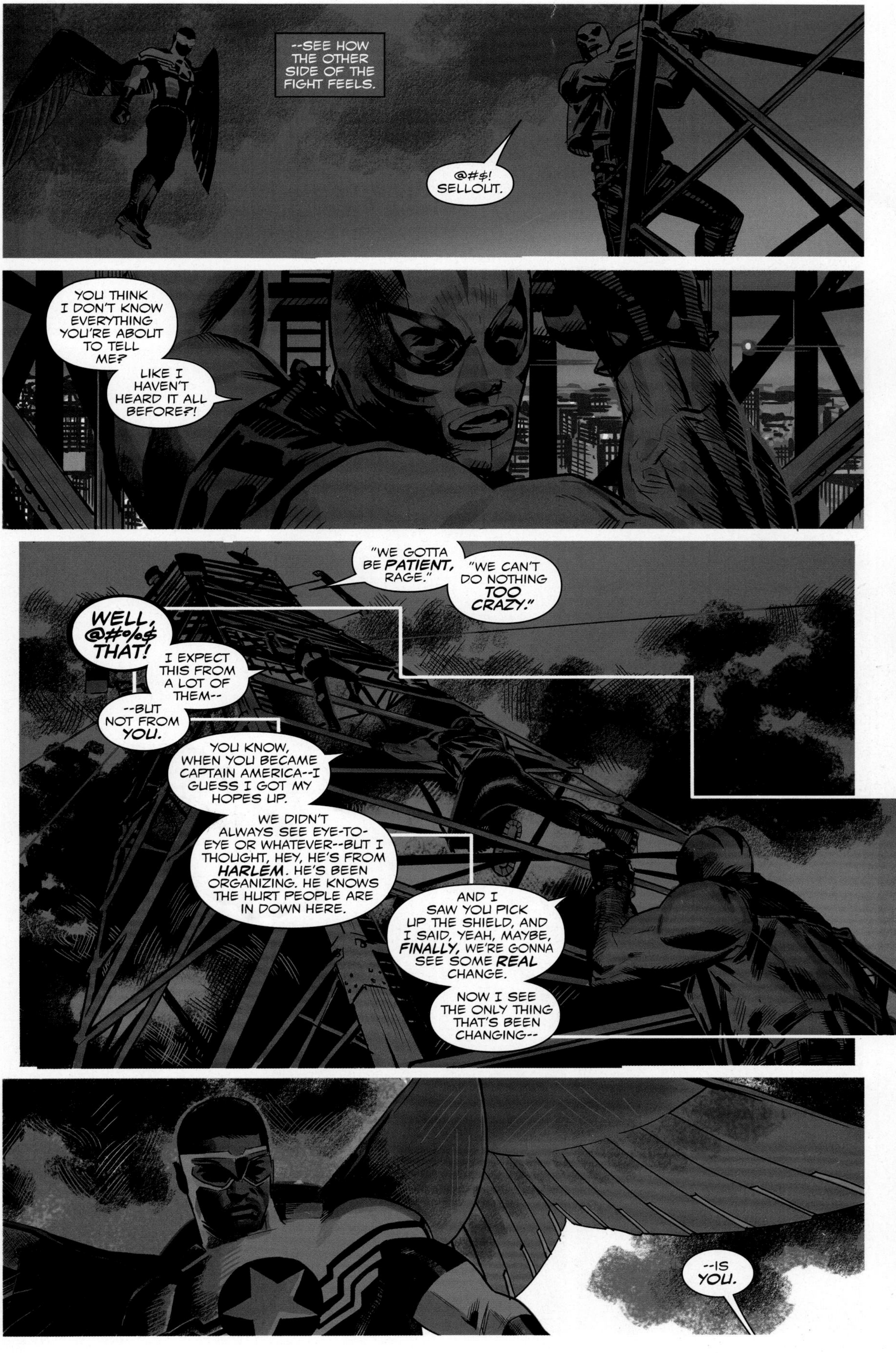
--SEE HOW THE OTHER SIDE OF THE FIGHT FEELS.
@#$! SELLOUT.
YOU THINK I DON'T KNOW EVERYTHING YOU'RE ABOUT TO TELL ME?
LIKE I HAVEN'T HEARD IT ALL BEFORE?!
"WE GOTTA BE PATIENT, RAGE."
"WE CAN'T DO NOTHING TOO CRAZY."
WELL, @#%$ THAT!
I EXPECT THIS FROM A LOT OF THEM--
--BUT NOT FROM YOU.
YOU KNOW, WHEN YOU BECAME CAPTAIN AMERICA--I GUESS I GOT MY HOPES UP.
WE DIDN'T ALWAYS SEE EYE-TO-EYE OR WHATEVER--BUT I THOUGHT, HEY, HE'S FROM HARLEM. HE'S BEEN ORGANIZING. HE KNOWS THE HURT PEOPLE ARE IN DOWN HERE.
AND I SAW YOU PICK UP THE SHIELD, AND I SAID, YEAH, MAYBE, FINALLY, WE'RE GONNA SEE SOME REAL CHANGE.
NOW I SEE THE ONLY THING THAT'S BEEN CHANGING--
--IS YOU.

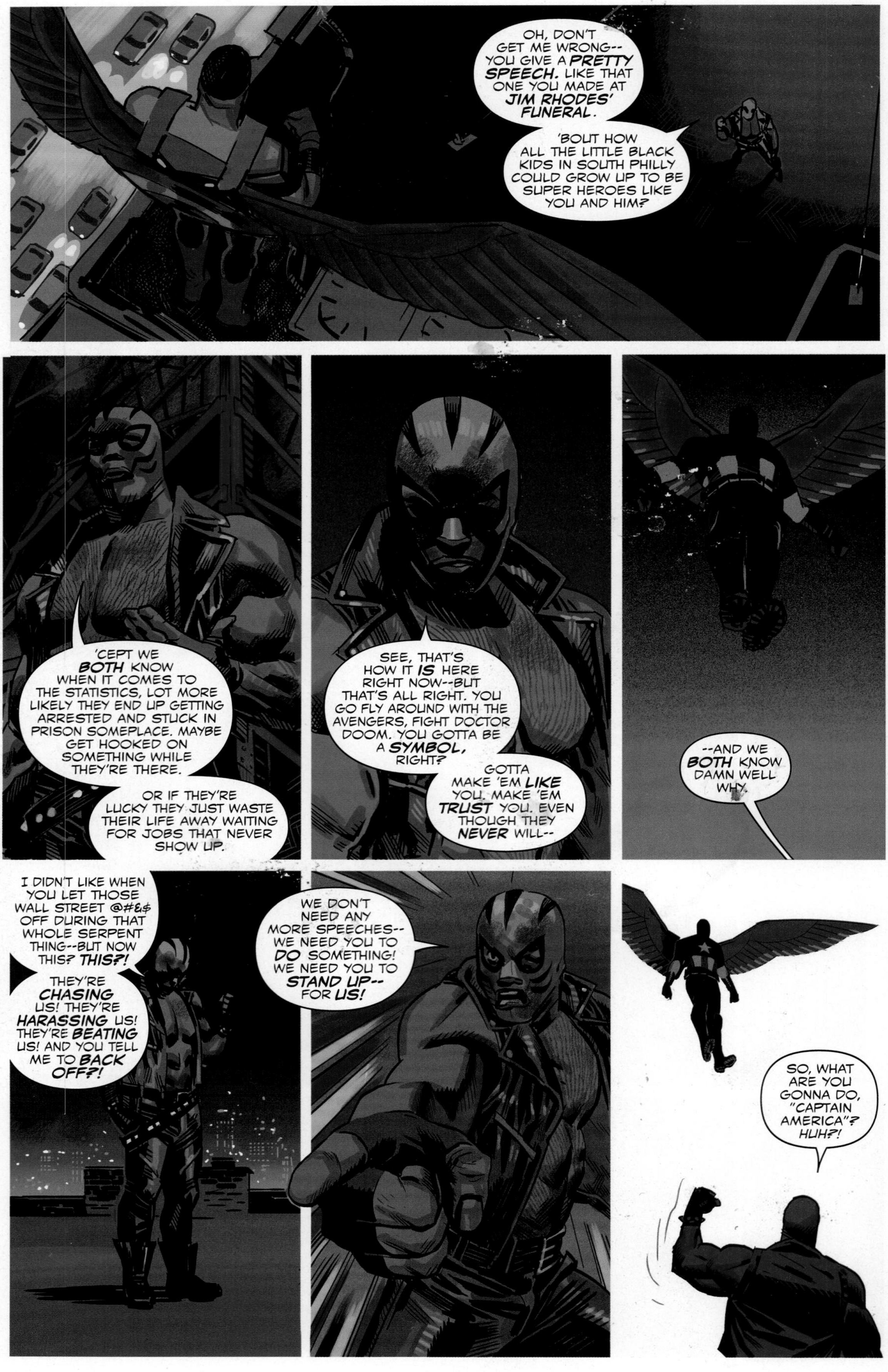
OH, DON'T GET ME WRONG-- YOU GIVE A PRETTY SPEECH. LIKE THAT ONE YOU MADE AT JIM RHODES' FUNERAL.
'BOUT HOW ALL THE LITTLE BLACK KIDS IN SOUTH PHILLY COULD GROW UP TO BE SUPER HEROES LIKE YOU AND HIM?
'CEPT WE BOTH KNOW WHEN IT COMES TO THE STATISTICS, LOT MORE LIKELY THEY END UP GETTING ARRESTED AND STUCK IN PRISON SOMEPLACE. MAYBE GET HOOKED ON SOMETHING WHILE THEY'RE THERE.
OR IF THEY'RE LUCKY THEY JUST WASTE THEIR LIFE AWAY WAITING FOR JOBS THAT NEVER SHOW UP.
SEE, THAT'S HOW IT IS HERE RIGHT NOW--BUT THAT'S ALL RIGHT. YOU GO FLY AROUND WITH THE AVENGERS, FIGHT DOCTOR DOOM. YOU GOTTA BE A SYMBOL, RIGHT?
GOTTA MAKE 'EM LIKE YOU. MAKE 'EM TRUST YOU. EVEN THOUGH THEY NEVER WILL--
--AND WE BOTH KNOW DAMN WELL WHY.
I DIDN'T LIKE WHEN YOU LET THOSE WALL STREET @#&$ OFF DURING THAT WHOLE SERPENT THING--BUT NOW THIS? THIS?!
THEY'RE CHASING US! THEY'RE HARASSING US! THEY'RE BEATING US! AND YOU TELL ME TO BACK OFF?!
WE DON'T NEED ANY MORE SPEECHES-- WE NEED YOU TO DO SOMETHING! WE NEED YOU TO STAND UP-- FOR US!
SO, WHAT ARE YOU GONNA DO, "CAPTAIN AMERICA"? HUH?!

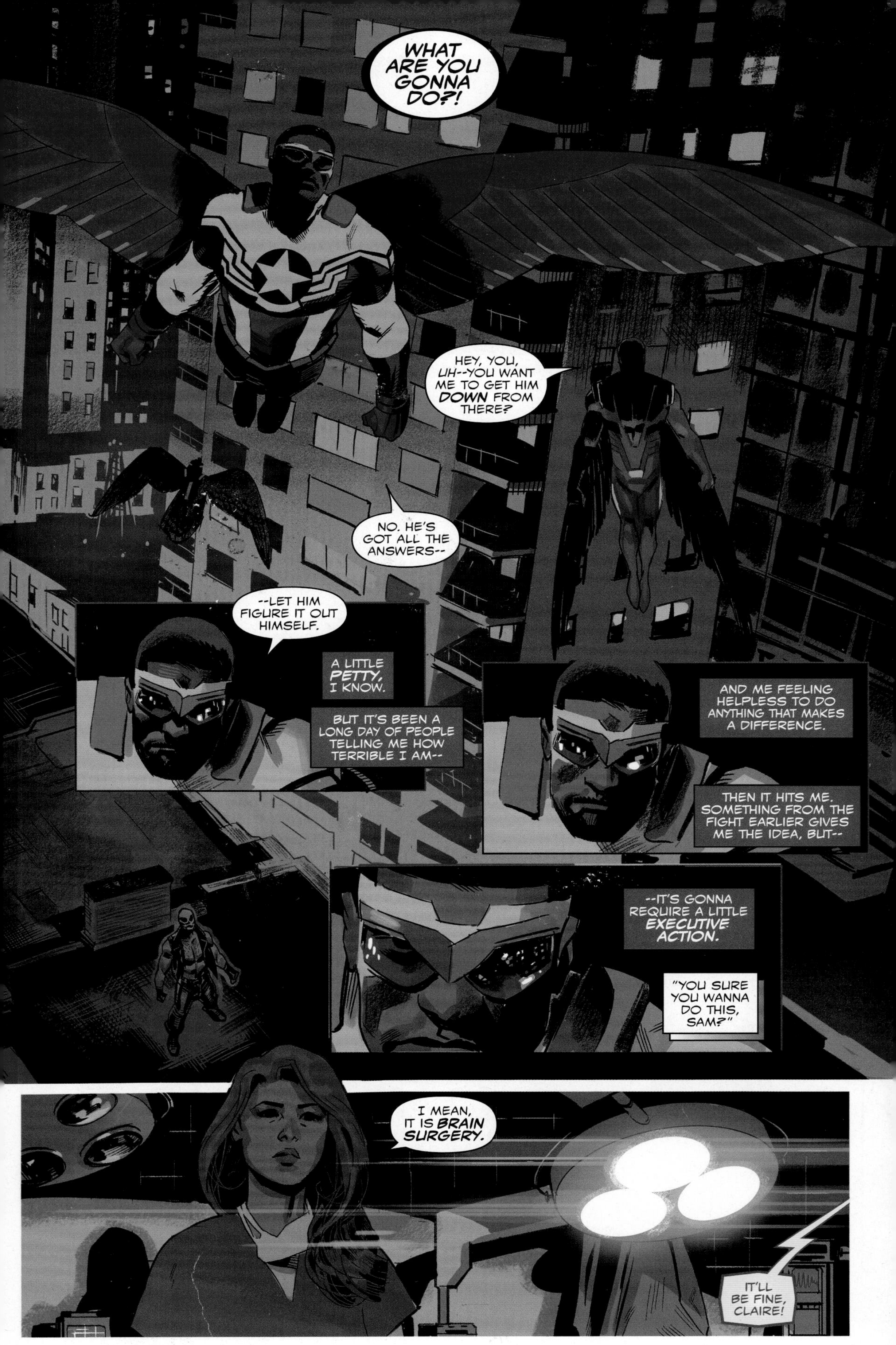
WHAT ARE YOU GONNA DO?!
HEY, YOU, UH--YOU WANT ME TO GET HIM DOWN FROM THERE?
NO. HE'S GOT ALL THE ANSWERS--
--LET HIM FIGURE IT OUT HIMSELF.
A LITTLE PETTY, I KNOW.
BUT IT'S BEEN A LONG DAY OF PEOPLE TELLING ME HOW TERRIBLE I AM--
AND ME FEELING HELPLESS TO DO ANYTHING THAT MAKES A DIFFERENCE.
THEN IT HITS ME. SOMETHING FROM THE FIGHT EARLIER GIVES ME THE IDEA, BUT--
--IT'S GONNA REQUIRE A LITTLE EXECUTIVE ACTION.
"YOU SURE YOU WANNA DO THIS, SAM?"
I MEAN, IT IS BRAIN SURGERY.
IT'LL BE FINE, CLAIRE!

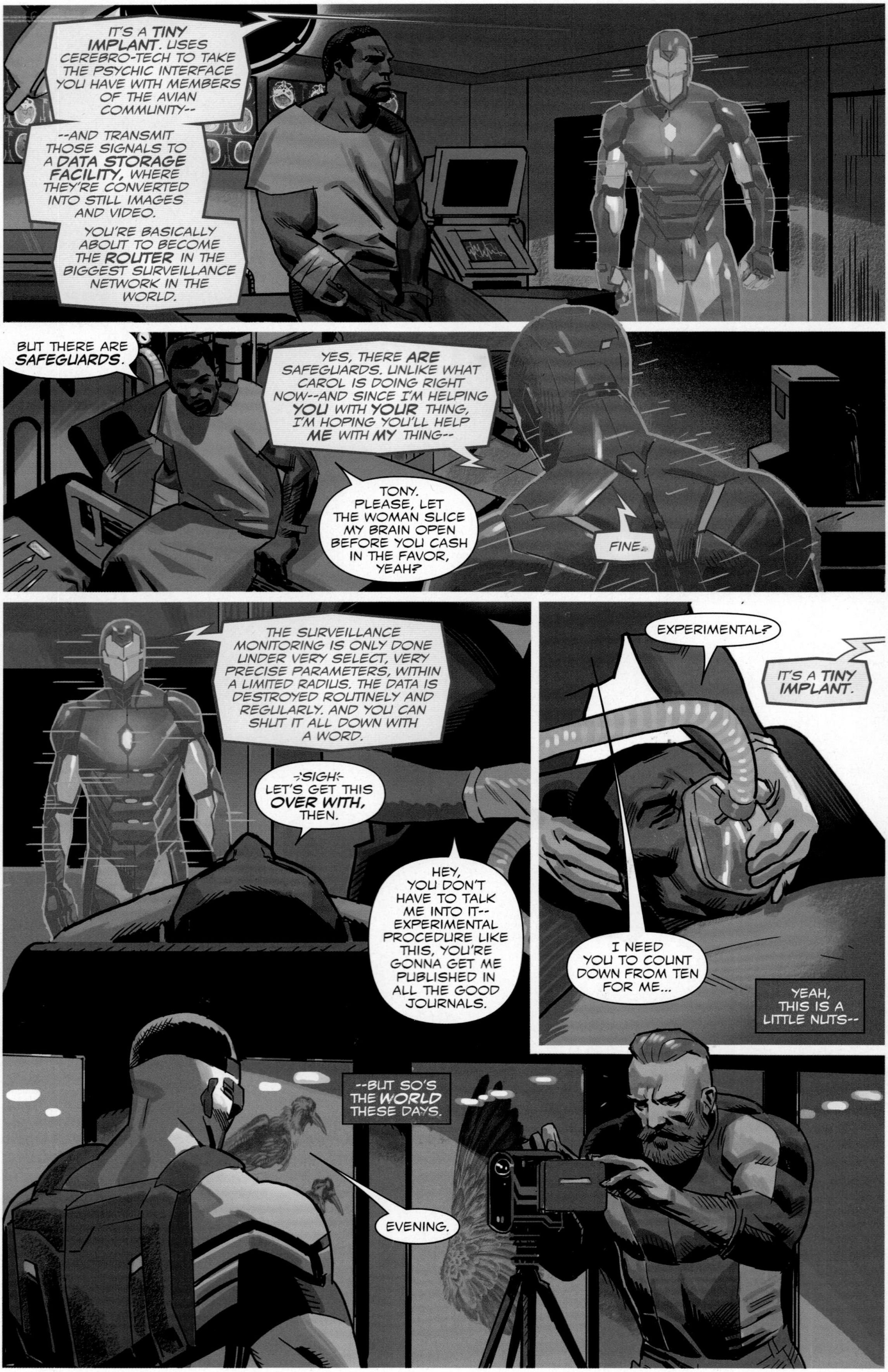
IT'S A TINY IMPLANT. USES CEREBRO-TECH TO TAKE THE PSYCHIC INTERFACE YOU HAVE WITH MEMBERS OF THE AVIAN COMMUNITY--
--AND TRANSMIT THOSE SIGNALS TO A DATA STORAGE FACILITY, WHERE THEY'RE CONVERTED INTO STILL IMAGES AND VIDEO.
YOU'RE BASICALLY ABOUT TO BECOME THE ROUTER IN THE BIGGEST SURVEILLANCE NETWORK IN THE WORLD.
BUT THERE ARE SAFEGUARDS.
YES, THERE ARE SAFEGUARDS. UNLIKE WHAT CAROL IS DOING RIGHT NOW--AND SINCE I'M HELPING YOU WITH YOUR THING, I'M HOPING YOU'LL HELP ME WITH MY THING--
TONY. PLEASE, LET THE WOMAN SLICE MY BRAIN OPEN BEFORE YOU CASH IN THE FAVOR, YEAH?
FINE.
THE SURVEILLANCE MONITORING IS ONLY DONE UNDER VERY SELECT, VERY PRECISE PARAMETERS, WITHIN A LIMITED RADIUS. THE DATA IS DESTROYED ROUTINELY AND REGULARLY. AND YOU CAN SHUT IT ALL DOWN WITH A WORD.
-SIGH- LET'S GET THIS OVER WITH, THEN.
HEY, YOU DON'T HAVE TO TALK ME INTO IT--EXPERIMENTAL PROCEDURE LIKE THIS, YOU'RE GONNA GET ME PUBLISHED IN ALL THE GOOD JOURNALS.
EXPERIMENTAL?
IT'S A TINY IMPLANT.
I NEED YOU TO COUNT DOWN FROM TEN FOR ME...
YEAH, THIS IS A LITTLE NUTS--
--BUT SO'S THE WORLD THESE DAYS.
EVENING.

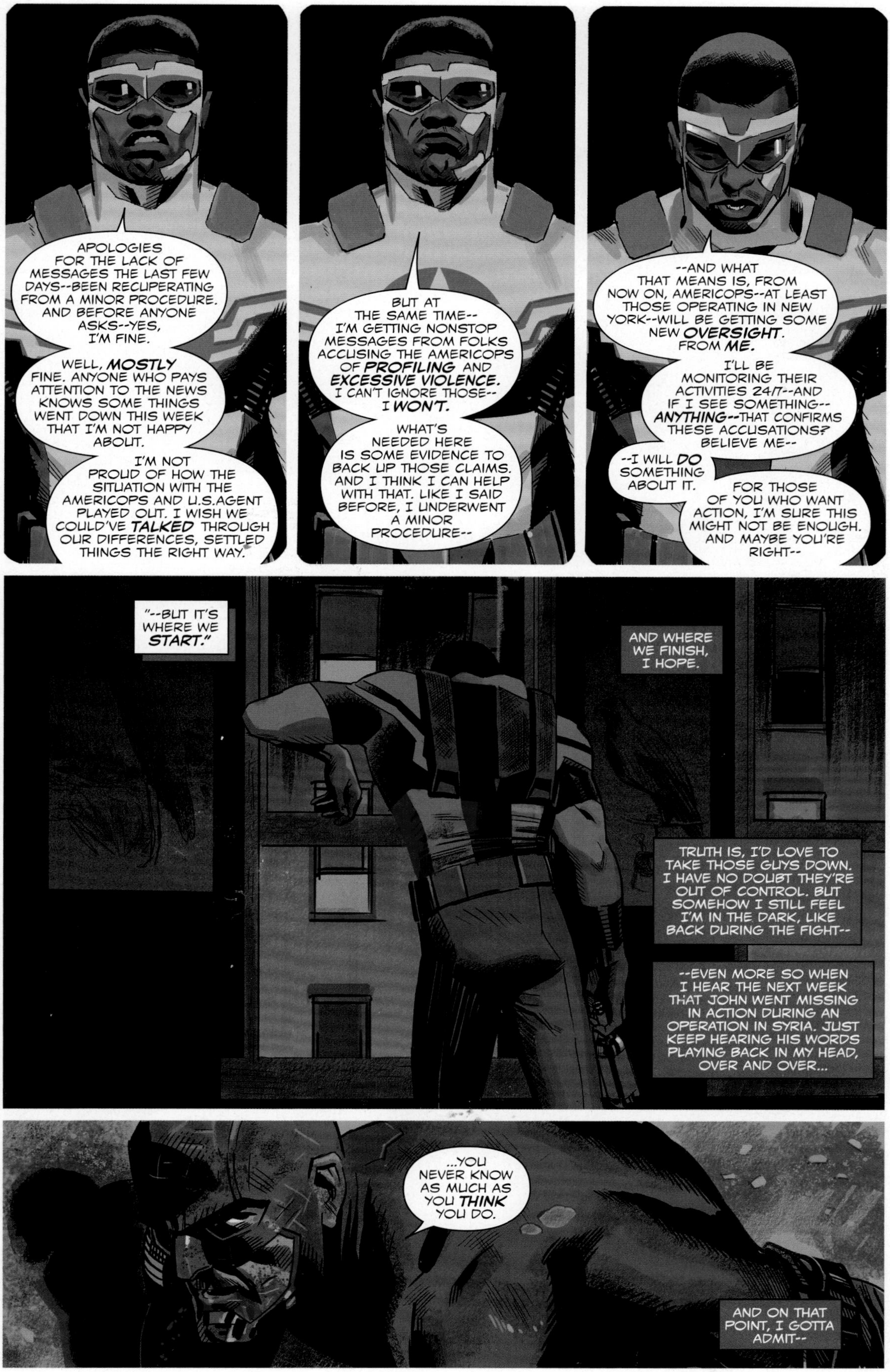
APOLOGIES FOR THE LACK OF MESSAGES THE LAST FEW DAYS--BEEN RECUPERATING FROM A MINOR PROCEDURE. AND BEFORE ANYONE ASKS--YES, I'M FINE.
WELL, MOSTLY FINE. ANYONE WHO PAYS ATTENTION TO THE NEWS KNOWS SOME THINGS WENT DOWN THIS WEEK THAT I'M NOT HAPPY ABOUT.
I'M NOT PROUD OF HOW THE SITUATION WITH THE AMERICOPS AND U.S.AGENT PLAYED OUT. I WISH WE COULD'VE TALKED THROUGH OUR DIFFERENCES, SETTLED THINGS THE RIGHT WAY.
BUT AT THE SAME TIME--I'M GETTING NONSTOP MESSAGES FROM FOLKS ACCUSING THE AMERICOPS OF PROFILING AND EXCESSIVE VIOLENCE. I CAN'T IGNORE THOSE--I WON'T.
WHAT'S NEEDED HERE IS SOME EVIDENCE TO BACK UP THOSE CLAIMS. AND I THINK I CAN HELP WITH THAT. LIKE I SAID BEFORE, I UNDERWENT A MINOR PROCEDURE--
--AND WHAT THAT MEANS IS, FROM NOW ON, AMERICOPS--AT LEAST THOSE OPERATING IN NEW YORK--WILL BE GETTING SOME NEW OVERSIGHT. FROM ME.
I'LL BE MONITORING THEIR ACTIVITIES 24/7--AND IF I SEE SOMETHING--ANYTHING--THAT CONFIRMS THESE ACCUSATIONS? BELIEVE ME--
--I WILL DO SOMETHING ABOUT IT.
FOR THOSE OF YOU WHO WANT ACTION, I'M SURE THIS MIGHT NOT BE ENOUGH. AND MAYBE YOU'RE RIGHT--
"--BUT IT'S WHERE WE START."
AND WHERE WE FINISH, I HOPE.
TRUTH IS, I'D LOVE TO TAKE THOSE GUYS DOWN. I HAVE NO DOUBT THEY'RE OUT OF CONTROL. BUT SOMEHOW I STILL FEEL I'M IN THE DARK, LIKE BACK DURING THE FIGHT--
--EVEN MORE SO WHEN I HEAR THE NEXT WEEK THAT JOHN WENT MISSING IN ACTION DURING AN OPERATION IN SYRIA. JUST KEEP HEARING HIS WORDS PLAYING BACK IN MY HEAD, OVER AND OVER...
...YOU NEVER KNOW AS MUCH AS YOU THINK YOU DO.
AND ON THAT POINT, I GOTTA ADMIT--

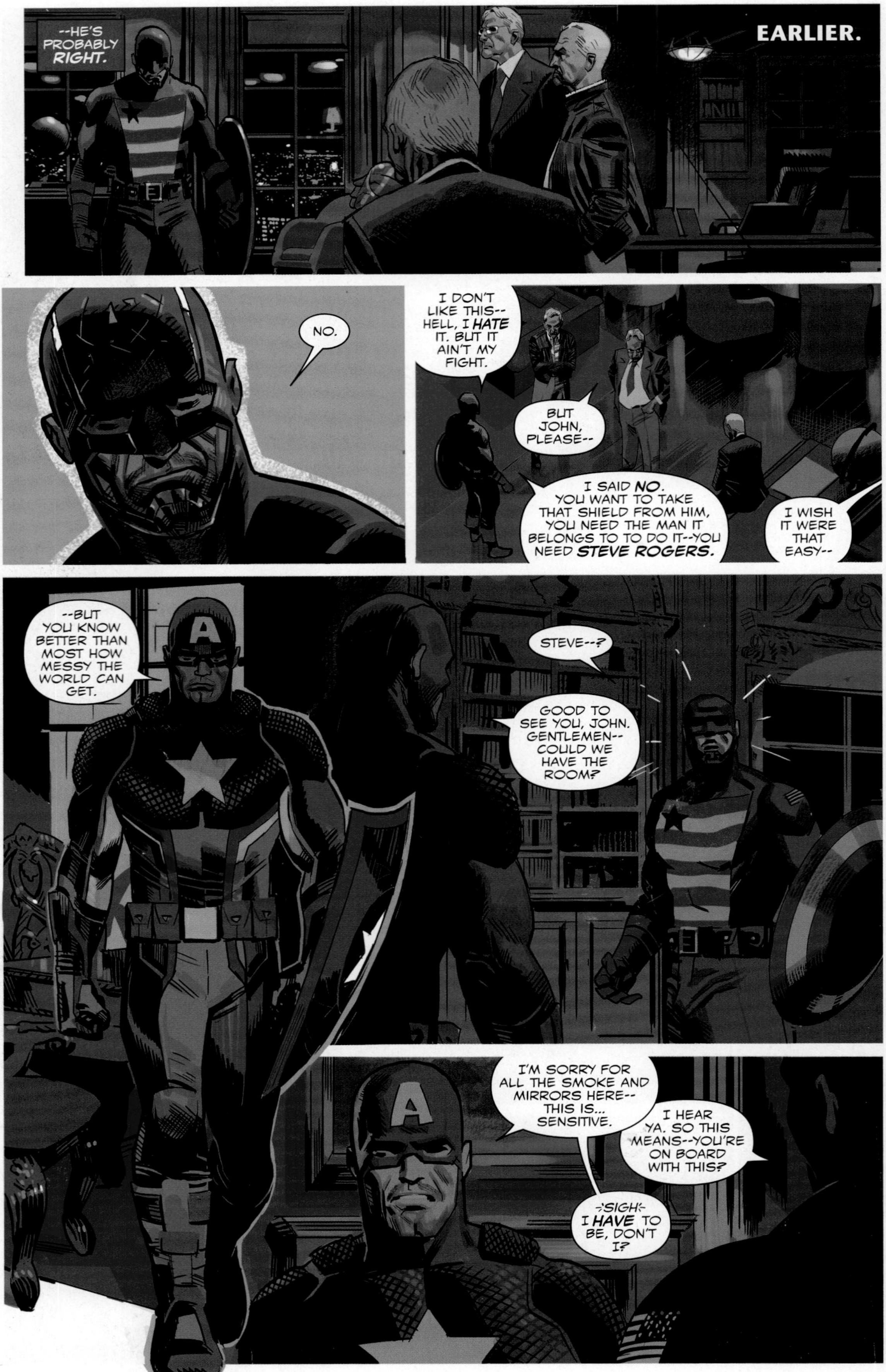

--HE'S PROBABLY RIGHT.
EARLIER.
NO.
I DON'T LIKE THIS--HELL, I HATE IT. BUT IT AIN'T MY FIGHT.
BUT JOHN, PLEASE--
I SAID NO. YOU WANT TO TAKE THAT SHIELD FROM HIM, YOU NEED THE MAN IT BELONGS TO TO DO IT--YOU NEED STEVE ROGERS.
I WISH IT WERE THAT EASY--
--BUT YOU KNOW BETTER THAN MOST HOW MESSY THE WORLD CAN GET.
STEVE--?
GOOD TO SEE YOU, JOHN. GENTLEMEN--COULD WE HAVE THE ROOM?
I'M SORRY FOR ALL THE SMOKE AND MIRRORS HERE--THIS IS... SENSITIVE.
I HEAR YA. SO THIS MEANS--YOU'RE ON BOARD WITH THIS?
SIGH I HAVE TO BE, DON'T I?

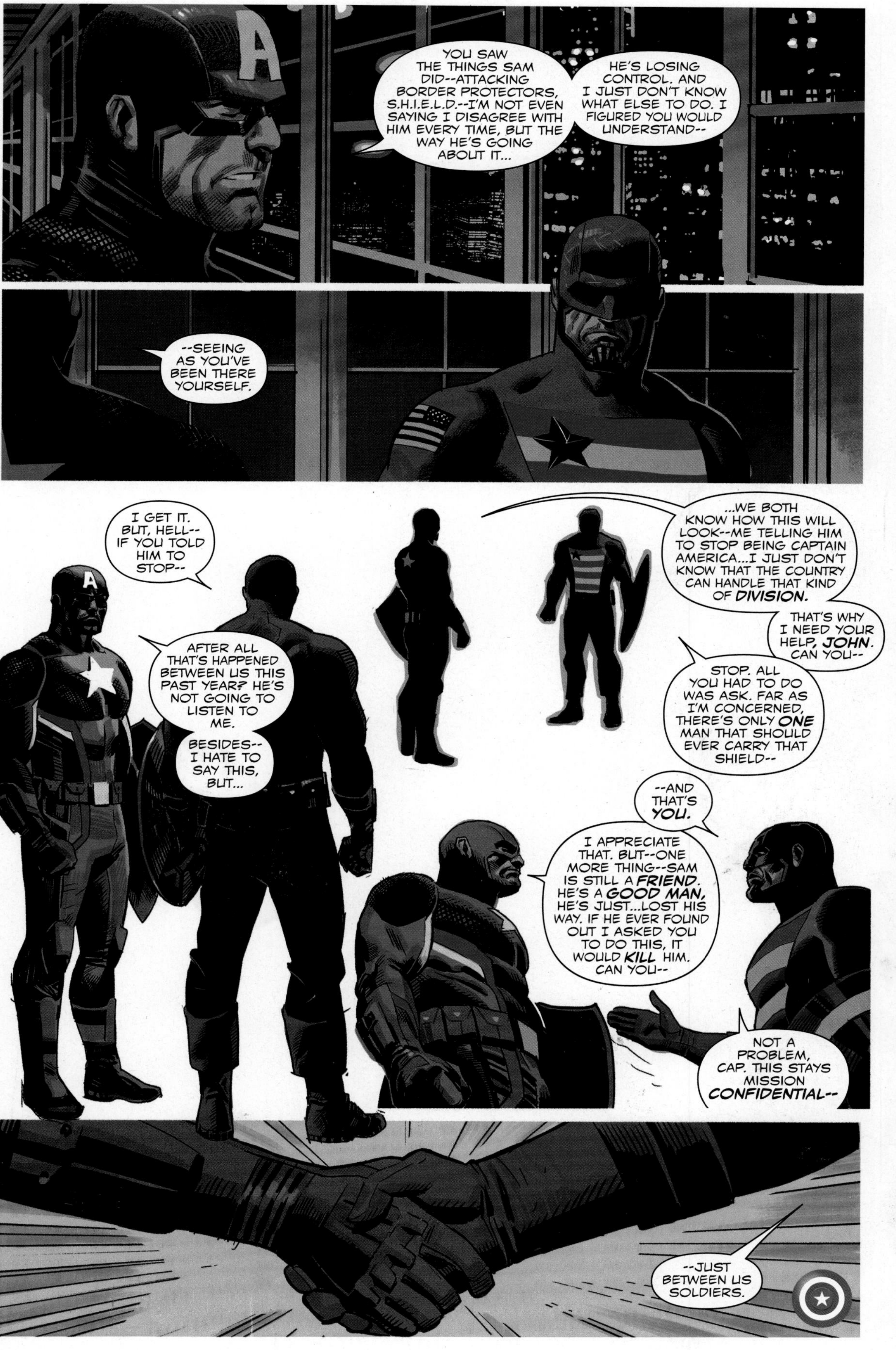
YOU SAW THE THINGS SAM DID--ATTACKING BORDER PROTECTORS, S.H.I.E.L.D.--I'M NOT EVEN SAYING I DISAGREE WITH HIM EVERY TIME, BUT THE WAY HE'S GOING ABOUT IT...
HE'S LOSING CONTROL. AND I JUST DON'T KNOW WHAT ELSE TO DO. I FIGURED YOU WOULD UNDERSTAND--
--SEEING AS YOU'VE BEEN THERE YOURSELF.
I GET IT. BUT, HELL-- IF YOU TOLD HIM TO STOP--
AFTER ALL THAT'S HAPPENED BETWEEN US THIS PAST YEAR? HE'S NOT GOING TO LISTEN TO ME.
BESIDES-- I HATE TO SAY THIS, BUT...
...WE BOTH KNOW HOW THIS WILL LOOK--ME TELLING HIM TO STOP BEING CAPTAIN AMERICA...I JUST DON'T KNOW THAT THE COUNTRY CAN HANDLE THAT KIND OF DIVISION.
THAT'S WHY I NEED YOUR HELP, JOHN. CAN YOU--
STOP. ALL YOU HAD TO DO WAS ASK. FAR AS I'M CONCERNED, THERE'S ONLY ONE MAN THAT SHOULD EVER CARRY THAT SHIELD--
--AND THAT'S YOU.
I APPRECIATE THAT. BUT--ONE MORE THING--SAM IS STILL A FRIEND. HE'S A GOOD MAN, HE'S JUST...LOST HIS WAY. IF HE EVER FOUND OUT I ASKED YOU TO DO THIS, IT WOULD KILL HIM. CAN YOU--
NOT A PROBLEM, CAP. THIS STAYS MISSION CONFIDENTIAL--
--JUST BETWEEN US SOLDIERS.

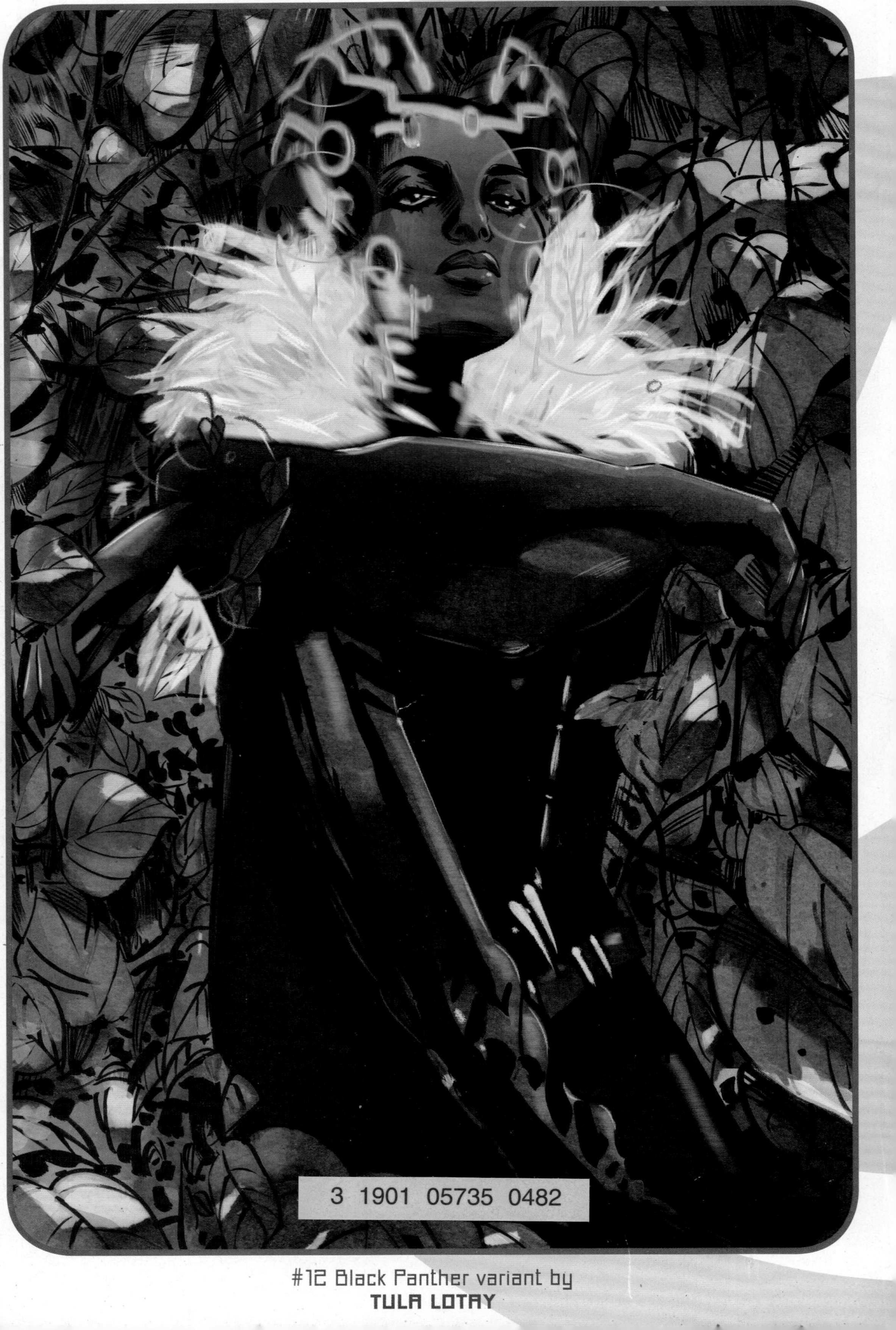

#12 Black Panther variant by
TULA LOTAY